#1231
Disability Statistics RRTC
Institute for Health and Aging
University of California, San Francisco
3333 Califonia Street, Room 340
San Francisco, CA 94118

91251
Disability Statistics RRTC
Institute for Health and Aging
University of California, San Francisco
3333 California Street, Room 340
San Francisco, CA 94118

Thinking About Answers

Thinking About Answers

The Application of Cognitive Processes to Survey Methodology

Seymour Sudman
Norman M. Bradburn
Norbert Schwarz

Jossey-Bass Publishers • San Francisco

Substantial discounts on bulk quantities of Jossey-Bass books are available to corporations, professional associations, and other organizations. For details and discount information, contact the special sales department at Jossey-Bass Inc., Publishers. (415) 433–1740; Fax (800) 605–2665.

For sales outside the United States, please contact your local Simon & Schuster International Office.

Manufactured in the United States of America.

Library of Congress Cataloging-in-Publication Data

Sudman, Seymour.
    Thinking about answers: the application of cognitive processes to survey methodology/Seymour Sudman, Norman M. Bradburn, Norbert Schwarz.
       p.   cm.
    Includes bibliographical references and index.
    ISBN 0-7879-0120-2 (alk. paper)
    1. Social surveys—Methodology.   2. Cognition.   I. Bradburn, Norman M.   II. Schwarz, Norbert, Dr. phil.   III. Title.
HN29.S6915   1996
300'.723—dc20

95-16504
CIP

FIRST EDITION
HB Printing   10 9 8 7 6 5 4 3 2 1

Contents

Preface

In the past decade, significant advances in understanding the survey process have been achieved with the help of cognitive psychology. Reports of these developments have appeared in a wide range of sources, including several books that contain collections of papers presented at conferences.

There now appears to be sufficient research to justify a book that attempts to integrate the work to date. Although we realize that the field continues to grow rapidly and that this book will certainly not be the last word on the subject, we still believe it is a good time to begin.

The book contains useful information that will help survey research practitioners write better questionnaires; however, its discussions are of a theoretical rather than a practical nature. For readers of some of our earlier works, this book resembles *Response Effects in Surveys* more than *Answering Questions*. We continue to believe that nothing is more practical than a good theory, and we are hopeful that the theoretical insights discussed in this book will ultimately lead to still better questionnaires.

In addition to students and practitioners of survey research, we hope that this book will be useful to the growing number of cognitive psychology researchers who are now using surveys as a method for testing their theories.

No single book can be exhaustive in a large and rapidly growing field. Our choice of topics and the emphasis we put on them are to some extent subjective. We have written most about the work that we know best, which means our own research and the research of others presented at a series of conferences that we organized. We recognize that our perspective is only one of several that might have been usefully developed.

Finally, a note on the order of the authors. As with our earlier books, this volume was a collaborative effort to which we all contributed equally. We rotate the order of the authors' names from book to book to reflect this fact.

Acknowledgments

We are deeply grateful to several of our colleagues who read and criticized earlier versions of this manuscript. Among them, we include Lu Ann Aday, University of Texas Health Center at Houston; Lawrence Barsalou, University of Chicago; Barbara Bickart, Rutgers University at Camden; Robert Groves, University of Michigan, Ann Arbor; Robert Fay, U.S. Bureau of the Census; Geeta Menon, New York University; Diane O'Rourke, University of Illinois, Urbana-Champaign; Stanley Presser, University of Maryland, College Park; Howard Schuman, University of Michigan, Ann Arbor; Eleanor Singer, University of Michigan, Ann Arbor; Judith Tanur, State University of New York, Stony Brook; and Roger Tourangeau, National Opinion Research Center.

Their suggestions have helped to improve this book but we, of course, are responsible for any errors or omissions. In addition, we tested earlier versions of this book in our classes and received invaluable feedback from our students. Our thanks go to graduate students at the University of Chicago, the University of Illinois, and the University of Michigan, as well as to participants in short courses taught at the University of Amsterdam, the Joint University of Maryland–University of Michigan Program in Survey Methods, the Summer Institute in Survey Research Techniques at

Michigan's Survey Research Center, and ZUMA's continuing education program. We are also grateful to Becky McGovern, Mary White, and Rachel Anderson, our editors at Jossey-Bass, for their useful comments.

Finally, we wish to thank the Alexander von Humboldt Stiftung and the Walter Stellner Fund at the University of Illinois, Urbana-Champaign, for the financial support that facilitated our collaboration on this book.

July 1995

Seymour Sudman
Urbana, Illinois

Norman M. Bradburn
Chicago, Illinois

Norbert Schwarz
Ann Arbor, Michigan

The Authors

Norman M. Bradburn, senior vice president for research and former director at the National Opinion Research Center, has served as provost of the University of Chicago and is the Tiffany and Margaret Blake Distinguished Service Professor in the department of psychology and the Harris Graduate School of Public Policy Studies. A survey methodologist, Bradburn chairs two important committees of the National Academy of Sciences' National Research Council: they are the Committee on National Statistics and the Panel to Evaluate Alternative Census Methods for Census 2000 and Beyond. From 1988 to 1992, he chaired the National Academy's Board on International Comparative Studies in Education. Bradburn is past president of the American Association of Public Opinion Research and is a fellow of the American Statistical Association. He has written extensively on cognitive aspects of survey response, asking sensitive questions, and recall error in surveys. He is the author (with Seymour Sudman) of four books on survey methodology, including *Asking Questions* (Jossey-Bass, 1982) and *Polls and Surveys* (Jossey-Bass, 1988).

Norbert Schwarz is professor of psychology at the University of Michigan, Ann Arbor, research scientist in the Research Center for Group Dynamics and the Survey Research Center of Michigan's Institute for Social Research, and research professor in the Joint

Program in Survey Methods at the University of Maryland, College Park. Prior to joining the University of Michigan, he was a program director at ZUMA, Mannheim, Germany. He has received doctoral degrees in sociology (University of Mannheim, Germany) and psychology (University of Heidelberg, Germany). His research interests focus on human judgmental processes, including their application to survey research. His recent books in the area of survey research include *Answering Questions* (Jossey-Bass, 1995), *Context Effects in Social and Psychological Research*, and *Autobiographical Memory and the Validity of Retrospective Reports* (all coedited with Seymour Sudman). He serves on the editorial boards of several journals in psychology and the social sciences.

Seymour Sudman is Walter H. Stellner Distinguished Professor of Marketing, professor of business administration and of sociology, and deputy director and research professor at the Survey Research Laboratory, University of Illinois at Urbana-Champaign. He received his Ph.D. degree in business administration from the University of Chicago. This is the sixteenth book he has authored, coauthored, or edited and the fourth he has coauthored or edited with Norbert Schwarz. Their other most recent book is *Answering Questions*, which was also published by Jossey-Bass (1995). Sudman also is author of more than two hundred articles and serves on the editorial boards of five professional journals. His current research interests are related to cognitive aspects of answering threatening questions, proxy reporting about others and organizations, and improving responses to autobiographical questions by interactive cognitive interviewing.

Thinking About Answers

1

Introduction

We are not yet ready—if we ever will be—for a grand theory of the survey process that explains all aspects of question answering with a limited number of powerful theoretical perspectives. In this book we present an eclectic theoretical framework drawn from psycholinguistics and social and cognitive psychology, and we review the growing literature on questionnaire design that uses this framework to study response errors in surveys.

We start with a dual conception of the survey. On the one hand, a survey is a social encounter. On the other hand, it is a series of cognitive tasks to be performed by respondents. When we call it a social encounter, we mean that interviewers conduct interviews in a form that is very similar to that of ordinary conversations and, as such, partakes of the linguistic and social rules that govern such conversations. To be sure, a survey is a special type of conversation with characteristics that set it apart from many other conversations, but it is a conversation nonetheless and needs to be understood as a conversation. A survey is also a voluntary social encounter between strangers and is subject to the rules that govern social relations between strangers. Thus, understanding the rules that govern conversations and social encounters in general should help us understand how survey questions are being understood and answered.

The vehicle through which survey questionnaires are delivered is language. Understanding how people comprehend speech and written material deepens our understanding of the ways in which questionnaire design affects people's answers. Language comprehension is based not only on formal structures like syntax, but more importantly, on pragmatic factors that may deeply affect meaning. A study of the effects of question wording has to focus on the factors that influence respondents' comprehension and on how the inferred meaning may differ from the researcher's intended meaning. Variations in contexts may result in different respondents answering, in effect, different questions (in such cases, the answers cannot be compared) or even questions that the researcher never intended to ask.

Trying to understand how respondents comprehend survey questions leads inevitably to a more basic search for information about how people understand the world around them and how they communicate with one another. Cognitive psychology has a rich research literature on memory and information processing, processes that are fundamental to understanding how respondents answer survey questions. It may seem as if a long distance separates the simple phenomenon of asking survey questions and the complex cognitive processes that individuals go through in answering them. But we maintain that only when the social and cognitive complexities of the response process are understood will we have a good understanding of the quality of survey data and know when response effects adversely affect the results of our surveys and when they can safely be ignored.

Outline of the Book

This book begins with an exploration of the methodological approaches researchers use to understand question characteristics, the cognitive processes, and respondents' difficulties in answering questions. Because these methods can be applied independently of the particular question answering process used and because they are very useful as supplements to traditional pretesting strategies, we review them in Chapter Two. Such methods as protocol analysis or cognitive interviews, in which respondents "think aloud" as they answer survey questions, give insight into the ways in which they understand questions, search their memories for relevant information, form judgments, and edit their answers. The limitations of these methods are also discussed. This chapter is likely to be especially useful to survey research practitioners.

Chapter Three presents an outline of cognitive theorizing, which underlies the empirical work reviewed in later chapters. Several very similar models of the survey process have been proposed. In the chapter, the models are described and their implications for survey practice explored. The basic concepts introduced are elaborated on in more detail as our discussion proceeds to more specific issues.

The subsequent three chapters deal with the context effects in question asking from a cognitive perspective. Chapter Four reviews different sources of context effects and describes their influence on the cognitive tasks involved in the question answering process. As many researchers have noted, however, context effects often seem inconsistent. Sometimes they move responses in the direction of previous information (usually referred to as "assimilation effects") and sometimes away from previous information (usually referred to as "contrast effects"). Chapter Five reviews in more detail why context effects may turn out to be assimilation effects or contrast effects and offers guidelines to help the researcher. Information that may affect responses is contained not only in previous questions and information but also in the response alternatives offered. Chapter Six examines context effects that arise from response alternatives and the order in which they are presented. Cognitive theory is used to explain why effects are sometimes based on the first items presented (primacy effects) and at other times on the last few items presented (recency effects).

The next four chapters relate to reports of behavior, or what is currently called "autobiographical memory." Chapter Seven deals with the storage and retrieval of autobiographical memories. In it we review some theories about how information is stored and how the organization of memory can affect accurate recall and then discuss some experiments that support these theories.

Many survey questions about behavior refer to events that occurred within a specified time period, such as, "How many times have you been to the doctor in the last three months?" Special cognitive effort is required in remembering not only that an event occurred but also when it occurred. Chapter Eight treats theories of memory for time and examines the reasons for systematic biases in reports on when events occurred.

When the memory task set by the survey questions is too difficult, respondents turn to estimation. In Chapter Nine we discuss when and how estimation occurs and some of the strategies respondents use to make estimates. We also discuss the ways in which behavior regularity may help or hinder retrieval of information about that behavior.

Reports on behavior come not only from respondents themselves but also from others who live in the same household or know them well. The task of reporting about others within a household or an organization adds still new cognitive complexities. In Chapter Ten we discuss these issues and present experiments describing comparisons of cognitive processes in self-reporting and proxy reporting.

Finally, in Chapter Eleven we summarize what we think we have learned from the application of cognitive theory to the survey process and review our social-cognitive framework of survey interviewing.

A Brief Research History

Before proceeding with the book, it is useful to set the stage with a short review of the research on survey questionnaire design. Since the earliest days of survey research, investigators have worried about the possible biasing effects of the data-collection process. The interviewers, the wording of questions, the order in which questions are asked—all have been seen as possible sources of measurement error. Indeed, it is probably fair to say that as survey research began in the 1930s and 1940s, more attention was given to these sources of error than to sampling error. This early work laid the foundations for some of the research described in this book.

Even with the relatively crude sampling methods of the time— quotas for respondents with different characteristics such as gender, age, and so on—the success of polls using these methods in the 1936 presidential race between Franklin D. Roosevelt and Alfred Landon established the superiority of scientific sampling over the self-selected methods typical of the media polls at that time. In 1936, the *Literary Digest,* using a huge but badly biased sample of ten million predicted a Republican victory. Yet the Democrats went on to win all but two states. At the same time, the new survey organizations such as Gallup, Roper, and Crossley, with a more "scientific" sample of only fifteen hundred, predicted the election's outcome correctly. Possible biases arising from different sampling methods, although discussed and known in the statistical literature, were not the subject of much research among the small group concerned with survey research as it grew during the late 1930s and early 1940s.

The failure of the polls to predict the outcome of the 1948 election—in which Harry Truman defeated Thomas Dewey—focused the attention of the academic community, as well as that of the media and the polling industry itself, on methodological problems. Attention to sampling methods was particularly sharp, and a lively debate about the relative merits of probability and quota sampling dominated the discussion. Interviewer bias, intertwined with the problems of quota sampling, was a source of great concern even before the 1948 debacle but gained renewed interest after it.

The Social Science Research Council (SSRC) sponsored several large projects to examine the methodology of surveys, particularly as practiced in the political arena. These efforts culminated in two important books. The first was a study done immediately after the 1948 election that looked at what went wrong with the polls in that election. While reviewing the most likely steps in surveys where errors may occur, the authors concluded that there were two primary causes of errors: sampling and interviewing methods and forecasting methods (Mosteller, Hyman, McCarthy, Marks, & Truman, 1949).

Because most early surveys were concerned with attitudes and opinions and such "subjective" topics were thought to be particularly susceptible to influence by interviewers, much of the methodological concern in the late 1940s was about possible interviewer effects. Did the interviewers' personal opinions influence the respondents? Were the interviewers consciously or unconsciously behaving in ways that biased the results? Did the personal characteristics of the interviewers make a difference? These questions lay at the heart of the second of the two SSRC projects and resulted in Hyman's classic work, *Interviewing in Social Research* (1954). The results of this project, which was based on a large number of individual studies at the National Opinion Research Center, laid to rest the worst fears of those who believed that opinion research was subject to rampant bias introduced by interviewers and effectively exhausted for some time any in-depth research on interviewer effects.

During the 1960s, with the rapid growth of a variety of governmental transfer and training programs designed as part of the War on Poverty campaign, demand for evaluation of these programs grew. A new industry of evaluation research that used the method of sample surveys to collect the necessary data was created. In these surveys, the focus shifted away from opinions and toward behaviors. Survey methods were used to chart the experiences of people enrolled in both demonstration and operational programs, and sophisticated social experiments were conducted to try out different policy ideas such as health insurance plans, housing allowances, early childhood education programs (notably Head Start), and income maintenance programs. The data's accuracy became of vital concern because large sums of money would be distributed on that basis. Thus methodological interest shifted toward sources of measurement error when measuring behavior rather than attitudes or opinions.

Studying Measuring Instruments

As a result of intensive methodological work, survey sampling developed into a scientifically based enterprise with clearly specified theoretical foundations and codified rules of application (Kish, 1965; Sudman, 1976). To a lesser extent, this was also true for survey interviewing. Although the theoretical basis of interviewing is still less rigorously developed than the theoretical basis of sampling, considerable agreement has been reached on the proper conduct of survey interviews and standardized training programs have been developed (Cannell and Kahn, 1968; Weinberg, 1983). In contrast, question wording and questionnaire design have largely remained an "art," governed by in-house traditions acquired by personal experience. Although many researchers explored the impact of question wording and question order on survey responses (for early reviews see the seminal volumes of Cantril, 1944, and Payne, 1951), the work conducted in this domain suffered from a lack of theoretical perspective. Articles appeared that demonstrated particular effects of particular question wordings and question orders, but no consistent body of findings or rules alerted the investigator to the types of situations in which wording or order effects were likely to appear. This resulted in a provocative collection of heterogeneous response effects yet their implications beyond the specific question under study remained uncertain. In the absence of a theoretical framework, it seemed that research on question wording and related factors had to start over with each new question asked.

Not surprisingly, many researchers lost interest in the issue and accepted that question wording would affect the distribution of the responses and that little could be done about it. Moreover, researchers hoped that question characteristics would primarily affect univariate distributions and not the observed relationship between variables. This hypothesis became known as the *form-resistant correlations assumption* (Stouffer & De Vinney, 1949). Accordingly, respondent characteristics and interviewer behavior seemed to provide more promising research arenas, whereas interest in questionnaire variables declined in the mid-1950s, not to be revitalized until the 1970s.

Several developments contributed to the revitalization. First, the assumption of form-resistant correlations did not hold up. In a seminal paper, Schuman and Duncan (1974) demonstrated that the relationship between variables *does* depend on the specific question asked, thus bringing question form back into focus. Second, increasing interest in tracking social change and determining the impact of social programs required interpretable longitudinal data, giving rise to concern about the comparability of answers given at different points in time to the same question in different questionnaires. This concern was compounded by the fact that univariate distributions were of crucial importance for many of the substantive issues addressed in evaluation studies.

In this context, in the early 1970s two of the authors of the present work (Bradburn and Sudman) began work on an extensive meta-analysis of the response effects literature (Sudman & Bradburn, 1974). In order to organize that review, they proposed a simple model for understanding the sources of response effects. The model started with the view that the survey interview is a special kind of conversation between individuals who speak the same language. It is a "conversation with a purpose," as Bingham and Moore (1934) described it, because it has a definite structure and particular rules that differentiate it from other conversational forms such as casual conversation between friends or instrumental conversation between colleagues, for example.

The interview structure consists of a social situation in which one person (the interviewer) has the role of asking the questions, a second person (the respondent) has the role of answering the questions, and a third person (the researcher) defines the task. The researcher has a particular purpose in mind, that is, to obtain information to answer some general practical or scientific questions. Thus the interview is in some ways like all conversations, in some ways like many conversations, and in some ways like no other conversation.

Methodological research on the survey process has tended to focus on aspects of the process that are unique to a particular survey or that resemble other surveys but ignore aspects of the process that are shared with other types of conversations. As we shall see in Chapter Three, the authors of the present work believe that consideration of the ways in which survey interviews adhere to the rules of general conversation helps us understand some response effects.

By conceptualizing the survey interview as a social system with two roles united by a common task, Bradburn and Sudman were able to identify three primary sources of response effects—those stemming from the interviewer, those coming from the respondent, and those coming from the task itself, particularly the questionnaire and the context within which it is perceived. The meta-analysis suggested that the largest effects were associated with the task itself, that is, the question asking and answering process. How powerful the impact of such task variables as question wording or question order could be was further illustrated by a series of split-ballot experiments on attitude questions by Howard Schuman and his collaborators, subsequently reviewed in Schuman and Presser's (1981) *Questions and Answers in Attitude Surveys*.

Together, these lines of work indicated that the most important part of the process is the wording of the question. The wording of the question is what the respondent must process in order to understand what information is being sought or, for that matter, that it is *information* that is being sought and not, say, an expression of affect or some other type of communication, as might be the case in another conversation.

This point is so fundamental that its importance is often overlooked. To take a vivid but trivial example, the questions "How old are you?" and "When were you born?" have only one word in common but are recognizably about the same topic. Estimates of the age distribution of the population based on responses to the two questions from a sample of that population will differ but not dramatically. However, if the two questions were "When were you born?" and "Where were you born?" the responses would be so different that the answers could not be compared even though these questions share more of the same words than do the two about age. The point is that the question's meaning is what is important. As Bateson (1984) pointed out, "A survey trades in meanings, and meanings are embodied in language. A survey consists of a transfer of meanings between the three participants through the medium of language."

Indeed, small changes in wording can alter the meaning fundamentally while extensive changes in wording may alter it only slightly. An early experiment by Rugg (1941) showed that small changes in wording, even in questions about the same topic, could produce dramatically different effects. He asked matched samples of respondents one of two questions: "Do you think the United States should allow public speeches against democracy?" or "Do you think the United States should forbid speeches against democracy?" When the question was one of "allowing" public speeches, 21 percent of respondents supported free speech. But when the question was one of "forbidding," 39 percent supported free speech. Rugg had no explanation for these findings except to note that "forbid" and "allow" were not exact opposites when used in these sentences even though they looked superficially as if they were. (For a cognitive explanation of this finding, see Hippler & Schwarz, 1986.) An adequate theory of response effects must be able to account for such differences.

Interviews entail much more than just questions, of course, including nonsemantic information. For example, there is the social context in which the interview takes place. It may take place in the home of a respondent who is selected as a member of a sample of the population. Or in the workplace with a respondent who is an employee of an organization about which the questions are asked.

Or in a researcher's office or laboratory with the respondent a "subject" in an experiment that is part of a study whose purpose is perceived to contribute to scientific knowledge.

In addition, social characteristics of the interviewer and the respondent, such as race or gender, may carry over into attitudes and affect relations in ways that are independent of the interview and reflect larger social beliefs. The mode of administration of the questions may also have important consequences on the responses: Is the interview conducted in person, on the telephone, or through self-administered questionnaires?

Many of these variables will have different effects depending on the interaction between their characteristics and the questionnaire's content. And, of course, there will be individual differences in the degree to which respondents are influenced by any of these factors. Nevertheless, task variables have the greatest impact on the responses obtained in survey interviews. In many ways, this is a fortunate state of affairs because it is the nature of the tasks presented to respondents that the researcher has the most control over.

The Application of Cognitive Theory to Questionnaire Construction

Focusing on the nature of the question asking and answering process naturally leads one to consider the cognitive processes involved in answering survey questions. Thus, interest turned to a more detailed conceptualization at the individual psychological level of what was involved in comprehending and answering survey questions, and by the late 1970s psychology was prepared to provide some reasonable information on these issues.

Having been dominated by the paradigm of behaviorism for nearly four decades, experimental psychology underwent a "cognitive revolution" in the 1970s, bringing mental processes back to center stage. In contrast to behaviorism's emphasis on stimulus-response sequences and the importance of rewards, the emerging paradigm of information processing emphasized complex mental processes. Experimental psychologists turned from animal learning, mazes, and food-dispensing levers to topics like information acquisition, storage, and retrieval, and the technology of reaction time measurement. (See Hunt, 1993, for a popular history of this development, and Lachman, Lachman, & Butterfield, 1979, for a more rigorous discussion.) Building on earlier work in nonbehaviorist traditions, this paradigm shift quickly resulted in the development of testable models of memory, language comprehension, inferential reasoning, and judgment, among others (see Lachman, Lachman & Butterfield, 1979). Although these topics are of key importance to an understanding of the question answering process, these developments went largely unnoticed by the survey research community. As work within the information processing paradigm progressed, however, some psychologists began to wonder how what they learned in the laboratory applied to human behavior in natural settings, giving rise to more naturalistic studies, in particular in the domain of memory. (For examples see the contributions in Neisser & Winograd, 1988.) This increasing interest in "everyday cognition" rendered applied issues a legitimate arena for cognitive research, setting the stage for cognitive psychologists' collaborations with other disciplines.

The collaboration between cognitively oriented psychologists and survey researchers can be traced to the late 1970s. One of the earliest instances, if not the earliest one, was a seminar held in 1978 by the British Social Science Research Council and the Royal Statistical Society on problems in the collection and interpretation of recall data in social surveys (see Moss & Goldstein, 1979).

The next two important events occurred in the United States in 1980. The first was a workshop convened by the Bureau of Social Science Research in connection with its work in the redesign of the National Crime Victimization Survey sponsored by the National Institute of Justice and the Census Bureau (see Biderman, 1980). This workshop brought together cognitive scientists, survey statisticians, and methodologists to discuss what contributions cognitive scientists could make to understanding response errors in behavioral reports. The second event was the establishment of a panel on the measurement of subjective phenomena by the Committee on National Statistics at the National Research Council/National Academy of Sciences. This panel produced two large volumes (Turner & Martin, 1982) that have stimulated considerable research on response effects involved in the measurement of subjective phenomena. This work complements the work that had been stimulated by the earlier seminars on measuring behavior or more "objective" phenomena.

Further impetus for the development of more cognitive approaches to the study of response effects came from a six-day seminar, "Cognitive Aspects of Survey Methodology" (Jabine, Straf, Tanur, & Tourangeau, 1984) in St. Michael's, Maryland, sponsored by the Committee on National Statistics and funded by the National Science Foundation.

In Europe, independent work was going on in parallel directions. Schwarz and his colleagues at the University of Heidelberg and ZUMA, a German social science research center, were beginning to carry out cognitive experiments related to questionnaires. A seminar involving European psychologists with some participation by American researchers took place at ZUMA in the summer of 1984 (see Hippler, Schwarz, & Sudman, 1987). Several cognitively based conceptions of the interview task came out of these conferences (for example, Strack & Martin, 1987; Tourangeau, 1984, 1987) and provided a basic conceptual framework for much of the subsequent empirical work.

In the decade since these initial conferences, the development of the field has been rapid and vigorous. Several U.S. Government statistical agencies including the Census Bureau, the Bureau of Labor Statistics, and the National Center for Health Statistics now have cognitive laboratories for questionnaire improvement. Schwarz and Sudman organized additional conferences: "Context Effects in Social and Psychological Research" in 1989, "Autobiographical Memory and the Validity of Retrospective Reports" in 1991, and "Methods for Determining Cognitive Processes Used to

Answer Questions" in 1993 (see Schwarz & Sudman, 1992, 1994, 1995). The Social Science Research Council organized the Committee on Cognition and Survey research, which sponsored a series of cognitive conferences (Tanur, 1992).

By now, several major survey centers, in the U.S. as well as in Europe, have established cognitive laboratories to help with questionnaire development, and the first degree-granting program in survey methodology (the University of Maryland–University of Michigan Joint Program in Survey Methods) offers courses in cognitive and social psychology as part of its curriculum.

Conclusion

The utility of applying cognitive psychology to the study of survey measurement error is now well established. The time seems right, therefore, to pull together some of the work that has been done and try to develop a theoretical basis for integrating the work to date. By so doing, we hope to set the stage for the kind of cumulative knowledge that is the hallmark of science.

2

Methods for Determining Cognitive Processes and Questionnaire Problems

This chapter describes the methods developed to determine the cognitive processes involved when respondents answer survey questions and the difficulties caused by the research instrument. Schwarz and Sudman's (1995) *Answering Questions* describes these and other methods in more detail. There are other ways in which the chapter could be organized (Forsyth & Lessler, 1991). The organization we use sets the stage for the framework we develop more fully in the next chapter. We discuss in separate sections the methods used by researchers to learn how respondents interpret a question, retrieve information, form judgments, and edit their answers.

For each of these cognitive tasks, we describe the procedures used and evaluate their quality. Some researchers (Nisbett & Ross, 1980; Nisbett & Wilson, 1977) have challenged the idea that individuals can provide accurate introspective reports about their cognitive processes and have presented examples of experiments where respondents' reports about their thought processes were misleading. We will discuss these criticisms but believe the evidence is very strong that the methods that have been developed to date provide useful, although not perfect, information for understanding respondents' cognitive processes and improving questionnaires. These methods generally do not rely on respondents' introspective insights into their cognitive processes but elicit material from which the researcher can infer the processes used. We are not surprised or dismayed that these procedures have their own measurement errors; measurements of all kinds do. We describe what is currently known about these errors. As with response effects in surveys, future research may help us reduce these errors or, at least, understand them better.

An important issue for consideration is whether there is a Heisenberg effect. That is, does the process of trying to measure cognitive activities change these activities? We believe, and shall try to show, that most of the procedures currently used are nonreactive, although it is certainly possible to prime certain cognitive processes with very specific probes. There is a fine line between probes that help less articulate respondents explain what they are thinking and probes that lead respondents to think or at least report thinking in a given way. Survey researchers will find our discussion of probes here to be similar to the discussion of probes' effects on the survey process itself.

Overview of Methods Used

Although we will describe a variety of methods, by far the most common methods besides experiments are verbal protocols—usually called "thinkalouds" or "talkalouds"—which are obtained either concurrently or retrospectively. The most widely cited source on these procedures is *Protocol Analysis* by Ericsson and Simon (1993). In addition to describing their own work on these procedures, the authors describe the earlier use of introspection by William James and others dating to the late nineteenth century as well as early criticisms of this method.

Although most of the examples in Ericsson and Simon describe verbal protocols given by college students solving problems, the results are relevant to the survey processes described in this book. We discuss more specific findings in the later sections. One difference between the work of Ericsson and Simon and that of many survey researchers is in the samples from whom protocols are obtained. Their college student samples are, in general, highly verbal and able to provide rich protocols with limited prompting. When developing questionnaires, survey researchers who obtain verbal protocols from less well-educated respondents have generally been forced to do more directive probing.

Because understanding what a question is attempting to discover is the first stage in the respondent's cognitive answering process, much attention in questionnaire development today is given to determining through retrospective protocols what the respondent thinks the question means. The retrospective think-aloud procedures used are similar to those that have been used by Belson for the past three decades (see Belson, 1968, 1981, 1986). Some of the other procedures, such as tape-recording interviews and coding the interviewer-respondent interactions, go back to earlier work by Cannell, Fowler, and Marquis (1968; see Fowler & Cannell, 1995, for a recent review).

It should be evident from this brief review that no single method for measuring cognitive processes in surveys is completely new or unique. What is new are the combinations of procedures that are used along with theoretical frameworks that integrate these procedures.

Researchers who utilize these procedures sometimes work together in what are called *cognitive laboratories*, a phrase that has become popular in the past few years. Such laboratories are not especially distinguished by equipment, although they often contain rooms with preinstalled audio- and videotape equipment and one-way observation mirrors, and sometimes computers for measuring response latencies. Many cognitive observations can be made with only a small tape recorder and pencils and paper. What distinguishes a cognitive laboratory is the theoretical perspective adopted by the researchers and the use of the range of procedures to develop and pretest questionnaires that are described in this chapter.

Table 2.1 shows the four cognitive processes that respondents perform in answering questions and the primary research methods used to determine these cognitive processes.

TABLE 2.1 Methods for determining cognitive processes by task.

Method	Task I Comprehend/ interpret	II Retrieve	III Form judgment	IV Edit answer
Verbal protocols (Thinkalouds, talkalouds)				
Concurrent		*	*	
Retrospective	*	*	*	*
Behavioral coding				
Coders	*			
Computer coding	*	*		
Cognitive experts	*	*	*	*
Response latency methods		*	*	
Sorting		*		
Focus groups		*		
Experiments		*	*	

Question Interpretation

The three primary methods used to determine respondents' comprehension and interpretation of a question are *retrospective protocols, behavioral coding of respondent-interviewer interactions,* and *evaluation of questionnaire drafts by cognitive experts.*

Retrospective Protocols

Retrospective protocols provide information about the respondent's understanding of either a single word in the question or the question in its entirety. Alternatively, respondents may be asked to paraphrase the question, to put it into their own words. The best way to describe the method is with examples.

EXAMPLE 1

Q. Do you think that children suffer any ill effects from watching programs with violence in them, other than ordinary Westerns?

When asked "Tell me exactly how you arrived at that answer . . . how did you work it out . . . how exactly did you get to it?" half the respondents included Westerns in their answer. The word "children" was interpreted to include babies to teenagers to young people of age twenty. There were also some exclusive interpretations, including "children who have been brought up properly," "your own grandchildren," "nervous children," and "children such as your own" (Belson, 1986).

EXAMPLE 2

Q. How long have you used a wheelchair, cane, hearing aid?

Many respondents who used these devices reported using them intermittently. Some reported the time since the first use while others tried to add the periods of time together (Royston, 1989).

EXAMPLE 3

Q. In the last few weeks, how often did you feel excited—never, not too often, pretty often, or very often?

After giving an answer, respondents were asked how many times a day or week they meant by their answer. There were large overlaps with many people who answered "pretty often" reporting the same number of times as those who answered "not too often" (Bradburn & Miles, 1979).

EXAMPLE 4

Q. After the war is over, do you think people will have to work harder, the same, or not so hard as before?

This was followed by, "When you said that people would have to work [answer] were you thinking of people everywhere and in all walks of life—laborers, white-collar workers, farmers, and businessmen—or did you have in mind one class or group of people in particular?"

About half the respondents thought the question referred to everybody (Cantril & Fried, 1944).

EXAMPLE 5

Q. During the past year, have you been bothered by pain in your abdomen?

Respondents were shown a figure (see Figure 2.1) and asked to indicate on it the blocks of areas covering the abdomen. No two respondents shaded in the same set of blocks. The revised question was "Please look at this diagram. During the past twelve months, have you had pain in this area (the area shaded in the diagram)?" (See Figure 2.2; taken from Sirken, 1989.)

EXAMPLE 6

Q. How many hours did you work last week at all jobs?

After the interview, respondents were questioned further:

People have different ideas about what counts as hours worked. I'm going to read you some examples of activities that might or might not be included as hours worked. For each one please tell me whether you would include it in hours worked.

1. Commuting time, that is, time spent traveling to and from a person's main place of work?
2. Other local travel time, such as time a salesman might spend driving to see a customer?
3. Travel time for out-of-town trips, such as time spent waiting in airports and flying to another city?

FIGURE 2.1 Figure used to determine respondent understanding of area covered by abdomen.

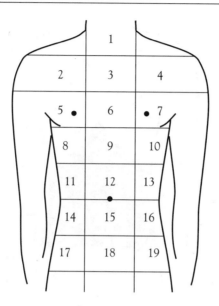

4. Time an analyst might spend working on a report in his office outside of normal working hours?
5. Time a teacher spends preparing lesson plans at home outside of normal working hours?
6. Time an engineer or doctor spends reading a professional journal at home?
7. Vacation time, sick leave, or other paid time off?

It may be noted that these questions range from general nondirective thinkalouds to more specific questions; the last example is perhaps the most detailed.

It is certainly possible that concurrent thinkalouds uncover some difficulties with understanding or interpreting questions, and, of course, such data are useful. However, we do not believe that concurrent thinkalouds can reliably replace retrospective thinkalouds.

Retrospective thinkalouds can be conducted with focus groups as well as with individuals but, aside from cost savings, those done

FIGURE 2.2 Revised figure used to determine abdominal pain.

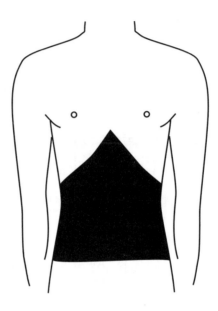

with focus groups offer little benefits; individual interviews provide more information per respondent and are not subject to group effects. Researchers who start with focus groups usually conduct individual thinkaloud interviews as a next step.

Coding Respondent-Interviewer Interaction

Cannell and his colleagues developed a procedure for coding tape-recorded interviews initially to evaluate interviewer performance (Cannell et al., 1968; Cannell & Oksenberg, 1988; Fowler & Cannell, 1995). The same procedure can be used for evaluating comprehension of the questionnaire (Morton-Williams & Sykes, 1984; Fowler, 1989) and it is usually used during pretests to improve the questionnaire. Essentially, ignoring the other interactions, coders look for two indications of problems with a question:

1. Respondents made remarks asking for clarification.

2. Respondents' answers to the question were inadequate.

The latter code indicates a problem with the question but the problem might or might not be related to comprehension. Some examples cited by Fowler (1989) are the following:

EXAMPLE 7

Q. What is the number of servings of eggs you eat in a typical day?

Almost one-third of respondents requested clarification. The main ambiguity lay in what constituted a serving of eggs. Respondents were also unclear on the term "typical day."

EXAMPLE 8

Q. What is the average number of days each week you have butter?

Initially, 18 percent of respondents requested clarification and 15 percent gave inadequate answers. The main point of ambiguity was whether margarine counted as butter. This question also caused retrieval problems.

EXAMPLE 9

After respondents reported on their last visit to a doctor, they were asked:
Q. Was that place a health maintenance organization or health care plan (that is, a place you go for all or most medical care, which is paid for by a fixed monthly or annual amount)?

About one out of six respondents had trouble understanding what constituted a health maintenance organization.

More recently, Bolton (1991) and Bolton and Bronkhurst (1995) have developed a procedure for coding some respondent difficulties automatically by computer. The procedure involves entering the tape-recorded interview verbatim into a computer, which searches for specified words or phrases that indicate respondents are having comprehension difficulties. Figure 2.3 shows the words and phrases. In addition, Bolton also coded, as did Cannell and his associates, when the respondent asked the interviewer a question.

Cognitive Experts

It has long been common for researchers developing survey questionnaires to seek input from fellow researchers, either individually or in group settings. More recently efforts have been made to evaluate draft questionnaires from a cognitive perspective using experts. A coding scheme has been developed by Forsyth, Lessler, and Hubbard (1992) (see also Lessler & Forsyth, 1995) and their colleagues at the Research Triangle Institute (RTI) using the four-stage framework described in this book, with one modification. Figure 2.4 shows the codes they use for problems with comprehension and definition of the cognitive task.

The authors illustrate the use of their coding procedure with the following example:

EXAMPLE 10

Q. On the average, during most of this period when you smoked daily, about how many cigarettes did you smoke per day? (IF NEEDED, READ ANSWER CHOICES.)

One to five cigarettes a day

About ½ pack a day (6–15 cigarettes)

About a pack a day (16–25 cigarettes)

About 1½ packs a day (26–35 cigarettes)

About 2 packs or more a day (over 35 cigarettes)

Forsyth, Lessler, & Hubbard, 1992

FIGURE 2.3 Coding categories used to indicate respondent cognitive difficulties.

Repeat	High frequency	No problems
repeat	always	no:problem
say:that:again	occasionally	no:problems
listen:to:&again	everyday	don't:have&problem
hear:that:again	frequently	only:problem
ask:that	repeatedly	not&problem
what&mean	daily	not&problems
explain	hourly	never&problem
interpret	every:day	haven't&problem
define	perpetually	haven't&problems
comment	continually	few&problems
I:don't:think:I:got:you	constantly	didn't:have:problem
what&looking:for	incessantly	didn't:have:problems
what:was&again	at:all:times	no:complaint
do:you:mean	night:and:day	no:complaints
are:you:talking	commonly	don't&complaint
are&talking:about	habitually	don't&complaints
asking	in:general	only:complaint
about:the:question	several	never:complaint
that:word	normally	never&complaints
is:that:what:you're:asking	usually	few&complaints
problem&question	all:the:time	not&complaints
in:terms:of	every:time	didn't&complaint
so:it:says	often	didn't&complaints
in:other:words		haven't&complaint
how&evaluate		haven't&complaints
how&rate		not&complaint
I:misunderstood		nothing:wrong
I:misunderstand		anything:wrong
I:thought:you:said		something:wrong
don't:understand		didn't&wrong
		nothing:wrong
		never&wrong
		not&wrong
		hasn't&wrong
		no:mistake
		no:mistakes
		didn't&mistake

FIGURE 2.3 Coding categories used to indicate respondent cognitive difficulties (*continued*).

Similar	Low frequency	Can't say
identical&question	seldom	I:can't:say
same&question	never	I:can't:tell
similar&question	sometimes	I:can't:rate
identical&answer	at:times	I:can't:evaluate
same&answer	every:now:and:then	I:can't:judge
similar&answer	once:in:a:while	tough&rate
answer&again	now:and:then	not:easy&rate
sound&alike	time:to:time	difficult&rate
question&close	often:enough	hard&rate
sound&identical	every:so:often	tough&evaluate
I&answered&that&question	few	not:easy&evaluate
like:I:said	rarely	difficult&evaluate
like:I:said&before	little	hard&evaluate
experience:again	one:or:two	tough:to:say
opinion:again	once	not:easy&to:say
there:again	one:time	difficult:to:say
repetitious	one:instance	hard:to:say
	one:incident	rough&judge
		not:easy&judge
		difficult&judge
		hard&judge
		tough&to:tell
		not:easy&to:tell
		difficult&to:tell
		hard&to:tell

Forget	Expect	Don't know
forget	I&assume	I:don't:know
don't:remember	I&expect	I:wouldn't:know
can't:think	assumption	not:know
I'm:trying:to:think	anticipate	
	predict	
	expectation	

FIGURE 2.3 Coding categories used to indicate respondent cognitive difficulties (*continued*).

No experience	Confidence	Certain
no:experience	probably	I'm:certain
never:experienced	approximately	definitely
not:experienced	maybe	I'm:sure
any:experience	perhaps	
never:experience	I:guess	
not:experience	kind:of	
haven't:experienced	assume	
not:familiar:with	unless	
no:need:for&service	somewhere:in:there	
no:need:for&option	I:reckon	
never:use	not:certain	
never:done	I&imagine	
never:used	depends	
don't:use	mostly	
haven't:used	sort:of	
	not:sure	
	whatever	
	or:something	

Problems	Difficult
problem	difficult&question
problems	hard&question
complaint	tough&question
complaints	that's:a:hard:one
mistake	that's:a:tough:one
mistakes	hard:to:deal:with
qualm	not:easy&question
qualms	isn't:easy&question
discrepancy	
discrepancies	
wrong	

FIGURE 2.4 Expert Questionnaire Appraisal Coding System.

Comprehension	Retrieval	Judgment	Response Generation
Establish reference set boundaries. Establish reference set period boundaries.	Retrieval of information.	Evaluate retrieved information.	Establish response set boundaries. Generate response.
Reference set	*Task requirements*	*Task requirements*	*Task requirements*
Task requirements	*Retrieval task*	*Type of judgment process*	*Response description*
Reference set type	Remember episode	Estimate total	Yes/no
Current characteristic/behavior	Remember set of episode	Determine +/−occurrence	Qualitative: category
Past characteristic/behavior	Remember general information	Determine +/−match	Qualitative: ordinal
Current attitude/opinion	Remember previous answer	Determine date/onset	Qualitative: open
Past attitude/opinion	Recall attitude	Determine age	Quantitative: count
General knowledge		Estimate duration	Quantitative: complex
	Memory process	Estimate average	Duration
Focus	Recall	Complex estimation	Time point
Self-report	Recognition		Age
Proxy report	Heuristic/inference	*Information integration*	Answer hidden question
	Mixed above	Count	
Reference set level		Qualitative judgment	*Potential problems*
Basic	*Memory content*	Quantitative judgment	*Instructions*
Subordinate	General self-knowledge		Hidden instructions
Superordinate	General world knowledge	*Potential problems*	Hidden definitions
Multilevel	Specific behavior (or try)	*Information evaluation*	
	Class of behavior	Accuracy evaluation	*Responses*
		Sensitive behavior	

Comprehension — Potential problems cont'd.

Question Structure:	*Problem summary*
Hidden question	Vague reference set
Complex syntax	Complex reference set
Implicit assumption	Constant behavior/implement
Several questions	Nonsalient attitude
Several definitions	
Unclear goal	
Q/A mismatch	
Violates con coven	

Reference set changes
Domain change
Level change
Abrupt change
Carry-over ref. set

Potential problems

Instructions
Conflicting instructions
Inaccurate instructions
Hidden instructions
Complex syntax
Unclear examples
Unclear layout

Questions
Technical Terms:
Present
Undefined
Ambiguous or vague

Reference period
Task requirements

Specified period
Lifetime
12-months
30-days

Potential problems

Instructions
Today
Tied to behavior/prev. Q
Undefined: e.g., currently

Reference period changes
Change from prior Q:
No change
Wider
Narrower
Distal boundary
Proximal boundary

Potential problems
Unanchored boundary
Nonfixed boundaries
Ill-defined period
Undefined period
Embedded period
Carry over ref. period

Affect/attitude
Time point/interval

Potential problems
High detail
Low detail
Unexpected detail
Shift: psychological reference
period

Sensitive attitude
Sensitive (general)
Socially undesirable

Consequence evaluation
Safety consequences
Legal consequences
Social consequences
Behavioral consequences

Information/response congruence
Incongruent

Terminology:
Technical terms
Undefined terms
Ambiguous/vague terms

Response Structure:
Boundary problems
Overlapping categories
Missing categories
Nondominant order

The staff at RTI coded several question characteristics that could interfere with comprehension:

1. The term "average" is a technical term that is not explicitly defined. It may also be ambiguous because it can be interpreted either according to its technical definition or more informally as "roughly."

2. The response categories refer to numbers of "packs" of cigarettes, which may be a vague term. The response categories are coded as ambiguous because a single respondent's conception of "packs" of cigarettes may not correspond to the parenthetical category definitions. The response categories also contain hidden definitions because the parenthetical definitions will not be read if the interviewer does not think they are needed.

3. The embedded clauses in the question give it a complex syntax.

Evaluation of Cognitive Procedures for Measuring Comprehension

The methods used for measuring comprehension and uncovering problems in questionnaires—retrospective protocols, coding respondent-interviewer interactions, and cognitive experts—all have desirable properties and no important drawbacks, which explains why they have already been widely adopted. Ideally, they should be used in combination, with the experts' evaluation first, the retrospective thinkalouds second, and the evaluation of tape-recorded pretests third.

However, the richest information comes from actual respondents. Of course, retrospective questions do not ask respondents to report whether they understood the question but to explain what the question meant to them. Often respondents who do not understand a question hesitate to report this to the interviewer or ask for clarification because they think it will make them look stupid. More important, respondents who misinterpret a question may never be aware of it. For this reason, misunderstandings are rarely identified in regular survey pretests unless they result in obviously inadequate answers. Similarly, the procedure for coding of pretest interviews may only identify some comprehension problems, picking up only a fraction of the total confusion.

In general, the methods described in this section allow researchers to identify cognitive difficulties but do not necessarily provide solutions. Moreover, attempting to solve one comprehension problem can sometimes lead to another. For example, explaining an ambiguous term (such as "butter") leads to additional clauses in the question (such as "not including margarine") that may make the question more complex or that respondents may forget or ignore. A possible solution is to split the now-complex question into two or more simpler questions.

It is often tempting, especially when there is time pressure, to assume that revised versions of questions do not need the same testing as the original questions did. But this can sometimes lead to even worse questions, as illustrated in an example reported by Fowler (1989).

EXAMPLE 11

ORIGINAL Q. During the past twelve months, that is, since January 1, 1987, about how many days did illness or injury keep you in bed more than half of the day? (Include days while an overnight patient in a hospital.)

In its initial form, 7 percent of respondents gave inadequate answers while 15 percent requested clarification about what was meant by "half of the day" and whether extra time in bed for vague illnesses rather than specific conditions should be included. As a result, the following revised version was asked:

REVISED Q. The next question is about extra time you have spent in bed because of illness or injury (including time spent in the hospital). During the past twelve months, since July 1, 1987, on about how many days did you spend several extra hours in bed because you were sick, injured, or just not feeling well?

The new version was significantly more complex. As a result, 30 percent of interviews had inadequate answers and 17 percent of respondents asked for clarification. This illustrates the necessity for continuing the testing process until the results are reasonably satisfactory. Of course, it should be noted that this question posed a difficult recall task in addition to the comprehension problem.

The procedures described in this section seem sufficiently powerful to detect most comprehension problems in survey questions but we need to be cautious in any efforts to quantify levels of miscomprehension. To date, we are not aware of efforts to measure the reliability, let alone the validity, of the cognitive coding used at RTI. Retrospective thinkalouds appear to have high face validity, but here also there have been no measures of reliability. There have been measures of intercoder reliability in the coding of pretest respondent-interviewer behavior and these intercoder reliabilities are high. Computer coding is still more reliable. As we have already pointed out, however, the measures used are only a partial indication of comprehension.

Interactions Between Cognitive Data and Substantive Results

It is clear that the procedures in this section do not have any effects on the substantive data. The coding of questionnaires by cognitive experts is completely noninteractive and the only possible effects of the coding of pretests would be in the use of a tape recorder. Tape-recording interviews, even those on very sensitive topics, has been done for decades with no evidence that it affects response. Virtually all interviewers report that respondents almost immediately forget the presence of the machine.

The retrospective thinkalouds are initiated either immediately after the interview is completed or during the interview after a question or series of questions is answered. If initiated after the interview, there can be no possible effects on the answers given during the interview, even if the questions are directive. If initiated after a question or series of questions, there can be no effect on the question(s) just answered but there is some possibility of effects on related, following questions. For this reason, we recommend conducting retrospective thinkalouds at the end of the interview or at the end of a section of related questions. Issues of memory are not as critical here as they are in retrieval processes (addressed in the next section). It is highly unlikely that respondents' understanding of a question or parts of a question will change in a few minutes unless subsequent questions provide additional information or cues. In the latter case, however, respondents' interpretation of the question may be affected by the new material, rendering unclear the extent to which their retrospective reports reflect their initial interpretation.

Retrieval Strategies

A variety of cognitive procedures are used to determine how respondents retrieve information from memory. A method that has received extensive attention and use in the past few years is concurrent or retrospective verbal protocols (thinkalouds or talkalouds). In conjunction with thinkalouds, measurements of response latencies provide information on how much cognitive processing is occurring and measurements of unstructured sorting tasks indicate how data are stored in memory. Preceding the development of a questionnaire, the use of cognitive ideas to structure and understand what occurs in focus groups has also become increasingly prevalent. Experiments, with and without thinkalouds, can sometimes be used to determine the cognitive processes used. Finally, cognitive experts are also useful in evaluating potential retrieval problems, as described in the preceding section.

Concurrent and Retrospective Thinkalouds

In the standard unprompted thinkaloud, respondents are told that the researcher is interested not only in their answers but also in the methods used to arrive at them. Here is a version that we have used that is very similar to the one used by most researchers: "We are interested in your answers, but also how you go about making them. I'd like to ask you to think aloud as you answer each question and tell me everything that comes to your mind in answering the question. The more you can tell us, the more useful it will be to us as we try to develop better questions. Okay? The first question is . . ."

Ericsson and Simon (1980) and others have suggested the use of warm-up exercises—asking subjects to think aloud while determining the number of windows in their homes, for example. We have found this an unnatural start to a thinkaloud interview. Instead we have used the first few questions on our questionnaire as natural warm-ups and provided feedback to respondents to encourage concurrent thinkalouds.

Some respondents, usually those with higher levels of education and greater verbal facility, find this an easy and interesting process and give rich protocols. Others, however, need prompting, turning what is intended to be a concurrent thinkaloud into a retrospective thinkaloud. That is, some respondents answer the question very quickly but do not report their thought processes. Our standard undirected probe is "How did you go about answering that question?" It should be noted that some respondents who provide unprompted verbal protocols do so after answering the question, thus muddying the distinction between concurrent and retrospective thinkalouds.

Even retrospective thinkalouds should come immediately after the question is answered. It is unrealistic to assume that respondents can remember how they retrieved information for one question after proceeding with additional questions.

For some purposes, we have found it necessary to use directed probes. Thus, for questions on autobiographical memory of frequency of behavior (see the discussion in Chapters Seven and Eight), we have attempted to determine whether respondents try to count individual events or estimate. If the thinkaloud response is insufficient, the interviewer uses the following probes:

"Did you try to count each time you did [event], or did you just make an estimate?"
IF ESTIMATE: "How did you make your estimate?"

Coding Thinkalouds

As with all open questions, it is necessary to have a coding procedure to summarize responses. We think it unlikely that a universal coding scheme can be developed because the topics of the questionnaire as well as the cognitive processes being studied will vary. Blair and Burton (1987) and Means and Loftus (1991) have given examples of procedures they have used. In our own work on proxies we have developed a similar but more detailed coding scheme (Bickart et al., 1989; Blair, Menon, & Bickart, 1991; Blair et al., 1991; Menon et al., 1990, 1995). For this purpose we developed a questionnaire dealing with a broad range of behavioral and attitudinal questions. Respondents reported about themselves and their spouses and gave concurrent and retrospective thinkaloud responses with some prompting.

The coding scheme we developed is given as Figure 2.5. Up to three codes were possible for each answer. Obviously some of the codes were conditional on the type of question and thinkaloud answer given. For example, event cues applied only if respondents reported using counting strategies; most anchoring strategy codes related to attitude questions about self and proxy.

FIGURE 2.5 Coding scheme for thinkaloud responses.

Code	Description
	10s: Automatic response
11	Automatic
12	Event did not occur/nonevent
13	Retrieveal of prior judgment
14	No probe, therefore no protocol
15	Don't know
16	Not applicable (for skips)
	20s: Counting strategies
21	General recall and count
24	Counting with adjustment for uncertainty
25	Counting with expression of uncertainty (no adjustment)
22	Counting by domain
26	Counting by domain with adjustment for uncertainty
27	Counting by domain with expression of uncertainty (no adjustment)
23	Counting by observation
	30s: Rate-based estimates
31	General rate-based estimation
33	Rate-based estimation with adjustment based on specific incident (addition/s to estimate)
34	Rate-based estimation with adjustment based on general knowledge
35	Rate-based estimation with adjustment based on non-occurrence (subtraction/s from estimate)
36	Rate-based estimation with adjustment for uncertainty
37	Rate-based estimation with expression of uncertainty (no adjustment)
32	Rate-based estimation by domain
38	Rate-based estimation by domain with adjustment for uncertainty
39	Rate-based estimation by domain with expression of uncertainty (no adjustment)

FIGURE 2.5 Coding scheme for thinkaloud responses (*continued*).

Code	Description
	40s: Enumeration-based estimates
41	General enumeration-based estimation
43	Enumeration-based estimation with adjustment based on specific incident (addition/s to estimate)
44	Enumeration-based estimation with adjustment based on general knowledge
45	Enumeration-based estimation with adjustment based on nonoccurrence (subtraction/s from estimate)
46	Enumeration-based estimation with adjustment for uncertainty
47	Enumeration-based estimation with expression of uncertainty (no adjustment)
42	Enumeration-based estimation by domain
	50s: Anchoring strategies
51	Same as self
52	Based on prior answer
53	Anchor on self and adjust
54	Anchor on norm and adjust
55	Anchor on another specific person and adjust
56	Anchor on proxy and adjust
	60s: Miscellaneous for attitude questions
61	Based on specific behavior/event
62	Based on discussions with other
63	Based on general knowledge
64	Based on attitude toward issue
	70s: Search strategies
71	No order/search
72	Forward search
73	Backward search

FIGURE 2.5 Coding scheme for thinkaloud responses (*continued*).

Code	Description
74	Anchor on date and forward search
75	Anchor on date and backward search
76	Search by domain
77	Based on another event
78	Based on regularity of behavior
	80s: Event cues (for counting strategies)
81	Person mentioned
82	Place mentioned
83	Emotional reaction to event mentioned
84	Time of event occurrence mentioned
85	Characteristic of event mentioned
86	Based on prior response (one answer triggers another)
87	Based on cues used from question
	90s: Reference period
91	Anchor date on public event
92	Anchor date on personal event
93	Anchor date on season of the year
	General characteristic of event/person (for estimation strategies):
94	"Always ..."
95	"Never ..."
96	"Nowadays ..."/"Usually ..."

In general, developing codes for verbal protocols is similar to coding open-ended questions in surveys (Bickart & Felcher, 1995). The researcher who develops the codes starts with a theoretical perspective and then examines samples of the protocols to establish preliminary codes. These codes are then modified, if necessary, to handle new protocols as they are processed.

Evaluation of Thinkalouds

Obviously, there are no direct ways to validate thinkalouds. The strongest claim that can be made for thinkalouds related to retrieval is that they have consistently given results that make good sense theoretically; that is, the results are not simply noise or artifacts of the method. Many of the findings given in subsequent chapters of this book were made through thinkaloud methods. Furthermore, other methods such as response latency methods (see the following section) tend to confirm thinkaloud reports. The findings of others using verbal protocols support these conclusions (Ericsson & Simon, 1984).

There is no evidence to suggest that respondents report retrieving information that they did not actually retrieve in answering a question. This does not necessarily mean that thinkalouds give complete explanations. We often observe that the process of responding to a survey question is so rapid that it is not surprising if some of the information retrieved remains unreported. As with other survey questions, using aided recall methods increases completeness.

The information retrieved from memory to answer a question must be readily accessible to a respondent to be reported in thinkalouds. If not, it may have a significant impact on judgment and not be mentioned. Many psychological experiments demonstrate that factors influencing responses, such as mood (Schwarz & Clore, 1983), context cues from earlier questions in the questionnaire (Schwarz & Sudman, 1992), and a variety of other factors (Nisbett & Bellows, 1977; Nisbett & Wilson, 1977) are not retrieved and reported by respondents.

Respondents are reasonably reliable informants about how successful their retrieval efforts have been. Respondents' confidence in their answers has usually been found to relate to accuracy when results are validated (for example, Blair et al., 1991). Confidence is also related to reported retrieval methods.

To date, we are unaware of attempts to measure the reliability of thinkalouds. To design such a reliability study would be difficult if the time period between protocols were short because people prefer not to repeat information in conversations. It is also difficult to know the effect of verbalizing thought processes about a particular question on later cognition about the topic. In contrast, with regard to coding processes, it is possible to measure intercoder reliability. In our proxy study described earlier, we found high intercoder reliability (0.8 or greater) for broad categorizations but, as expected, somewhat lower reliabilities for the finer ones.

Interactions Between Verbal Protocols and Substantive Results

As far as anyone has been able to determine, neither concurrent nor retrospective thinkalouds change the *kinds* of strategies used by respondents to retrieve information. The one possible effect is that thinkalouds may spur respondents to make a greater cognitive effort to retrieve information. Most survey respondents are cognitive misers (Krosnick, 1991), doing just enough retrieval to come up with an answer that they think is acceptable. Questions about the process they use may increase this level of effort, a possible Hawthorne effect. There was some indication of this in our proxy study but the results were inconclusive. Although it is possible to design response latency experiments to test this effect, we are unaware of any such studies.

Other Methods

In this section we describe a few other methods, including coding respondent-interviewer interactions, response latency measures, sorting tasks, and focus groups.

Coding Respondent-Interviewer Interactions. Bolton (1991), as described earlier, transcribed interviews and then used a computer to code words and phrases to indicate cognitive difficulties. The words and phrases she used as indicators of retrieval difficulties are given in Figure 2.3. As with comprehension, this procedure gives only a partial indicator of retrieval difficulties, although it is very useful in spotting hard questions and in determining whether the difficulty of revised questions is lower.

Response Latency Measures. When respondents enter answers into a computer, available programs allow measurement of how long it takes them to answer a question from the time it appears on the screen to the time a key on the keyboard is activated. Fazio (1990) and Bassili (1995) provide excellent introductions to this methodology, which has recently been successfully adopted for use in telephone interviews (see Bassili, 1995). Response latency time, adjusted at an individual level for the respondent's normal speed of reaction, is a measure of the level of cognitive effort used by the respondent. Response latency measures have been used widely in studies of information processing (see Aaker et al., 1980; MacLachlan, Czepid, & LaBarbera, 1979; Tyebjee, 1979).

It is difficult when using response latency measures to distinguish between time spent in retrieving information and time spent in forming a judgment. One would expect to find that the response time would be lowest for an answer stored in memory that requires no additional processing—the respondent's date of birth or address, for example. Estimation procedures should usually take less time than counting individual episodes because fewer distinct events must be retrieved. When estimating, regular events require less time to retrieve than do irregular events because again there is less to retrieve (see Menon, 1991, 1994).

An alternative procedure used by Bolton (1991) was to tape-record the interview and code pauses of more than three seconds or broken utterances. A broken utterance is when a respondent stops in the middle of a sentence and begins a new one ("I've never—oh! I remember!"). Pauses and broken utterances are mainly indications of retrieval difficulties.

Evaluation of Response Latency Measures. As physical measures of response time, response latencies are highly reliable and valid. The problem in using them is in interpreting what they tell us about the underlying cognitive processes. Although some researchers have used response latencies as their only measure in carefully designed experiments, we believe that for measuring cognitive responses to survey questions they are best used in conjunction with thinkalouds. This use of two quite different methods increases the convergent validity of both procedures. One highly desirable characteristic of latency measures is that they are completely invisible to the respondent and, thus, nonreactive.

An alternative procedure is to count pauses and broken utterances when interviews are tape-recorded. Along with other methods used simultaneously, this procedure is useful in identifying questions with problems and testing the value of revised questions.

Sorting Tasks. Survey researchers often search for cues that will aid respondents' recall. For aided recall to be effective, researchers need to know what kinds of information are linked together in memory networks so that retrieving one piece of information makes it easier to retrieve something else that the researcher is looking for. Sorting tasks and focus groups (described in the next section) are procedures for obtaining information on these mental networks. Again, the method is best illustrated with an example (see Brewer & Lui, 1995, for a comprehensive introduction).

Brewer, Dull, and Jobe (1989) studied how chronic illnesses are categorized by respondents using free sort and dimensional sorting tasks. In the free sort task, respondents were given a stack of sixty-eight cards listing specific chronic conditions. (If they indicated they had not heard of a condition, a standardized definition was read.) They were then asked to sort the conditions into "piles based on how you think they should go together," with no limit on the number of piles. There were no time constraints.

The individual clusters were subjected to a hierarchical cluster analysis program and twelve clusters emerged. These are shown in Figure 2.6. It was then possible to compare this clustering with the clusters used by experts in the International Classification of Diseases, 9th Revision (ICD-9) and in the National Health Interview

FIGURE 2.6 Chronic conditions, by organization resulting from hierarchical cluster analysis—twelve-cluster solution.

Cluster 1

Arthritis or rheumatism
Lumbago
Sciatica
Bursitis
Migraine
Neuralgia or neuritis

Cluster 2

Slipped disk
Bunions
Curvature of spine
Cleft palate
Clubfoot

Cluster 3

Eczema or psoriasis
Acne
Dermatitis
Herpes
Syphilis

Cluster 4

Gallstones
Cirrhosis
Hepatitis
Jaundice
Nephritis
Kidney stones

Cluster 5

Ulcer
Hernia
Gastritis
Enteritis
Diverticulitis
Colitis
Hemorrhoids

Cluster 6

Bronchitis
Asthma
Hay fever
Sinusitis
Tonsilitis
Emphysema
Pleurisy
Tuberculosis

Cluster 7

Rheumatic fever
Hardening arteries
Coronary heart disease
Hypertension
Stroke
Brain hemorrhage
Angina pectoris
Myocardial infarction—
    heart attack
Damaged heart valve
Tachycardia
Heart murmur
Aneurysm

Cluster 8

Anemia
Blood clots
Varicose veins
Phlebitis

Cluster 9

Cataracts
Glaucoma

Cluster 10

Cerebral palsy
Diabetes
Epilepsy
Multiple sclerosis

Cluster 11

Skin cancer
Cancer of the stomach, etc.
Breast cancer
Cancer of prostate
Cancer of uterus
Lung cancer
Leukemia

Cluster 12

Gout
Goiter

Survey. Respondent sortings matched the ICD-9 closely but there were interesting exceptions. Because they were lay people, respondents focused more on external symptoms than on underlying physiological systems.

Following the free sort, participants were asked to sort the conditions again in a set of structured-sorting tasks for seven different scales. The seven scales were the following:

1. Perceived incidence (four points from extremely common to extremely rare)
2. Perceived painfulness (four points from very painful to not at all painful)
3. Perceived seriousness (four points from major to minor)
4. Perceived severity (four points from disabling to not at all disabling)
5. Embarrassment (three points from definitely embarrassing to not at all embarrassing)
6. Perceived controllability (three points from definitely controllable to definitely not controllable)
7. Perceived likelihood of contracting the condition (four points from very unlikely to already has the condition or has had it in the past)

Although sorting was used here, these are simply rating scales that could be obtained in other ways on a computer or paper questionnaire. Again, the conditions were clustered using profile analysis. Brewer and her colleagues concluded that although the clusters obtained in this way had some meaning, the procedure was inferior to the free sort procedure in capturing how people perform natural sorting.

Evaluation of Sorting Procedures. As the example illustrates, free sort procedures appear to tap into the way that many people store things in memory, although it is also clear that not everyone does so in the same way. Dimensional sorting is less effective because it imposes constraints on sorting that do not match natural techniques.

The value of knowing how information is stored is that it should help develop questionnaires that use this information to improve retrieval. To date, however, we are unaware of any surveys where this has been attempted.

Focus Groups. Focus groups have been widely used for a long time as a method for developing meaningful questionnaires. Although they are used for a variety of purposes, we believe that focus groups are most useful in conjunction with thinkalouds for determining how respondents retrieve information.

In a typical focus group, a moderator working from a discussion guide raises a series of broad topics for discussion with a group of about six to twelve participants. The moderator then lets the participants answer without any directed prompting, stepping in only if the discussion strays too far afield. Focus groups normally last from about one and a half to two hours. We illustrate with an example from some recent work on health prevention procedures (Sudman et al., 1993). Krueger (1994) and Stewart and Shamdasani (1990) provide general introductions to the use of focus groups.

EXAMPLE 12

As part of a supplement to the National Health Interview Survey, female respondents are asked questions about several cancer screening procedures including Pap smears, breast examinations, and mammograms. Each of the procedures is treated separately with a series of questions.

In focus groups, women over the age of fifty were asked questions about what they did to prevent illnesses and the procedures they used for early detection of diseases. For many but not all participants Pap smears, breast examinations, and mammograms were mentioned as being part of a general physical or gynecological examination. In drafting a questionnaire for use with thinkalouds, the researchers started with questions related to physical and gynecological examinations as a method for cueing respondents to the procedures they were interested in.

Evaluation of Focus Groups. Although a few researchers have argued that focus groups are sufficient by themselves, we do not agree. Focus group results cannot be quantified and are not completely trustworthy because of the small number of participants and the unrepresentative nature of those who are willing to participate. Also, there are always potential problems with group interactions. Some particularly verbal persons in a group may dominate the discussion and lead its direction even if the moderator tries to get everyone to participate equally.

Nevertheless, researchers listening to focus groups are often alerted to issues that they might otherwise have ignored. These are issues that can then be explored in thinkaloud interviews. That is why we believe that combining focus groups with other methods, especially thinkalouds, increases the value of all of the methods.

Experiments. The traditional method of understanding cognitive processes has been through experimentation where the experimental measures are the responses given by subjects to the experimental stimuli, which can, of course, include survey questions. It is also possible to use the other measures discussed in this section such as thinkalouds and response latency measures as measures of experimental effects.

The key difference between experimental and nonexperimental methods is that experiments are designed to provide information on the cognitive processes over and above what respondents report in verbal protocols. We do not give examples here since many of the results reported in the other chapters in this book are based on experiments.

Evaluation of Experiments. The strengths and weaknesses of experiments have been discussed extensively. The obvious power of experiments is the use of designs to eliminate alternative explanations of the cognitive behavior observed. The primary potential weakness of experiments is that they may be unrealistic and not generalizable to other situations and populations.

The typical psychological experiment has been conducted with college students. We believe students are a good population to start with because these subjects are both available and able to follow complicated instructions. For many situations, however, we believe it is necessary to continue experiments with more representative samples selected from the general population. This is especially the case when there may be differences in cognitive methods used by different subjects with different cognitive abilities. For example, Knäuper and Wittchen (1994) observed that older respondents had more difficulty understanding some of the questions of a standardized medical interview than did younger respondents, resulting in misdiagnoses.

Cognitive Experts.   Continuing the discussion begun in the previous section, cognitive experts can be used to identify potential retrieval methods and problems respondents might have with these methods. Figure 2.4 gives the RTI codes developed for this stage.

Judgment Formation

Judgments are of two kinds. Respondents can make judgments about their behavior or about their attitudes toward persons, groups, or things. Most of the psychological research that has been done concentrates on attitudes. There are really only two ways in which researchers can attempt to measure judgment formation, through thinkalouds and through experimentation. As we discuss in the following section, using thinkalouds for describing judgment formation is widespread but remains somewhat controversial. Our view on the issue is a tempered one; that is, we believe that in some situations respondents can report how they made a judgment and in other situations they cannot. The task is to specify the situation in which thinkalouds are useful. We do not discuss experiments specifically in this section. As for retrieval processes, the use of experiments to determine judgment formation is described in other chapters. It is also possible for cognitive experts to speculate about how judgments are formed but at this stage in our knowledge the ways in which people make judgments are still far from fully understood. Except to refer to Figure 2.4, we say nothing more about cognitive experts in this section. As we indicated earlier, latency measures are used to measure both retrieval and judgment times, and it is generally not possible to separate the two processes using time measures.

Thinkalouds

Behavioral questions. When asking behavioral questions, we start with the assumption that the respondent does not have the answer already stored in memory. When the answer is simply retrieved, no one can be expected to recall how that answer was formed since it was formed at a much earlier time. Nor do we pay much attention to a question such as "Did you ever do . . . ?" Here the process appears to be obvious; respondents search through their memories for any example of the event and stop when they find one. If they can recall no example after their limited search, they report that no event occurred.

The judgment process becomes more complex when respondents are asked about frequencies of events, such as "How many times did you . . . in the past week?" We believe, however, that most respondents can report with reasonable accuracy how they combined the information they have just retrieved. We give examples of the kinds of answers respondents give that have good face validity. It should be noted, however, that this does not mean that the behavior report is correct, because the data retrieved may be incomplete or the schema selected may be inappropriate.

EXAMPLE 13

1. *Reports of simple addition.* "I went to the doctor last week for a regular checkup and once before for an attack of flu. So that's twice in the last year." "I read two *News-Gazettes* last

week, one *New York Times,* and three *Daily News.* So that's
six newspapers in the last week."
2. *Rate-based estimation.* "I read the newspaper every day so I
   read it seven times last week."
3. *Rate-based estimation with addition or subtraction.* "He normally reads the newspaper every day but last week he was
   out of town for a day. So he must have read six newspapers."
4. *Enumeration-based estimation.* "I ate in a restaurant for lunch
   yesterday and dinner on Monday. So that's twice a week. I'd
   say that I ate in a restaurant about eight times last month."

It is tempting in trying to determine the judgment rules used by
respondents to consider prompting questions but we believe that
only nondirective questions are appropriate. Any suggestion to
respondents about methods they might use to make judgments is
likely to cause these methods to be overreported.

In addition to the strategies, respondents may rely on other
heuristics to determine an answer. One is to pick an initial value
that is subsequently adjusted. This strategy is known as "anchoring
and adjustment" (Tversky & Kahneman, 1974). We identified the
use of this strategy in our coding of proxy reporting (see Figure 2.6).

EXAMPLE 14

Some examples of anchoring strategies are the following:
1. *On self.* "She watches the same amount of TV as I do."
2. *On self and adjust.* "She is more in favor of women's rights
   groups than I am."
3. *On prior answer.* "I said three for labor unions so I'll rate
   environmental groups five."

Evaluation of Thinkalouds to Measure Judgment Formation.   A
major challenge to thinkaloud methods has come from researchers
such as Nisbett and his colleagues (Nisbett & Bellows, 1977; Nisbett
& Ross, 1980; Nisbett & Wilson, 1977; for a recent extension, see
Wilson, LaFleur, & Anderson, 1995). They show that certain attributes not mentioned by the respondents affect judgment formation;

we have discussed this situation earlier and believe that it relates to imperfect reports of memory retrieval. They also provide examples of situations where respondents claim that certain attributes influenced their judgments although the experimental design demonstrates that this was not the case; this error is explained by Nisbett and colleagues as resulting from respondents simply choosing a plausible judgment rule. To us, this is another way of saying that respondents sometimes use schemata, with possible adjustments, to retrieve their judgment processes just as they may have used schemata at the previous stage to retrieve rates of behavior and schemata to select a judgment rule. The issue then becomes how well the retrieved schemata (with adjustments, if any) represent what the respondent actually did in a specific instance. In many cases, the retrieved schemata are a good representation of what occurred in the specific judgment formation. We are not surprised, however, that there is measurement error in reports of judgment rules so that sometimes rules reported by respondents are not identical to the rules they actually followed.

One common error that we have observed in our proxy study and in several examples in the literature is that respondents may confuse ease of retrieval of information with influence in judgment formation. That is, respondents report retrieving some information about a person or product and assume that "if I can remember it, it must have influenced my judgment." Although often true, this generalization is not always true.

Defenders of thinkalouds provide other examples of cases where there is close or reasonably close agreement between the reports of the judgment rules and the other data indicating how the judgment was formed. In such studies, respondents are usually asked for overall evaluations, for evaluations of specific aspects of the person or object, and for the rule believed to have been followed in making the judgment. The correlation between the overall evaluation based on combining aspects according to the respondent's rule and the actual overall evaluation is the measure of how well the respondent reported the rule (for example, Weitz & Wright, 1979; Cook & Stewart, 1975).

Researchers such as Ericsson and Simon who support think-alouds also point out that in many of the studies cited by Nisbett and colleagues there is a fairly long time lapse so that significant memory loss is not surprising. In contrast, defenders of thinkalouds usually are willing to admit that not all cognitive processes can be retrieved even with concurrent thinkalouds.

To summarize our view, we believe that useful information on processes of judgment formation may be obtained from respondents, whether the responses are generated on the spot or based on retrieved schemata. Nevertheless, we believe that these reported judgment rules are subject to significant error, usually higher than those for any of the other stages in answering survey questions. The errors of omission are essentially retrieval errors that we discussed earlier. The false positives are probably the results of improper use of schemata.

Editing Answers

As has often been pointed out, an interview is a social interaction and respondents are reluctant to give answers that they believe to be socially undesirable. Questions that require such answers are seen as threatening and respondents may well edit their answers before giving them to the interviewer or putting them on a self-administered questionnaire. It is possible to get some indication of how threatening a question is by asking respondents about it at the end of an interview.

There have been no recently reported studies measuring threat, but in our earlier work (Bradburn, Sudman, & Associates, 1979) we observed that direct questions about threat were also seen as threatening. It was possible, however, to obtain reasonable reports of threat by asking the question in a projective fashion, as in the next example.

EXAMPLE 15

Q. (asked after the interview was completed) Questions some-times have different kinds of effects on people. We'd like your opinions about some of the questions in this interview. As I mention groups of questions, please tell me whether you think those questions would make most people very uneasy, moderately uneasy, slightly uneasy, or not at all uneasy?

Evaluation of the Use of Postinterview Projective Methods

As with the other measures of cognitive activity discussed, postinterview questions about threat appear to have good face validity. Thus, we found that virtually no respondents thought that questions about leisure time activities were threatening whereas questions about sexual activities, drug use, and income were perceived as threatening by many respondents. We were also able to demonstrate a relationship between perceived threat and underreporting.

This does not mean that the projective measures obtained necessarily reflect perceived threat and editing behavior at an individual level. Measurement errors in both directions are possible. Some respondents who are themselves threatened by a question may not report that others would be; some who are not bothered may believe that others would be. We speculate that reported threat, like reports of not understanding the question, is more likely to be underestimated than overestimated but there are no hard data to support or disprove this speculation.

Threatening questions refer to socially desirable and to socially undesirable behavior. We believe that respondents are less likely to report as threatening questions about socially desirable behavior such as voting in a recent election than questions about socially undesirable behavior such as drug use, even though they are likely to overstate desirable behavior. This hypothesis has not yet been tested.

Summary

In this chapter, we have presented the methods currently used to uncover the cognitive processes used by respondents when they answer questions. We believe that these methods provide useful information both for understanding the process and for improving survey questions and questionnaires. These methods are far from perfect, however. As with the survey questions themselves, measures of cognitive processes all have their own measurement errors. Future research should lead either to new methods for reducing these measurement errors or to a better understanding and measurement of these errors.

Practical Implications for Questionnaire Designers

In questionnaire design, we strongly recommend the use of think-aloud interviews for determining what respondents think the questions mean and how they retrieve information to form a judgment. This technique is already being used by federal data-collection agencies and other large survey organizations at the beginning stages of questionnaire development before pretesting in the field. Although such interviews increase the time required to develop a questionnaire, they are an efficient means for identifying questions that are difficult to understand or answer.

Thinkaloud questions and prompts range from nondirective to very specific. Although there can be no general rule, we believe that some directive probing is necessary for general population samples but urge that the probes not be too directive since respondents would then be unduly affected by the researcher's suggested cognitive processes.

Even after problem questions have been identified and modified, some respondents may still interpret a question differently than the researcher intended. For selected behavioral questions we think it may be useful to ask respondents what they think the question means, even during the main interview. If the respondent interprets the question in a way other than intended, a well-trained interviewer should be able to explain the question in his or her own words to the respondent. The interviewer variability introduced by this technique may well be less serious than the variability resulting from respondent misinterpretation.

Unfortunately, the problems are more difficult with attitude questions. If a respondent does not already have an answer stored in memory, the judgment will be strongly affected by context and interviewer cues. Here, giving the interviewer flexibility to explain the question can significantly change a respondent's answer in unknown and uncontrollable ways so that interviewer flexibility cannot be recommended.

Before the thinkaloud interviews, several other methods may be useful. Focus groups are always an efficient initial step to determine how some of the key concepts being studied are understood and retrieved by potential respondents. Because they are conducted in group settings, they are cheaper per person than thinkaloud interviews but also provide less detailed information. We believe focus groups and thinkaloud interviews are most effective when used together, but if time and costs do not permit both we recommend the thinkaloud interviews over the focus groups. Nonverbal techniques such as sorting may also be useful in special situations.

Using cognitive experts to examine a questionnaire before interviewing is a low-cost efficient way of identifying potential problems. Obviously, this is more practical if the experts are available locally or are known to the researcher.

Tape-recording pretest interviews and analyzing respondent difficulties with the questionnaire are useful additional steps. It is important to remember that questionnaire development is not a single-stage process. When problems are discovered with a questionnaire, either through thinkaloud interviews or pretest response analysis, the questionnaire designer will usually modify the questionnaire. It is then necessary that the redesigned questionnaire also be evaluated. If not, the revision may turn out to introduce problems as serious or more serious than those in the initial questionnaire.

3

Answering a Survey Question

Cognitive and Communicative Processes

Several researchers have offered conceptual models of the question asking and answering process. Initially these models presented straightforward extensions of general information processing models developed in cognitive psychology (for example, Bodenhausen & Wyer, 1987; Hastie, 1987), described in detail by Lachman, Lachman, and Butterfield (1979). However, as the collaboration of cognitive psychologists, social psychologists, and survey researchers progressed, it became increasingly obvious that the information processing paradigm could only capture some of the key aspects of survey interviews.

Most important, mainstream information processing models share an exclusive focus on individual thought processes. As many critics noted, this concentration on individuals as isolated information processors fostered a neglect of the social context in which human judgment occurs (Forgas, 1981; Schwarz, 1994; Schwarz & Strack, 1991c). The survey interview, however, is best considered as an ongoing conversation in which respondents conduct their own share of thinking and question answering in a specific social and conversational context. Hence, conceptualizations of the question answering process in survey interviews need to consider conversational as well as cognitive processes and pay close attention to the complex interplay of social communication and individual thought processes (see Clark & Schober, 1992; Schwarz, 1994; Strack & Schwarz, 1992, for more detailed discussions).

In the present chapter we begin by summarizing respondents' tasks. We then discuss in some detail each of these tasks and the cognitive and communicative processes involved in their performance, providing a conceptual framework for the following chapters. Those chapters will elaborate on different aspects of the processes introduced here as they become relevant to different issues of survey research.

Overview of Respondents' Tasks

From a cognitive perspective, answering a survey question requires that respondents accomplish several tasks. There is wide agreement among researchers on the substantive nature of these tasks although different researchers use somewhat different labels (see, for example, Feldman, 1992; Feldman & Lynch, 1988; Schwarz, 1990a; Schwarz & Bless, 1992a; Strack, 1992, 1994; Strack & Martin, 1987; Tourangeau, 1984, 1987, 1992; Tourangeau & Rasinski, 1988). In the following paragraphs we discuss the various tasks as if they were sequentially ordered. This facilitates the exposition; however, respondents may in fact go back and forth between different tasks. The sequential order of our presentation should not, therefore, be taken too literally.

Not surprisingly, respondents' first task consists in interpreting the question to understand its meaning. If the question is an opinion question, they may either retrieve a previously formed opinion from memory or may "compute" an opinion on the spot. To do so they need to retrieve relevant information from memory to form a mental representation of the target they are to evaluate. In most cases, they also need to retrieve or construct some standard against which they can evaluate the target. After they form a "private" judgment they have to communicate it to the researcher. To do this, they may need to format the judgment to fit the response alternatives provided as part of the question. In addition, they may wish to edit their response before they communicate it because of social desirability and situational factors.

Similar considerations apply to behavioral questions. Again, respondents first need to understand the question and the kinds of behavior they are supposed to report. Next, they have to recall or reconstruct relevant instances of the behavior from memory. If the question specifies a reference period, they must also determine if the instances occurred during that period. Similarly, if the question refers to "usual" behavior, respondents have to determine if the recalled or reconstructed instances are reasonably representative or if they reflect a deviation from their usual behavior. If they cannot recall or reconstruct specific instances of the behavior or if they are not sufficiently motivated to engage in this effort, respondents may rely on general knowledge or other salient information to help them come up with an estimate. Finally, respondents have to provide the answer to the researcher. They may need to map the estimate onto a response scale provided to them and, again, they may want to edit it for reasons of social desirability.

Accordingly, interpreting the question, retrieving information, generating an opinion or a representation of the relevant behavior, formatting a response, and editing it are the main psychological components of a process that starts with respondents' exposure to a survey question and ends with their overt report. Figure 3.1, which we adapted from Strack and Martin's (1987) discussion of attitude questions, summarizes these steps.

Although the actual question answering sequence ends with the respondent's answer, the processes involved in answering a question may themselves change a respondent's cognitive representation of the issue and affect their subsequent behavior. Feldman and Lynch (1988) referred to this possibility as *self-generated validity*. This term means that the measurement process can sometimes generate the very thing it is supposed to assess. We address this consequence of survey participation as the final step of the question answering process.

FIGURE 3.1 Model of information processing in a survey situation.

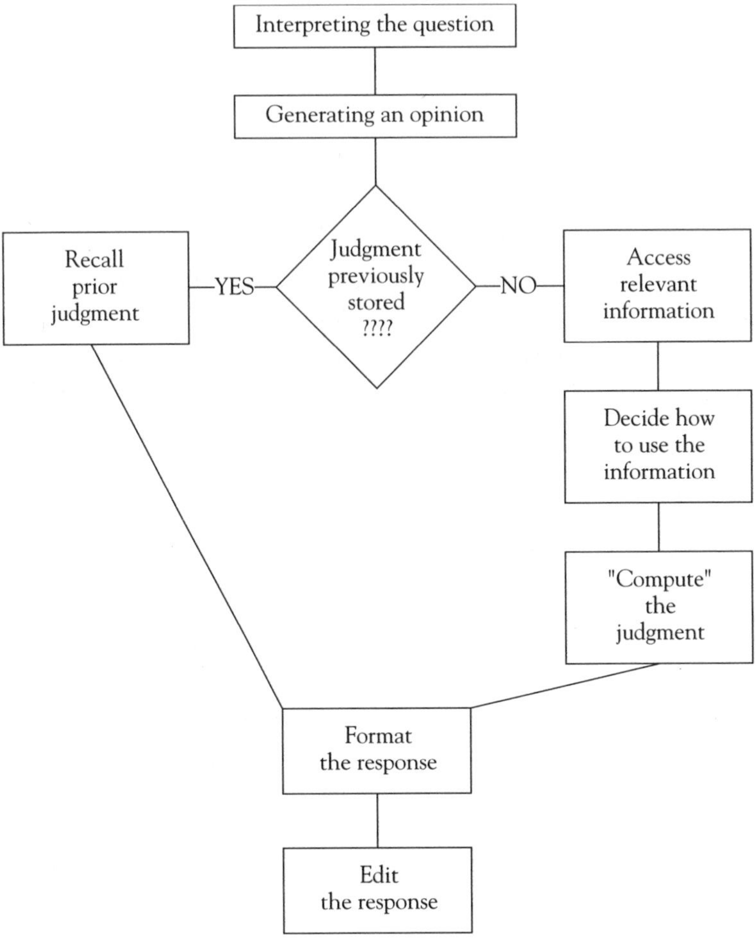

Understanding the Question

The key issue in question comprehension is whether the respondent's understanding of the question matches what the researcher
had in mind. Is the attitude object—or the behavior—that the respondent identifies as the target of the question the one that the
researcher intended? Does the respondent's understanding tap the
same facet of the issue and the same evaluative dimension?

From a psychological point of view, question comprehension

reflects the operation of two intertwined processes (Clark & Schober, 1992; Strack, 1992; Strack & Schwarz, 1992). The first involves semantic understanding of the utterance. If the words used are ambiguous or unfamiliar, for example, respondents need to disambiguate their meaning. However, mere understanding of the words is not sufficient. For example, if respondents are asked "What have you done today?" they are likely to understand the meaning of the words. However, they still need to determine the kinds of activities the researcher is interested in. Should they report, for example, that they took a shower? Hence, understanding a question in a way that allows an appropriate answer requires understanding not only the *literal meaning* of the question but involves inferences about the questioner's intention. To infer the questioner's intention, that is, the *pragmatic meaning* of the question, respondents rely on the tacit assumptions that govern the conduct of conversation in everyday life. Next, we consider the processes involved in question comprehension in more detail.

Understanding the Literal Meaning

Language comprehension begins with a perceptual process that transforms the sounds of an utterance or the symbols of written language into words. Next, the string of words is "parsed" into meaningful units, and the lexical meaning of the identified words is recalled from semantic memory (see Anderson, 1980; Glass, Holyoak, & Santa, 1979, for more detailed discussions). Performance of each of these steps is very context-dependent, although we are usually not aware of the degree to which we use context in apparently simple tasks of comprehension.

At the perceptual level, word recognition is relatively context-independent if the word is presented in writing. However, spoken words are more difficult to recognize and numerous studies demonstrate that a given spoken word is easier to recognize in a meaningful context than in isolation (for example, Lieberman, 1963; see Marslen-Wilson, 1984, for a review). Moreover, the same string of letters or sounds may acquire different meaning, depending on the syntax of the sentence. Thus, the correct meaning of a word can only be identified after the sentence is parsed into meaningful syntactic units. Consider the sentence "The man pushed through the door fell" (taken from Smyth, Morris, Levy, & Ellis, 1987). Most readers will need to revise their initial interpretation when they reach the end of the sentence. As Anderson (1980, p. 413) noted, listeners "select only one interpretation (their best guess) for a pattern and carry it through to the end of the sentence. If the best guess turns out to be wrong, their comprehension suffers and they have to backtrack and try another interpretation."

Most comprehension problems arise because of either lexical or structural ambiguities. In the sentence "John went to the bank," the word "bank" is a source of lexical ambiguity because it can refer to a financial institution or a riverbed. In contrast, the sentence "Flying planes can be dangerous" is structurally ambiguous because "flying" may be interpreted as a verb or as an adjective.

Whereas structural ambiguities can be avoided by careful question wording, lexical ambiguities are inherent in language and reflect the multiple meanings of words. In most cases, these multiple meanings are constrained by the context in which words appear. If these constraints allow for several different meanings, the interpretation used is the one that comes to mind most easily. In general, individuals do not entertain different interpretations simultaneously but select the most accessible one and carry it through until potentially proven wrong.

Which of the multiple meanings of a word comes to mind most easily in a survey interview is a function of questionnaire and respondent variables. At the questionnaire level, the content of preceding questions may increase the accessibility of a concept, rendering it likely that this concept rather than another is used in resolving subsequent lexical ambiguities. For example, Lackner and Garrett (1972) asked subjects to interpret the sentence "The spy put out the torch as our signal to attack." In this case, "put out" could be interpreted as either "switched off" or "made visible." Subjects were more likely to choose the former meaning when a simultaneous second task primed the concept "extinguished" and the latter meaning when it primed the concept "displayed." When asked, however, subjects were not aware of any influence of the accompanying second task, illustrating the unconscious and automatic nature of semantic priming effects. However, not all question order effects at the comprehension stage reflect such an automatic encoding process. Rather, the impact of preceding questions may also reflect conscious inferences about intended meaning, addressed in the following section.

Independent of question context, different meanings may be differentially accessible to different respondents because of the frequency with which they employ them in daily life. In an amusing example, Billiet (cited in Bradburn, 1992, p. 317) observed that some respondents offered numbers between twenty and thirty in response to the question "How many children do you have?" Closer inspection revealed that these respondents were teachers who interpreted the question to refer to the children in their classes, the meaning that was most accessible in their memories.

The problem of differential lexical meanings is further compounded by the existence of idiosyncratic meanings and by differences in meanings across regions and subcultures. In addition, many of the terms used in public opinion research do not have clearly defined lexical meanings to begin with and respondents who ask the interviewer to provide a definition are usually instructed to define the concept for themselves. As a result, it often remains unclear what a term meant to a respondent. A study by Fee (1979) nicely illustrates these ambiguities. Exploring the meaning of common political terms, Fee observed at least nine different meanings for the term "energy crisis." Similarly, the term "big government" elicited at least four distinct representations: one referred to welfare and overspending, another to big business and government for the wealthy, a third to federal control and diminished states' rights, and a fourth to bureaucracy and a lack of democratic process. Needless to say, it is nearly impossible to interpret the responses to a question about "big government" without knowing which interpretation the respondents chose. Finally, the meaning of a term may change over time, posing considerable problems for trend analyses.

Not surprisingly, these problems are compounded when we want to compare survey data from different countries. In designing comparative surveys, researchers usually try to word questions in the same way across languages, using iterations of translation into and back out of other languages (see Brislin, 1980; Paarek & Rao, 1980, for discussions of cross-cultural surveys). To the extent that similar terms have different meanings in different countries, however, different questions may be needed to convey a single meaning.

In summary, the comprehension of the literal meaning of an utterance involves the identification of words, the recall of lexical information from semantic memory, and the construction of a meaning of the utterance, which is constrained by its context. However, understanding the literal meaning of a question is often not sufficient to answer it. As cooperative participants in a conversation, we also need to identify the intended meaning of the question to determine the information the questioner actually desires.

Inferring the Intended Meaning: The Logic of Conversation

To understand how respondents infer the intended meaning of a question, we need to consider the assumptions that govern the conduct of conversation in everyday life. These tacit assumptions were systematically described by Paul Grice (1975), a philosopher of language (see Levinson, 1983, for a detailed introduction; Sperber & Wilson, 1986, for a recent extension; and Clark & Schober, 1992; Schwarz, 1994; Schwarz & Hippler, 1991; Strack, 1994; Strack & Schwarz, 1992, for applications to survey research).

According to Grice's analysis, conversations proceed according to a "cooperativeness" principle. This principle can be expressed in the form of four maxims. A *maxim of quality* enjoins speakers not to say anything they believe to be false or lack adequate evidence for. A *maxim of relation* enjoins speakers to make a contribution relevant to the aims of the ongoing conversation. A *maxim of quantity* requires speakers to make their contribution as informative as required but not more informative than required, and *a maxim of manner* holds that the contribution be clear rather than obscure, ambiguous, or wordy. Thus, according to Grice, speakers are supposed to be truthful, relevant, informative, and clear.

As a result, "communicated information comes with a guarantee of relevance" (Sperber & Wilson, 1986, p. vi) and listeners interpret the speakers' utterances "on the assumption that they are trying to live up to these ideals" (Clark & Clark, 1977, p. 122). These tacit assumptions have important implications for survey research, implications to which we shall repeatedly return throughout this book.

To begin with an extreme example, the assumption that speakers try to be truthful, relevant, informative, and clear implies that they are unlikely to ask meaningless questions. If a survey researcher does so nevertheless, as is the case with questions about highly obscure (for example, Schuman & Presser, 1981) or completely fictitious issues (for example, Bishop, Oldendick, & Tuchfarber, 1986), respondents are unlikely to assume that the researchers violated each and every principle that usually governs the conduct of conversation. Hence, they will operate on the default assumption that the question is meaningful and do their best to determine what the researchers might have had in mind when they wrote it. In doing so, respondents turn to the context of the question and the response alternatives for relevant clues. This strategy is licensed by the maxims of conversation.

Even if comprehending the literal meaning of the question poses no problem, respondents still have to infer what the specific information is that the researchers are interested in. Speakers are supposed to provide information that the recipient needs rather than reiterate information that the recipient already has—or may take for granted anyway (Haviland & Clark, 1974). Accordingly, determining the intended meaning of a question and the kind of response that is adequate requires a considerable degree of inference, including inferences about the information that the recipient already has and the kind of additional "new" information that the recipient may need. In making these inferences, respondents not only rely on the wording of the question but also consider the response alternatives, the context in which the question is presented, and their own previous answers.

Response Alternatives

Suppose, for example, that respondents are asked in an open response format, "What have you done today?" To give a meaningful answer, respondents must determine which activities are of interest to the researcher. In an attempt to be informative, respondents are likely to omit activities that the researcher is already aware of, such as "I participated in a survey interview," or probably takes for granted, such as "I took a shower." But if respondents are given a list of activities that includes being interviewed and taking a shower, most respondents will endorse them. However, presenting such a list would reduce the likelihood that respondents report activities that are not represented on it (see Schuman & Presser, 1981; Schwarz & Hippler, 1991, for a review of relevant studies). Both of these question-form effects reflect the fact that response alternatives can clarify the intended meaning of a question, in the present example by specifying the activities the researcher is interested in. Whereas this example may seem rather obvious, more subtle influences are frequently overlooked.

Suppose that respondents are asked how frequently they felt "really irritated" recently. To answer this question, they again must determine what the researcher means by "really irritated." Does the term refer to major or to minor annoyances? To identify the intended meaning, they may consult the frequency response alternatives provided by the researcher. If the response alternatives offer low-frequency categories (for example, ranging from "less than once a year" to "more than once a month") they may conclude that the researcher has relatively rare events in mind and that the question does not refer to minor irritations, which are likely to occur more often. Accordingly, Schwarz, Strack, Müller, and Chassein (1988) observed that respondents who were asked to report the frequency of irritating experiences on a low-frequency scale assumed that the question referred to major annoyances whereas respondents who had to give their report on a high-frequency scale assumed that the question referred to minor annoyances. Thus, respondents inferred a different meaning for the question based on the response alternatives provided.

Similarly, Schwarz, Knäuper, Hippler, Noelle-Neumann, and Clark (1991) observed that respondents may use the specific numeric values provided as part of a rating scale to interpret the meaning of the scale's labels. In this study, a representative sample of German adults was asked, "How successful would you say you have been in life?" This question was accompanied by an 11-point rating scale, ranging from "not at all successful" to "extremely successful." However, in one condition the numeric values of the rating scale ranged from 0 ("not at all successful") to 10 ("extremely successful"), whereas in the other condition they ranged from −5 ("not at all successful") to +5 ("extremely successful"). The results showed a dramatic impact of the numeric values presented to respondents. Whereas 34 percent of the respondents endorsed a value between 0 and 5 on the 0 to 10 scale, only 13 percent endorsed one of the formally equivalent values between −5 and 0 on the −5 to +5 scale. Subsequent experiments indicated that the results reflected differential interpretations of the term "not at all successful." When this term was combined with the numeric value 0, respondents interpreted it to reflect the absence of success. However, when the same term was combined with the numeric value −5 and the scale offered a 0 as the midpoint, they interpreted it to reflect the presence of failure.

This differential interpretation of the same term as a function of its accompanying numeric was also reflected in the inferences made by judges based on a report given along a rating scale. For example, in one experiment a fictitious student reported his academic success along one of the above scales, checking either a −4 or a 2. Judges who were asked to estimate how often this student had failed an exam assumed that he had failed twice as often when he checked a −4 than when he checked a 2, although both values are formally equivalent along 11-point rating scales of the type described.

Extending this line of work, Grayson, Schwarz, and Hippler (1995) asked respondents to provide behavioral frequency reports on a rating scale ranging from "rarely" to "frequently." Depending on experimental conditions, the verbal label "rarely" was coded with the numeric value 0 or the numeric value 1. As expected, respondents provided higher frequency ratings when "rarely" was coded 0 rather than 1. The numeric value 0 induced them to interpret the verbal label "rarely" as meaning "never," thus requiring the assignment of higher numbers for a given behavioral frequency.

In combination, such findings demonstrate that respondents use the response alternatives in interpreting the meaning of a question. In doing so, they proceed on the tacit assumption that every contribution is relevant to the aims of an ongoing conversation. In the survey interview, these contributions include apparently formal features of questionnaire design, such as the numeric values given on a rating scale. Hence, identically worded questions may acquire different meanings depending on the response alternatives by which they are accompanied (see Schwarz & Hippler, 1991, for a more extended discussion).

Question Context

Respondents' interpretation of a question's intended meaning is further influenced by the context in which the question is presented. Not surprisingly, this influence is more pronounced as the wording of the question becomes more ambiguous. From a theoretical point of view, some contextual influences may reflect the operation of semantic priming, as discussed earlier, as well as the operation of conscious inference processes on the basis of conversational assumptions.

For example, Strack, Schwarz, and Wänke (1991, Experiment 1) asked German students to report their attitude toward an ambiguous issue: the introduction of an undefined "educational contribution." For some respondents, this question was preceded by a question about the tuition students have to pay in the United States; for others it was preceded by a question about the financial support Swedish students receive from their government. As expected, respondents reported a more favorable attitude toward the educational contribution when the preceding question referred to money students receive rather than to money they have to pay. (It should be noted that university education is free in Germany.) This finding may indicate that the preceding questions primed different concepts that were subsequently used automatically in the encoding of the ambiguous question or that the respondents deliberately searched the context of the ambiguous question to make sense of it. Although we cannot distinguish these processes in the Strack, Schwarz, and Wänke study, other studies have demonstrated that questions that follow rather than precede an ambiguous question may result in similar disambiguations in self-administered questionnaires (see Schwarz, Strack, Hippler, & Bishop, 1991). This suggests that respondents deliberately search the context of the ambiguous question to make sense of it, even to the extent of returning to the question after they encounter a subsequent one that allows a meaningful interpretation. How often such backtracking occurs in self-administered questionnaires is unknown. We assume that it is most likely to occur when respondents encounter a question that does not make sense to them until a subsequent question allows for a reasonable interpretation.

Moreover, a question's context may influence its interpretation even under conditions where the literal meaning of the question does not seem especially ambiguous. Two examples may illustrate this point. Schwarz, Strack, and Mai (1991) asked respondents to report their general life satisfaction, which did not pose a particular comprehension problem. However, in one condition of their experiment, this question was preceded by a question about the respondent's marital satisfaction and both questions were introduced by a joint lead-in. This lead-in read, "We would first like to ask you to report on two aspects of your life that may be relevant to people's overall well-being." In this case, respondents interpreted the general life satisfaction question as if it were worded, "Leaving aside the life domain that you already told us about, how satisfied are you currently with other aspects of your life?" This shift in the interpretation of the general life satisfaction question reflects the impact of the "given-new" contract (Haviland & Clark, 1974) that requests that participants provide information that is new to the recipient rather than to reiterate information already given. Accordingly, respondents deliberately excluded their marriage in answering the general question because they had reported on it earlier. (We return to this study in more detail in Chapters Four and Five.) In a similar vein, Bachman and Alcser (1993) asked respondents to report their satisfaction "with the current U.S. health care system" and their satisfaction with their own health insurance plans. Most respondents who had health insurance reported high satisfaction with their insurance plans, independently of the order in which both questions were presented (77.8 percent were very or somewhat satisfied when the question was asked first and 76.4 percent when it was asked second). Their reported satisfaction with the U.S. health care system in general, however, showed a pronounced order effect. When the question about the U.S. health care system was asked first, 39.6 percent of the respondents reported being very or somewhat satisfied whereas only 26.4 percent did so when this question was preceded by the question about their own insurance plans. This pattern of findings suggests that respondents who had just reported on their own health insurance plans, with which most were satisfied, excluded this information from consideration when they were asked to evaluate the U.S. health care system in general. Having already provided information about their own situation, they apparently interpreted the general question as if it were worded, "Aside from your own health insurance, how satisfied are you with the U.S. health care system in general?" resulting in reports of lower satisfaction.

As these findings illustrate, question comprehension is not merely a function of the wording of the question itself. Respondents use information provided by the context of the question to determine its intended meaning. In making these pragmatic inferences, they rely on the principles that govern the conduct of conversation in daily life. Accordingly, models of the question comprehension process must include pragmatic as well as semantic processes (see Clark & Schober, 1992; Schwarz, 1994; Strack, 1994; Strack & Schwarz, 1992, for more detailed treatments).

Recalling or Computing a Judgment

Once respondents determine what the researcher is interested in, they need to recall relevant information from memory. In some cases, respondents may have direct access to a previously formed relevant judgment that they can offer as an answer. In most cases, however, they will not find an appropriate answer readily stored in memory and will need to compute a judgment on the spot.

Recalling a Judgment

Whether respondents can recall a previously formed relevant judgment from memory depends on whether such a judgment has been formed in the first place and whether it is accessible at the time of the interview. In the case of attitude questions, a key determinant is the personal importance of the issue and the degree of personal experience with the attitude object. Not surprisingly, issues of personal importance are more likely to elicit spontaneous judgments than are less important ones. Moreover, some daily activities, such as major purchasing decisions, require the evaluation of different objects, and if the decision was made recently the evaluations formed at that point may still be accessible in memory. In addition, the likelihood that a respondent has access to evaluative judgments of an attitude object increases with the degree of the respondent's personal experience with the object. (See Fazio, 1989, for a review of attitude accessibility research, and Bassili, 1995, for an application to survey research.) Finally, if respondents have been asked a related question before, the judgment formed at that time may still be accessible in memory, provided that little interfering information has been activated in the meantime.

In the case of behavioral questions, a relevant answer is most likely to be directly accessible if the behavior is of personal importance and has a low frequency of occurrence, as we shall see in the chapters on behavioral reports (see Bradburn, Rips, & Shevell, 1987; Schwarz, 1990a; Strube, 1987, for reviews). If the behavior is a frequent one, respondents are only likely to have direct access to a judgment if the behavior is highly regular, in which case they may remember a rate of occurrence, such as "once a week" (see Menon, 1994).

Computing a Judgment

Usually, respondents need to compute a judgment when asked a question. In the case of attitude questions, this is because issues are complex whereas survey questions are necessarily simple, as Schuman and Kalton (1985) noted. Thus, even under conditions where respondents can retrieve an opinion on the issue from memory, the opinion may not exactly match the facet tapped in the question. Similarly, respondents are unlikely to have an appropriate answer to most behavioral questions stored in memory. Even if they can recall relevant instances, they will still need to determine if these instances fit the reference period, and so on. As a result, most of the answers that we record in surveys reflect judgments that respondents generate on the spot in the specific context of the specific interview. They are therefore strongly influenced by the information that is accessible at that time and this is in part a function of the preceding questions.

This context-dependency of human judgment results from the fact that humans are "cognitive misers" (Taylor, 1981), who follow a "satisficing" rather than an "optimizing" strategy (see Simon,

1957, for an introduction to these concepts, and Krosnick, 1991, for their application to survey responding). When asked to form a judgment, individuals first need to form a mental representation of the target to which the question pertains, as we shall discuss in more detail in Chapter Five. To do so, they do not retrieve all potentially relevant information. Rather, they truncate the search process as soon as enough information has come to mind to form a representation that is sufficient for the judgment at hand. (See Bodenhausen & Wyer, 1987, for a more detailed discussion.) An extensive search of memory is only likely when individuals are highly motivated because the judgment has important personal consequences (Kruglanski, 1980). This is rarely the case in survey interviews. Moreover, searching memory takes time and the time pressures that characterize most survey interviews (see Groves & Kahn, 1979) further contribute to individuals' tendency to truncate the search process early. Accordingly, respondents' judgments are usually based on the information that comes to mind most easily while other potentially relevant information that is less accessible in memory is unlikely to be considered. How easily a given piece of information comes to mind depends on the recency and frequency of its use and the degree to which it is linked to other pieces of information (see Bodenhausen & Wyer, 1987; Higgins, 1989; Schwarz & Sudman, 1995; Wyer & Srull, 1989, for reviews).

Information that has just been used to answer the preceding question is particularly likely to come to mind when a related question is asked. The information has been rendered "temporarily accessible" by the preceding question and is likely to serve as a basis for later judgments to which it may be relevant. This priming function of preceding questions is the procedural basis of many context effects in survey measurement, which we consider in more detail in Chapters Four and Five. In addition to the recency of its use, the accessibility of a given piece of information is further influenced by the frequency of its use. For example, a respondent who is concerned about the threat of unemployment may frequently think about this issue, rendering it "chronically accessible" in memory. As a result, this respondent may think of unemployment spontaneously if a relevant political question is asked whereas other respondents may think of unemployment only if it was addressed in a preceding question. As we have already discussed in the context of lexical meanings, the *temporary accessibility* of information is largely a function of questionnaire variables, whereas the *chronic accessibility* of information is largely a function of respondent variables.

Finally, a given piece of information is proportionately more accessible in memory the more it is integrated into a larger knowledge structure. Most cognitive psychologists portray memory as an extended network, in which individual pieces of information are represented as nodes (see Anderson, 1980, for a textbook length introduction, or Hastie, 1987, for a short summary). A search of memory proceeds along the pathways that connect these nodes, and a given node is more likely to be accessed if more pathways lead to it. In terms of the previous example, a respondent who is concerned about unemployment may have thought about this problem with regard to many aspects of his personal life, thus establishing many pathways. As a result, unemployment may come to mind when any of the aspects to which it has been linked is activated.

Whereas the accessibility of information in memory determines *which* information is used in forming a judgment, what exactly respondents do with the information that comes to mind depends on the inferential procedures that they apply to it. Not surprisingly, the procedures that are used to generate an opinion or to generate a behavioral report differ substantially, and we shall explore these procedures in the respective chapters. For the time being, we note that survey responses are based on the information that is most accessible at the time of judgment. Respondents use this information to form a mental representation of the attitude object or of the relevant behavior and base their reports on the implications of this representation. Some of the information that enters this representation is chronically accessible in memory and likely to come to mind whenever the respondent thinks of the issue. This chronically accessible information contributes to the stability of reports at different points in time and in different contexts. Other information, however, is only temporarily accessible, for example, because it was used to answer a preceding question. This information contributes to the instability of reports over time and underlies the emergence of context effects in survey measurement. We shall repeatedly return to these issues throughout this book.

Formatting the Response

Once respondents have formed a judgment, the interviewer usually does not allow them to report it in their own words. Rather, they are asked to endorse one of the response alternatives provided. In order to do this, they must format their response in line with the options given. Accordingly, the researcher's choice of response alternatives may strongly affect survey results (see Schwarz & Hippler, 1991, for a review).

From a theoretical point of view, however, it is important to note that the influence of response alternatives is not limited to the formatting stage and that response alternatives are likely to influence all steps of the question answering sequence. As an illustration, consider the case of categorical scales that offer a number of discrete opinions or behaviors, of which the respondent is supposed to check the appropriate one. If respondents cannot identify a response alternative that reflects their judgment, they are unlikely to report it, even if a generic "other" category is offered for such cases (for example, Schuman & Presser, 1981). This well-documented finding, for example, may reflect constraints at the formatting stage as well as differences in respondents' inferences about the intended meaning of the question, as discussed previously. Similarly, the range of the frequency categories that accompany a behavioral question may influence question comprehension (for example, Schwarz, Strack, Müller, & Chassein, 1988) as well as respondents' judgmental strategy (for example, Schwarz, Hippler, Deutsch, & Strack, 1985), in addition to the formatting process.

The only scale effects that seem to occur unequivocally at the formatting stage pertain to the use of rating scales, as described by Ostrom and Upshaw's (1968) perspective theory and Parducci's (1983; Parducci & Perrett, 1971) range-frequency theory. As numerous studies demonstrate, respondents use the most extreme stimuli to anchor the endpoints of a rating scale. As a result, a given stimulus will be rated as less extreme if presented in the context of a more extreme stimulus than if presented in the context of a less extreme one. In Parducci's model, this impact of the range of stimuli is referred to as the "range effect." In addition, if the number of stimuli to be rated is sufficiently large, respondents attempt to use all categories of the rating scale about equally often. Accordingly, the specific ratings given also depend on the frequency distribution of the presented stimuli, an effect that is referred to as the "frequency effect." Daamen and de Bie (1992) provide an introduction to the logic of these processes and report several studies that illustrate their impact on survey results. We return to these issues in Chapter Four.

Editing the Response

Finally, respondents may want to edit their responses before they communicate them, reflecting considerations of social desirability and self-presentation. Not surprisingly, the impact of these considerations is more pronounced in face-to-face interviews than in self-administered questionnaires (for example, Smith, 1979). DeMaio (1984) reviews the survey literature on this topic.

It is important to emphasize, however, that the size of response effects reflecting influences of social desirability is usually modest and these effects are limited to potentially threatening questions. Moreover, what constitutes a socially desirable response depends on the situation. For example, several researchers (see Smith, 1979, for a review) observed that respondents report higher levels of happiness and satisfaction in face-to-face interviews than in self-administered questionnaires. In contrast, Strack, Schwarz, Chassein, Kern, and Wagner (1990) obtained a reversal of this effect under specific conditions. In their study, respondents reported deflated levels of happiness when they were questioned by a disabled interviewer, presumably because it seemed inappropriate to tell an unfortunate other how wonderful their own lives were. In contrast, the sheer presence of a disabled confederate while respondents filled out a self-administered questionnaire resulted in increased reports of happiness, indicating that the disabled person served as a salient standard of comparison inflating the respondents' private judgments. As this example illustrates, understanding issues of social desirability requires close attention to the actual social situation, which determines what is desirable and what is not.

Self-Generated Validity:
Consequences of Survey Participation

Although the question answering sequence ends with the respondent's report, it is useful to consider the impact of the measurement process on the respondent's subsequent attitudes, intentions, and behaviors. Feldman and Lynch (1988; see also Feldman, 1992) provide a detailed discussion of the underlying processes, which we shall address in more detail in our discussion of context effects in attitude measurement. In principle, answering a question about one's behavioral intentions increases the accessibility of these intentions in memory and hence the likelihood that they may come to mind in a situation in which one may act on them.

Sherman and his colleagues (Sherman, 1980; Sherman, Zehner, Johnson, & Hirt, 1983) observed that the very act of making a prediction about one's future behavior can induce behavioral change that brings the future behavior in line with one's predictions. In one of their experiments, college students were asked to predict whether they would volunteer three hours for a cancer society's fundraising campaign. These subjects typically overestimated their willingness relative to the actual behavior of a control group that was simply asked to volunteer three hours. But these errors were "self-erasing" in the sense that subjects who made a prediction subsequently acted on the basis of their predictions, resulting in a higher level of actual volunteer behavior. Similarly, Gregory, Cialdini, and Carpenter (1982) found that consumers who were induced to consider a scenario in which they were cable television subscribers subsequently were more likely actually to subscribe to cable television service. Moreover, Greenwald, Carnot, Beach, and Young (1987) demonstrated that asking respondents whether they intended to vote increased their actual participation in an election.

At present, the most dramatic evidence of the impact of survey measurement on subsequent behavior has been reported by Morwitz, Johnson, and Schmittlein (1993). Using data from a consumer panel survey with more than forty thousand households, the authors observed that being asked a question about one's intention to buy a car or a personal computer increased the likelihood of actual purchase. Whereas 2.4 percent of the households surveyed in that study bought a car within a six-month time period when they were not asked an intention question in the previous wave, 3.3 percent of the households did so when they were asked an intention question. This reflects an increase of 37 percent over the baseline of 2.4 percent as a result of being asked a single question, namely, "When will the next new car be purchased by someone in your household?" Similarly, 3.8 percent of the households reported the purchase of a personal computer without having been asked an intention question, whereas 4.5 percent did after having been asked in a preceding wave, "Do you or does anyone in your household plan to acquire a (another) personal computer in the future for use at home?" This reflects an increase of 18 percent over the baseline. Thus, "the proportion of households that acquired a product was greater for households whose intentions were measured once than for those whose intentions were never measured" (Morwitz, Johnson, & Schmittlein, 1993, p. 52). Additional analyses indicated that the impact of measurement was more pronounced for households that had no prior experience with the respective product than for households that had.

Finally, repeated intent measures over several waves resulted in a polarization of respondents' intentions, increasing the intentions of respondents who initially reported a high intent and significantly decreasing the intentions of those who initially reported a low intent. These analyses also revealed that repeated intent questions increased actual purchases for households with a high initial purchase intent but decreased purchases for those with a low initial intent, in particular those with no prior product experience. Thus, thinking about purchase intent in response to survey questions increased the likelihood of corresponding actual behavior.

In summary, these studies illustrate that answering survey questions may influence not only responses to subsequent questions but also the actual behavior of respondents. The data suggest that such behavioral effects, if they occur, confirm the response provided in the survey, resulting in what Feldman and Lynch (1988) have termed "self-generated validity."

Summary

In this chapter we discussed what respondents must do to answer a question. For ease of exposition, we presented respondents' tasks in a sequential order. We assume that this sequential order is, in fact, a correct portrayal of the sequence respondents go through in many cases. But it is equally plausible that respondents may switch back and forth between these tasks. They may notice, for example, that their initial interpretation of a question was not the one the researcher intended when they try to report their answer and cannot find an appropriate response alternative. Or they may realize that the researcher is interested in a more detailed behavioral report than they initially assumed when they encounter highly detailed response alternatives that may prompt them to engage in more detailed recall efforts. Hence, thinking of these tasks as sequentially ordered is plausible but may not always capture respondents' actual actions. Nevertheless, the sequential ordering of the tasks provides a useful framework for our purposes.

To reiterate, respondents first have to interpret the question to understand what is meant. If the question is an opinion question, they may retrieve a previously formed opinion from memory or "compute" an opinion on the spot. To do so, they need to retrieve relevant information from memory to form a mental representation of the target that they are to evaluate. In most cases, they will also need to retrieve or construct some standard against which the target is evaluated. Once respondents form a "private" judgment, they have to communicate it to the researcher. To do so, they may need to format the judgment to fit the response alternatives provided or they may wish to edit their responses before communicating them, because of influences of social desirability and situational factors.

Similar considerations apply to behavioral questions. Again, respondents first need to understand what the question refers to and which behavior they are supposed to report. Next, they have to recall or reconstruct relevant instances of this behavior from memory. If the question specifies a reference period, they must also determine if these instances occurred during the reference period or not. Similarly, if the question refers to "usual" behavior, respondents have to determine if the recalled or reconstructed instances are reasonably representative or if they reflect a deviation from their usual behavior. If they cannot recall or reconstruct specific instances of the behavior or are not sufficiently motivated to engage in this effort, respondents may rely on their general knowledge or other salient information that bears on the task to compute an estimate. Finally, respondents have to provide their estimate to the researcher. They may need to map it onto a response scale provided and they may want to edit it for reasons of social desirability.

To understand how respondents infer the intended meaning of a question, we need to consider communicative as well as cognitive processes. The communicative processes reflect the fact that respondents bring the assumptions that govern the conduct of conversation in everyday life to the survey interview. These tacit assumptions were systematically described by Paul Grice (1975).

Drawing on these assumptions, respondents use cues provided by the context of the question and the response alternatives to determine the question's intended meaning. In addition, the content of preceding questions increases the cognitive accessibility of information that was used to answer them. It therefore affects what is likely to come to mind later on and influences which information respondents draw on in answering subsequent related questions.

Finally, answers to survey questions not only influence other answers in the survey but also may influence future behavior.

4

Psychological Sources of Context Effects in Survey Measurement

Survey research methodologists have long been aware and concerned that survey responses are context-dependent. Most important, early questions may influence responses to subsequent ones (see Bradburn, 1983; Payne, 1951; Schuman & Presser, 1981; Schwarz & Strack, 1991a; Schwarz & Sudman, 1992; Tourangeau & Rasinski, 1988, for research examples and reviews). However, the conditions under which context effects occur are not well understood, and when they do occur, it is difficult to predict their direction.

In this and the following chapter, we explore the different processes that underlie the emergence of context effects. In the present chapter, we discuss their various psychological sources and review selected findings from the survey methodology literature. In Chapter Five we focus on variables that determine whether responses to subsequent questions become similar to or different from responses to preceding questions, exploring the conditions that elicit assimilation or contrast effects in attitude measurement. The final section of Chapter Five links our observations on context effects to traditional theorizing in the domain of attitude research, asking what the implications of context effects are for how we think about the nature of attitudes in general. Finally, in Chapter Six we address a specific issue in attitude measurement, namely, the impact of the order in which response alternatives are presented.

Context Effects

Before exploring the nature of context effects, it is important to emphasize that researchers always set contexts that influence some aspect of the question answering process. Sometimes we do so deliberately—for example, to clarify the meaning of a question or encourage respondents to consider an issue in the context that is of interest to the researcher—but often we do so unintentionally. What has been called "response effects" or "response errors" in the survey methodology literature may be thought of as those cases where we unthinkingly affect the context and thus, for the purpose at hand, create "error."

However, the concept of "error" is quite problematical in attitude measurement. Whereas reports about behaviors or events can, at least in principle, be verified, attitude reports reflect subjective evaluative judgments. Yet human judgment is *always* context-dependent; in essence, context-free judgments do not exist. Accordingly, if we want to talk of "errors" in attitude measurement, we can only do so in relation to what we are trying to do in a questionnaire: there is no objective standard that reflects respondents' "true" attitudes. Thus, to avoid the "error" terminology when we address attitude measurement, we speak of context effects instead.

Many context effects are the result of the influence of question order. They have often been referred to as question order effects in the survey methodology literature. However, from a theoretical point of view, question order is simply a technical aspect of the questionnaire and does not by itself constitute a meaningful psychological variable. Rather, the content of a preceding question may affect any of the steps of the question answering process (outlined in Chapter Three) and involve a number of different psychological processes. Moreover, any given order effect observed in a survey may reflect the impact of several of these processes. Disentangling the relative contribution of different processes in a given case presents a difficult task, and some of the more robust "classic" context effects are likely to be overdetermined. Furthermore, we can only speak of order effects in the strict meaning of the term when the questions are presented in a face-to-face or telephone interview. In mail surveys and other self-administered question-naires, respondents may read later questions before answering earlier ones or backtrack and change previous responses, thus oblit-erating the presentation order. In such cases, later questions may influence responses to earlier ones. Although systematic informa-tion on how often respondents read ahead or return to previous questions is not available, several studies found an impact of subse-quent questions on the answers given to previous ones (for exam-ple, Bishop, Hippler, Schwarz, & Strack, 1988; Schwarz & Hippler, 1995), as we shall see in some of the examples reviewed in the fol-lowing paragraphs. Before addressing any examples in detail, how-ever, let us look at the cognitive processes that are likely to be involved in the emergence of context effects.

First, the content of preceding questions may influence respon-dents' interpretation of later questions (or subsequent ones may influence interpretation of earlier ones, in the cases noted earlier), resulting in context effects at the comprehension stage, as we dis-cussed in Chapter Three.

Second, answering a preceding question may render the infor-mation used to answer it more accessible in memory and thereby increase the likelihood that it be used in forming subsequent judg-ments to which it may be relevant. As a result we may obtain con-text effects at the judgment stage. In most cases, the information rendered more accessible in memory will be substantive informa-tion, typically some feature of the target of judgment. For example, answering a question about the president's performance on eco-nomic issues increases the likelihood that this aspect of his perfor-mance will be considered in evaluations of his overall performance. In other cases, the information rendered accessible may be a gen-eral norm, which may subsequently be applied to other issues. Both cases have been given considerable attention in survey methods research.

However, our judgments do not depend only on *what* comes to mind. Consideration of an issue may include a variety of phenomenal experiences, such as our affective reaction to the content we are thinking about or the ease with which that content comes to mind. Such phenomenal experiences constitute a source of information in their own right, and different preceding questions may elicit different phenomenal experiences. To date, this source of context effects has received only limited attention in survey research.

Answering a question may also increase the accessibility of cognitive procedures, thereby increasing the likelihood that the same procedure will be employed later on. Whereas the activation of substantive or normative information and differences in the phenomenal experiences that accompany the thought process all influence *which* information respondents use in computing a judgment, the activation of procedural knowledge influences *how* respondents use the information, that is, which strategy they employ.

In addition, preceding questions may influence what comes to mind when respondents anchor a rating scale, thus influencing the response formatting process. Finally, preceding questions may increase or decrease respondents' concerns about self-presentation and social desirability, affecting the editing stage of the question answering sequence. In the following sections, we explore each of these processes in turn.

Context Effects at the Comprehension Stage

We have already addressed context effects at the comprehension stage in Chapter Three, noting that they may reflect the operation of semantic priming processes as well as the operation of pragmatic inferences (see Strack, 1992, for a detailed discussion). If respondents encounter an ambiguous question, they are likely to interpret it in terms of the applicable concept that is most accessible at that point in time (see Higgins, 1989; Wyer & Srull, 1989, for reviews). Moreover, they may deliberately refer to preceding questions to infer the intended meaning of the ambiguous one, as we have seen in the Strack, Schwarz, and Wänke (1991) study reviewed in Chapter Three. In that study, German students interpreted a question about a fictitious "educational contribution" to mean that students would have to pay money when the question was preceded by another about tuition fees and to mean that students would receive money when it was preceded by a question about student support payments. (See also Tourangeau & Rasinski's [1988] discussion of an obscure monetary control bill, first introduced by Schuman & Presser, 1981.)

In general, the more ambiguous the question the more likely context effects are to emerge at the comprehension stage. It is under this condition that respondents are most likely to turn to the context to make sense of a question (see Schwarz, 1994; Strack & Schwarz, 1992, for reviews). However, there is an important exception to this generalization. As we discussed in Chapter Three, according to the rules that govern the conduct of conversation in everyday life speakers must provide information that is new to the recipient rather than reiterate information that the recipient already has (see Clark, 1985). Application of this rule to the survey interview may result in different interpretations of questions that are not in themselves particularly ambiguous. For example, Schwarz, Strack, and Mai (1991; see also Tourangeau, Rasinski, & Bradburn, 1991) first asked respondents to report their happiness with their marriage and subsequently their satisfaction with their lives as a whole. When these questions were presented on different pages of the questionnaire, respondents interpreted the question about their life as a whole to include their marriage, much as one would expect. For other respondents, however, both questions were placed in the same conversational context by a joint lead-in that read, "We now have two questions about your life." In this case, respondents interpreted the general life-satisfaction question as if it were worded, "Aside from your marriage, which you already told us about, how satisfied are you with *other* aspects of your life?" We will return to this study in more detail in the next chapter. For now we note that preceding questions may change the interpretation of subsequent ones even under conditions where the wording of the question is not particularly ambiguous. This is to be expected when the two questions form a part-whole relationship, such that a specific preceding question renders a subsequent more general question partially redundant. In that case, the general question may be interpreted as excluding the specific aspect that has already been assessed.

Context Effects at the Judgment Stage

Most context effects at the judgment stage reflect the increased accessibility of information that was used to answer preceding questions. They may take different forms depending on whether the information rendered accessible is a previously formed judgment, a feature of the target of judgment, or a general norm. In addition, the process of answering a question may elicit subjective experiences, such as whether the question is easy or difficult to answer, and these experiences may themselves provide information that is used in making subsequent judgments. We elaborate on these processes in the following section, and we return to some of them in more detail in the next chapter.

Previously Formed Judgments

In some cases, a question may prompt respondents to form a judgment that may bear on a subsequent related question. If the previously formed judgment is still accessible in memory, respondents may recall this judgment and use it to derive an answer to the second question without retrieving much additional information. This possibility is nicely illustrated in a study by Carlston (1980). He asked subjects to form an impression of a student who allowed a fellow student to cheat on an exam by copying his answers. Some subjects were first asked to evaluate if the target person was "honest," whereas others were asked if he was "kind." The answer is obviously "no" to the honesty question but "yes" to the kindness question. Yet when subjects who first evaluated the target's honesty were later asked to rate his kindness, they judged him to be less kind than did subjects who evaluated his kindness first. Conversely, those who had first evaluated his kindness went on to rate him as more honest than did those who evaluated his honesty first. This pattern of findings suggests that subjects did not recall the behavioral information they had used to form the first judgment when they were asked to make the second judgment. Rather, they seemed to use the evaluative implications of the first judgment to derive the second one, assuming that "good (or bad) traits go together." Therefore, if he is kind he must be honest, and vice versa (for additional examples, see Schwarz & Bless, 1992b).

In general, respondents who have formed a judgment are unlikely to start from scratch when asked to make a second, closely related judgment; rather they will probably derive the second judgment from the implications of the first, without reconsidering the original information used to form the initial judgment.

Features of the Target of Judgment

When respondents cannot recall a previously formed related judgment to derive a subsequent one, they need to start from scratch by recalling relevant information. The information most likely to come to mind is the information they used in answering related preceding questions. Accordingly, preceding questions may influence the information respondents use in constructing a mental representation of the target. We address the complexities of this process in greater detail in the next chapter, where we discuss how it determines the emergence of assimilation and contrast effects.

General Norms

A context effect that reflects the activation of a general norm was first reported by Hyman and Sheatsley (1950). In 1948, they asked

Americans if "the United States government should let Communist reporters from other countries come in here and send back to their papers the news as they see it." When this question appeared in the first position, only 36 percent of the American sample supported freedom of press for such reporters. However, when respondents were first asked if "a Communist country like Russia should let American newspaper reporters come in," a proposition that most respondents endorsed, support for Communist reporters in the United States increased to 73 percent. Endorsing freedom of the press for American reporters in Russia apparently made respondents aware that the same principle should hold for Communist reporters in the United States.

In subsequent research, Schuman and colleagues (see Schuman & Ludwig, 1983; Schuman & Presser, 1981) traced this and related findings to the operation of a norm of "reciprocity" or "evenhandedness." Although the empirical evidence is currently limited to the impact of reciprocity norms, we may expect that any question or sequence of questions that draws respondents' attention to a general norm is likely to elicit an application of the norm in making subsequent judgments to which the norm is applicable.

Subjective Experiences

The processes considered so far have focused on the *content* that is brought to mind when one answers a question. Sometimes, however, answering a question may elicit a variety of feelings. For example, thinking about a happy or sad event may induce a happy or sad mood (for example, Strack, Schwarz, & Gschneidinger, 1985). If so, the mood may itself influence subsequent judgments, even about targets that are unrelated to the specific content that elicited the mood in the first place. In a large number of studies, being in an elated or depressed mood has been shown to influence a wide range of judgments, from satisfaction with consumer goods (for example, Isen, Shalker, Clark, & Karp, 1978) to feelings toward other people or estimates of risk (for example, Johnson & Tversky, 1983). In general, respondents provide more positive evaluations when they are in a good mood (see Forgas, 1992; Schwarz, 1990b; Schwarz & Clore, 1988, for reviews). In such cases respondents may simplify the judgmental task by using their affective reaction to the target as a basis of judgment. Asked, for example, if one likes something, one may consult one's feelings about the target, essentially asking oneself, "How do I feel about it?" In so doing, however, it is difficult to distinguish between one's affective reaction to the target and one's preexisting mood. As a result, the target is evaluated more positively when people are in good moods than when they are in bad moods. Such mood effects are not obtained, however, when people are aware that their feelings may not reflect their reaction to the target but may be the effect of something else.

A study by Schwarz and Clore (1983, Experiment 2) serves as an illustration. Respondents who were interviewed by telephone reported higher general life satisfaction when they were called on sunny days than when they were called on rainy days. Asking themselves, "How do I feel about my life as a whole?" they evaluated their life more positively when they felt good rather than bad. The impact of the weather, however, was eliminated when the interviewer opened the conversation with a private aside, asking the respondent, "How is the weather down there?" Drawing attention to the weather made respondents aware that their current mood might not reflect how their lives were going in general but only the impact of a transient cause, namely, the weather. Thus, the informational value of their current mood was called into question and its impact was eliminated (see Schwarz & Strack, 1991b, for a more detailed discussion).

In general, questions that change respondents' current mood by bringing positive or negative material to mind are likely to affect subsequent judgments even if the target of judgment is completely unrelated. However, the less respondents are aware that their current feelings may have been caused by the question asked the more their mood is likely to have an impact on unrelated judgments. If the question is blatant, respondents may become aware that thinking about the question has affected their feelings and may disregard such feelings when asked to make another judgment, much as they did in the weather study. But if the affect-eliciting question is more subtl , respondents may see no reason to discount their feelings, resulting in mood-congruent judgments on subsequent questions (see Schwarz & Clore, 1988). Similar considerations hold when respondents are aware that a certain thought may come to mind because of a preceding question, as we will see in Chapter Five.

Although the role of subjective experiences in judgment has been most extensively studied in the domain of moods and emotions, other experiences may affect judgments in a similar way (see Banaji, Blair, & Schwarz, 1995; Clore, 1992). For example, respondents may find it easy or difficult to answer a certain question. This subjective experience alone may provide relevant information for making certain judgments. This assumption is at the heart of Tversky and Kahneman's (1973) availability heuristic, which holds that people estimate the frequency, likelihood, or typicality of events by the ease with which they can bring relevant examples to mind. Moreover, the ease or difficulty of recall may change the conclusions that respondents draw from the content they recall. A study by Schwarz, Bless, Strack, Klumpp, Rittenauer-Schatka, and Simons (1991) illustrates this possibility. They asked respondents to describe either six or twelve situations in which they behaved assertively. Whereas describing six examples was easy, it was difficult for respondents to call twelve examples to mind, although all could complete this task. Subsequently, they had to rate their own assertiveness. Theoretically, if the respondents relied solely on the examples they brought to mind they should have rated themselves as more assertive the greater the number of examples. However, this was not the case. Respondents rated themselves as more assertive when they had to recall only six examples. Apparently, the difficulty of recalling twelve examples suggested to them that they couldn't be all that assertive if it was so difficult to bring twelve examples to mind. Thus, the conclusions that respondents drew from the recalled examples depended primarily on whether the recall task was experienced as easy or difficult. In a similar vein, Bishop (1987) observed that respondents were less likely to report that they followed public affairs if the question was preceded by a difficult knowledge question. Specifically, the knowledge question asked that they report what their United States representative had done for the district. Knowing little about the representative's record, respondents apparently concluded that they didn't follow what was going on.

It should be noted, however, that these findings should only be obtained when respondents attribute the experienced difficulty to their own inadequacy. These findings should not be obtained when they attribute the difficulty to another cause. In such cases, the experienced difficulty is not informative, much as we have seen for one's mood in Schwarz and Clore's (1983) weather study. In line with this assumption, Schwarz, Bless, et al. (1991) found that respondents reported higher assertiveness after recalling twelve rather than six examples when they were able to attribute the experienced difficulty to the impact of a distracting task. Similarly, Schwarz and Schuman (1992) observed in an extended replication of Bishop's (1987) studies that asking respondents to evaluate the public relations work of their U.S. representative eliminated the otherwise obtained negative effect of the knowledge question on their reported political interest, as shown in Table 4.1.

Confirming Bishop's (1987) results, Schwarz and Schuman (1992) found that asking a knowledge question about the performance record of the respondents' U.S. representatives increased the percentage of respondents who reported that they follow politics only "now and then" or "hardly ever," from 21 percent to more than 39 percent. Respondents apparently concluded from the difficulty they experienced in answering the knowledge question that they didn't follow politics very closely. In a third condition, however, respondents had to evaluate the quality of their representative's public relations work before they reported on how closely they follow politics. In this case, respondents could conclude that their lack of knowledge reflected the representative's poor job of keeping the

TABLE 4.1 Impact of a knowledge question on reported political interest.

Question order		
Political interest Knowledge	Knowledge Political interest	Knowledge Public relations Political interest
21.0%	39.4%	29.6%

Source: Schwarz and Schuman, 1992.

Note: Shown is the percentage of respondents who reported following politics "now and then" or "hardly ever."

public informed rather than their own lack of interest. As a result, the impact of the knowledge question was cut by half, and only about 30 percent of the respondents reported that they followed politics only "now and then" or "hardly ever."

The latter finding is particularly interesting because Bishop (1987) observed that the impact of the knowledge question on reported political interest was largely unaffected by filler items, even under conditions where the two questions were separated by a full 101 unrelated buffer items. In contrast, a single intervening question was sufficient to reduce the effect to nonsignificance in the present study. This one question, however, was targeted to undermine the psychological process that drives the observed context effect. In combination, the differential impact of 101 versus 1 buffer items demonstrates that researchers need to understand the psychological processes that underlie a given context effect. Purely technical analyses, focusing on the sheer number of buffer items, for example, are unlikely to advance an understanding of survey response.

As these examples show, early questions may affect subsequent judgments by influencing not only what comes to mind but also the manner by which things come to mind. Feelings—that it is easy or difficult to answer a question, or that one is in a good mood—may themselves influence the conclusions drawn. However, respondents will only use these experiences as a basis for judgment if they seem relevant to the judgment at hand. If they attribute the experienced feelings to a source that renders them irrelevant to the judgment at hand, they will disregard them. (See Clore, 1992; Schwarz, 1990b, for more detailed discussions of the informational value of feelings and subjective experiences.)

Context Effects at the Formatting Stage

Preceding questions may also influence how respondents use the response scales provided to them, resulting in context effects at the formatting stage. This is particularly likely to happen when the response has to be provided along a rating scale, as described in the following section. In addition, the order in which the response alternatives of a categorical scale are presented may influence the likelihood that a given alternative is endorsed. However, this reflects the impact of the ordering of the response alternatives themselves rather than the impact of preceding questions. Accordingly, we address response order effects on categorical scales separately in Chapter Six.

Rating Scales

Numerous studies in psychophysics demonstrate that ratings of a stimulus are context-dependent (see Poulton, 1989, for a review). For example, a given square is rated as larger when presented in the context of smaller squares than when presented in the context of larger squares. This suggests that respondents anchor the rating scale on the extremes of the stimulus continuum, as shown in Figure 4.1.

Suppose that respondents were asked to rate the size of square C along a four-point scale, ranging from one (very small) to four (very large). If only squares A to D were presented to them, thus constituting the relevant "perspective" for this task (Ostrom & Upshaw, 1968), they would use A and D to anchor the scale. In this case, square C would receive a rating of three. Suppose, however,

FIGURE 4.1 Anchoring a rating scale.

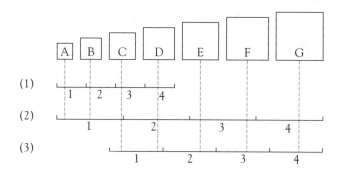

that squares A to G were presented, extending the relevant per-spective. In this case, anchoring the rating scale on A and G would essentially stretch the scale and square C would now receive a rat-ing of two. Moreover, more than one square would be assigned to the same rating scale category, decreasing the discrimination between stimuli. Finally, suppose that only squares C to G were pre-sented to respondents. In this case, anchoring the scale on C and G would result in a rating of one for square C, again reflecting a change in perspective.

Perspective effects of this type are most pronounced when all stimuli are rated along the same scale, as in this example. However, respondents can only anchor the scale on the extremes of the pre-sented stimulus continuum when they are aware of what the extremes are. If only one stimulus is presented at a time, respon-dents will anchor the scale on extremes recalled from memory, reflecting whatever perspective is accessible to them at the time of judgment. To enter into the perspective, the extreme stimulus must seem relevant to the task at hand. Two studies from different domains illustrate this point.

In a classic study in psychophysics, Brown (1953) asked subjects to rate the weight of different blocks they were asked to lift. Not surprisingly, a given block was rated as heavier when preceded by a light block than when preceded by a heavy block. However, this was only the case when the heavy block was perceived as being part of the series of blocks to be rated. When the subjects were asked to lift a tray—a dissimilar object—of equivalent weight, their judgment of the target objects remained unaffected. Apparently, the tray was not perceived as part of the stimulus series. Accordingly, it did not enter the subjects' representation of the relevant "perspective," and was ignored when anchoring the rating scale. As this example illustrates, even psychophysical judgments, which are often thought to depend primarily on sensory inputs, are strongly affected by the cognitive representation of the stimuli.

Although the Brown (1953) study demonstrates that an extreme stimulus must be perceived as relevant to the set of target stimuli in order to affect their ratings, it is not necessary that the extreme stimulus itself be rated. For example, Schwarz, Münkel, and Hippler (1990; see also Noelle-Neumann, 1970) asked German respondents to rate how "typically German" a variety of drinks were. Before this task, some respondents had to estimate how many Germans drink beer (a typical drink in that country), whereas others had to estimate how many Germans drink vodka (an atypical drink). Their subsequent ratings of wine, milk, and coffee showed the expected contrast effect, as seen in the first row of Table 4.2.

Respondents who had estimated the consumption of beer rated all beverages as "less typically German" than respondents who had estimated the consumption of vodka, indicating that all used the highly accessible extreme stimuli brought to mind by the preceding

TABLE 4.2 Impact of extreme stimuli on subsequent ratings.

	Context stimulus	
	Vodka	Beer
Preceding question		
Consumption	5.4	4.4
Calorie content	4.4	4.5

Source: Adapted from Schwarz, Münkel, and Hippler, 1990.

Note: N = 25 to 27 per cell; 9 = "very typical." Shown is the mean of ratings of three beverages (milk, wine, and coffee).

question to anchor the rating scale. It should be noted that this shift in ratings occurred even though the extreme stimuli themselves were not rated along the scale; this suggests that their sheer accessibility in memory was sufficient to change respondents' perspective. Reiterating the theme of Brown's (1953) study, however, this conclusion comes with one important qualification. In this example, respondents had to estimate the frequency with which Germans consume beer or vodka; this judgment was relevant to the typicality dimension because a drink is only "typically German" if Germans drink it frequently. But other respondents had to estimate the caloric content of a glass of beer or vodka. Whereas this task also served to increase the accessibility of the extreme stimuli in memory, it did not bear on the typicality issue. As a result, these respondents did not show a shift in their subsequent ratings, as seen in the second row of Table 4.2. Hence, we conclude that extreme stimuli brought to mind by preceding questions will only be used in anchoring the response scale if the content of the preceding question links them to the underlying dimension of judgment. If it does, these stimuli are likely to affect subsequent ratings even if they themselves are not rated along the same scale. (In Chapter Five we discuss additional variables that determine the use of information in constructing scale anchors and standards of comparison.)

The impact of scale anchoring discussed so far is referred to as the *perspective effect* in Ostrom and Upshaw's (1968) perspective theory and as the *range effect* in Parducci's (1982, 1983) range-frequency theory. Both theories maintain that respondents anchor the scale in a way that accommodates the range of stimuli presented to them. In addition, respondents try to discriminate between stimuli as best they can given the limits of the rating scale. Suppose, for example, that additional small squares, let us say A' to A''', were inserted between squares A and B in the sequence of A to D squares shown in Figure 4.1. If respondents used the rating scale as shown in line 1, all four squares A to A''' would be assigned to the same rating category, resulting in limited discrimination. To be most informative, however, respondents would be unlikely to assign four stimuli to one category of the response scale and one stimulus each to each of the remaining categories. Rather, they would most likely attempt to assign a roughly equal number of stimuli to each rating category, because "assigning the same number of stimuli to each category maximizes the number of bits of information transmitted (in the information theory sense)" (Parducci, 1983, p. 269). Parducci calls this the *frequency effect* in his range-frequency theory, and it is not addressed by Ostrom and Upshaw's model.

In sum, the use of rating scales is a function not only of the extreme stimuli that are used to anchor the scale (resulting in a range effect) but also of the number and distribution of stimuli (resulting in a frequency effect). Accordingly, a given stimulus will receive different ratings depending on the extremity, frequency, and distribution of context stimuli introduced in the questionnaire. Daamen and de Bie (1992) provide a detailed discussion of these issues and explore their implications for survey research.

Effect of Rank-Ordering Scales on Subsequent Ratings

A special complication may arise at the formatting stage when a rating task is preceded by a rank-ordering task: the direction of rank-ordering may affect the subsequent use of numerical rating scales. In a series of studies, Schwarz and Wyer (1985) asked respondents to rank-order a set of environmental issues from most important to least important or from least important to most important. Subsequently, respondents had to evaluate along a rating scale other environmental issues that were not included in the rank-ordering task. When respondents rated the importance of the issues, they rated all issues as more important if the earlier rank-ordering had progressed from most to least important than from least to most important. However, when they rated triviality of issues, they also rated all issues as more trivial when the preceding ranking had progressed from most to least important than least to most important. Moreover, the same pattern was obtained when the rankings pertained to triviality, as shown in Table 4.3.

TABLE 4.3 Mean ratings of environmental issues as a function of ranking criterion.

| | Previous ranking of other issues by importance or triviality | | | |
| | Importance | | Triviality | |
	Most to least	Least to most	Most to least	Least to most
Rating of new items				
Importance	65.5	52.2	65.5	49.6
Triviality	47.4	42.6	49.5	29.5

Source: Adapted from Schwarz and Wyer (1985), Experiment 2.

Note: The possible range of ratings is from 0 ("not at all important" or "not at all trivial," respectively) to 100 ("extremely important" or "extremely trivial," respectively). $N = 18$ to 20 per condition.

In essence, respondents assigned higher ratings following the most-to-least sequence, independent of both the substantive implications of these ratings (importance or triviality) or the content of the rank-ordering task. Indeed, ranking desirable attributes in a spouse from most to least important also resulted in higher ratings of the importance and the triviality of environmental issues than did ranking desirable spousal attributes from least to most important.

That the impact of the direction of rank-ordering on the obtained ratings was unrelated to the content of the ranking task or to the substantive meaning of the ratings suggests that the observed effect was not driven by any substantive information that the rank-orderings may have brought to mind. Rather, the direction of rank-ordering influenced respondents' subsequent use of a rating scale. Apparently, respondents who first had to rank-order unrelated stimuli from most to least important (trivial, or whatever) subsequently focused on the end of the rating scale that reflected a high standing on the rating dimension, essentially the end equivalent to "most." In contrast, respondents who had to rank-order stimuli from least to most important (or trivial) subsequently focused on the low end of the rating scale, essentially the end equivalent to "least." As a result, the obtained ratings were displaced toward the end of the scale that the respondents focused on, resulting in higher ratings when the ranking task elicited a focus on the high end and in lower ratings when it elicited a focus on the low end. Consistent with this assumption about the use of numeric rating scales, additional studies showed that the direction of preceding rankings did not affect evaluations along verbal response scales.

Context Effects at the Editing Stage

Finally, preceding questions may draw respondents' attention to issues of social desirability and self-presentation, resulting in biases in responses to subsequent questions to which these concerns may be relevant. This seems particularly likely to occur when the issue is not sufficiently sensitive to elicit these concerns spontaneously. We would expect different reports of tranquilizer consumption, for example, when the context questions pertain to medical issues or to issues of drug abuse. An amusing example of such effects was reported by Sherman and Golkin (1980). They told subjects about a father and son who were involved in a car accident. The father died on the spot but the son was rushed to the hospital and prepared for surgery. The surgeon came in, saw the patient, and exclaimed, "I can't operate on him; he's my son." This scenario seemed impossible to most people until they realized that the surgeon was the patient's mother, which many did only after the explanation was offered by the experimenter. However, following this involuntary confrontation with their own sexist biases, respondents went on to express particularly liberal attitudes on questions pertaining to gender-based discrimination.

Summary

The context in which a question is asked can influence respondents' cognitive processes at each stage of the question answering process. Moreover, the various processes are not mutually exclusive;

a given context effect may reflect the simultaneous operation of several processes. Finally, it is important to keep in mind that in some modes of administration context effects are not necessarily limited to the impact of preceding questions on subsequent ones. Under self-administered questionnaire conditions, for example, where respondents may read ahead or return to previous questions, questions asked later on may affect responses to preceding ones (see Schwarz & Hippler, 1995).

In the next chapter, we offer a more detailed exploration of context effects at the judgment stage. We will pay particular attention to the conditions under which information that is brought to mind by preceding questions results in assimilation or contrast effects in subsequent responses.

5

The Direction of Context Effects

What Determines Assimilation or Contrast in Attitude Measurement?

In Chapter Four we reviewed a number of different sources of context effects in attitude measurement. In the present chapter, we focus in more detail on one particular source, namely, substantive information that is brought to mind by preceding questions. This information may affect the judgment stage of the response answering process and result in assimilation or in contrast effects. To conceptualize the underlying processes, we draw on the inclusion/exclusion model proposed by Schwarz and Bless (1992a). This model specifies the conditions under which question order effects emerge at the judgment stage and predicts their direction, size, and generalization across related issues.

Although the model has received a fair amount of empirical support in psychological experimentation (see again Schwarz & Bless, 1992a, for a review), we emphasize at the outset that its predictions go far beyond the data given. We consider this an advantage rather than a shortcoming. Traditionally, research on context effects in surveys has been hampered by a lack of theoretical frameworks and has been characterized by a more or less ad hoc nature. In this as in other areas of research, however, we are likely learn useful lessons from a comprehensive model, even if empirical work eventually proves parts of it wrong.

The Inclusion/Exclusion Model

The key assumptions of the inclusion/exclusion model draw heavily on recent research in cognitive psychology that emphasizes the dynamic nature of knowledge representations (see Barsalou, 1989; Kahneman & Miller, 1986; and the contributions in Martin & Tesser, 1992). Moreover, the model's assumptions and predictions regarding the emergence of assimilation effects are compatible with the belief sampling model proposed by Tourangeau and colleagues (Tourangeau, 1987, 1992; Tourangeau, Rasinski, & Bradburn 1992). In contrast to the belief sampling model, however, the inclusion/exclusion model explicitly identifies the conditions that give rise to contrast effects. For that reason, our discussion in this chapter draws on the conceptualization offered by the inclusion/exclusion model, although this model is largely identical with the belief sampling model of Tourangeau, Rasinski, & Bradburn (1992) with regard to the conceptualization of assimilation effects and the stability of attitude reports over time.

Constructing Targets and Standards

Schwarz and Bless (1992a) assume that when individuals are asked to form a judgment about some target stimulus they first must retrieve some cognitive representation of it. In addition, they need to determine some standard of comparison to evaluate the stimulus. Both the representation of the target stimulus and the representation of the standard are, in part, context-dependent. Individuals do not retrieve all knowledge that may bear on the stimulus, nor do they retrieve and use all knowledge that may potentially be relevant to constructing a standard. Rather, they rely on the subset of potentially relevant information that is most accessible at the time of judgment (Bodenhausen & Wyer, 1987; Higgins, 1989; Higgins & King, 1981). Accordingly, their temporary representation of the target stimulus as well as their construction of a standard includes information that is chronically accessible—hence, context-independent—as well as information that is only temporarily accessible due to contextual influences.

Whereas differences in the chronic accessibility of information reflect respondent characteristics, differences in the temporary accessibility of information are primarily due to questionnaire variables. Most important, information that has been used for answering a preceding question is particularly likely to come to mind when respondents are later asked a related question. How the information that comes to mind influences the judgment depends on whether it is used to construct a representation of the target, a representation of a standard or scale anchor against which the target is evaluated or whether it is excluded from all of these.

Assimilation Effects

Information that is included in the temporary representation that individuals form of the target of judgment will result in assimilation effects because the judgment is based on the information included in the representation used. Accordingly, the addition of information with positive implications results in a more positive judgment, whereas the addition of information with negative implications results in a more negative judgment.

The size of context-induced assimilation effects increases with the amount and extremity of the temporarily accessible information and decreases with the amount, extremity, and evaluative consistency of chronically accessible information included in the representation of the target. Hence, the size of assimilation effects is a function of context as well as of respondent variables. On the one hand, the size of assimilation effects increases the more, or the more extreme, information the preceding question brings to mind. On the other hand, the impact of the temporarily accessible information is limited by the chronically accessible information. For example, adding positive information to a representation that includes only one piece of negative information will have more impact than adding it to a representation that includes numerous negative attributes. By the same token, adding a piece of positive information to a representation that includes, for example, two positive and two negative attributes will have more impact than adding it to a representation that includes four negative attributes. Thus, the size of assimilation effects decreases as more chronically accessible information and more evaluatively consistent information is included in the representation of the target.

This conceptualization has important implications for the impact of respondents' expertise on the emergence of context effects. In addition, it bears on how one versus several preceding questions affect the size of context effects. We address each of these issues in turn.

Expertise. Survey researchers have often assumed that respondents who are highly knowledgeable about an issue should be less susceptible to context effects than those who are less knowledgeable, but relevant empirical findings are mixed (see Bickart, 1992; Schuman & Presser, 1981). The present model allows us to specify the crucial conditions in more detail. First, let us suppose that a respondent has a large amount of evaluatively consistent information about target X that is chronically accessible in memory. Increasing the temporary accessibility of some additional information about X through preceding questions should have little impact on the respondent's evaluation of X. This is the case in which the usual assumption of experts' resistance to context effects should hold. But if the expert's chronically accessible information is evaluatively mixed, the temporarily accessible information is still likely to make a difference. Hence, the evaluative consistency of the expert's chronically accessible information is the crucial boundary condition.

As a second possibility, let us suppose that the respondent's expertise pertains to the general content domain rather than to the specific target addressed in the question of interest. For example, a market research survey could ask respondents to evaluate a new car with which they have not yet had any experience. If the survey draws attention to price, this information would probably have more meaning for respondents who know more about cars in general (see Herr, 1989). For example, experts could infer features that a car in the $40,000 price range is likely to have whereas the same information would hold less meaning for novices. In terms of our model, a question pertaining to the adequacy of the $40,000 price tag would render more information temporarily accessible for experts than for novices. As a result, this question should produce stronger context effects among experts than among novices. Thus, the crucial issue is what respondents' expertise pertains to: if they are experts on the specific car under study we would not expect them to show strong context effects. In the present example, however, respondents are experts on the general domain (cars), but not on the specific target (this particular car) and thus may bring more domain knowledge to bear on the target, allowing for the emergence of stronger context effects.

In general terms, these considerations predict that experts on target X are less likely to show strong context effects in judgments of X than novices provided that their chronically accessible information is evaluatively consistent. But if information about X is relevant for evaluating target Y, experts on X should show stronger context effects in their judgment of Y than novices, reflecting that questions about X bring more information to the experts' mind. Because most studies have only assessed respondents' general domain expertise without considering the relationship of this expertise to the target under study, it is not surprising that the available findings are mixed.

As this discussion illustrates, how we define expertise is of crucial importance. On theoretical grounds, expertise may pertain to the general content domain or to the specific issue under study. Both forms of expertise have different implications for the emergence of context effects. Unfortunately, many discussions of respondents' expertise not only ignore this distinction but also draw solely on global proxy variables, such as years of schooling or self-reported interest. Such variables are unlikely to moderate the size of context effects unless they are confounded with the actual amount of knowledge about the target issue. It should come as little surprise then that formal education or self-reported interest have been found to show inconsistent relationships with the emergence and size of context effects (see Bradburn, 1983; Schuman & Presser, 1981).

Number of Preceding Questions. Whereas our discussion of expertise on target issue X pertained to the amount of chronically accessible information about it, similar considerations hold for the amount of information rendered temporarily accessible by preceding questions. Specifically, the impact of a piece of information brought to mind by one question is reduced as additional information is brought to mind by other questions. Hence, the impact of a given question decreases as the number of related context questions increases. For example, answering a question about marital happiness had a pronounced impact on subsequent reports of general life satisfaction when respondents' marriage was the only specific domain addressed. This impact was significantly reduced, however, when respondents had to answer questions about their leisure time and their job in addition to questions about their marriage before reporting their general life satisfaction (Schwarz, Strack, & Mai, 1991). In addition, the increased accessibility of information used to answer a preceding question wears off over time, further reducing its impact on questions that are separated by a sufficient number of intervening items (see Tourangeau & Rasinski, 1988; Tourangeau, 1992).

Contrast Effects

According to the inclusion/exclusion model, the same piece of information that elicits an assimilation effect may also result in a contrast effect. The inclusion/exclusion model (Schwarz & Bless, 1992a) holds that a contrast effect occurs when the information is excluded from rather than included in the cognitive representation formed of the target.

For example, let us suppose that a given piece of information with positive (or negative) implications is excluded from the representation of the target category. In this case, the representation will contain less positive (or negative) information, resulting in less positive (or negative) judgments. We call this possibility a *subtraction-based contrast effect* (see Bradburn, 1983; Schuman & Presser, 1981, for a related discussion). The size of subtraction-based contrast effects increases with the amount and extremity of the temporarily accessible information excluded from the representation of the target, and it decreases with the amount, extremity, and evaluative consistency of the information that remains in the representation of the target, paralleling our discussion of assimilation effects. Hence, we would again expect experts to show less pronounced subtraction-based contrast effects because they have a larger amount of chronically accessible information to use in constructing the representation of the target.

However, respondents may not only exclude accessible information from the representation formed of the target but also may use this information in constructing a standard or scale anchor. If the implications of the temporarily accessible information are more extreme than the implications of the chronically accessible information used in this construction, the process will result in a more extreme standard and elicit contrast effects for that reason. The size of such *comparison-based* contrast effects increases with the extremity and amount of temporarily accessible information used in constructing the standard or scale anchor and decreases with the amount and extremity of chronically accessible information used in making this construction.

Which of these processes drives the emergence of a contrast effect determines whether the contrast effect is limited to a single target or generalizes across related targets. If the contrast effect is based on the mere subtraction of information from the representation formed of the target, it is limited to the evaluation of that particular target. This simply means that the evaluation is based on the information "left" in the representation of the target. But if the information excluded from the representation of the target is used in constructing a standard or scale anchor, contrast effects are likely to emerge on each judgment to which this standard or scale anchor is relevant.

Because the model provides two related mechanisms for the emergence of contrast effects, a logical question is raised. Under which conditions are we likely to obtain subtraction-based effects and under which are we likely to obtain comparison-based effects? The model holds that information that is excluded from the representation of the target is only used in constructing a standard or scale anchor if it has been thought about with regard to the relevant judgmental dimension. In Chapter Four, we reviewed a study on scale anchoring by Schwarz, Münkel, and Hippler (1990) that illustrates this point (see Table 4.2). Respondents were asked to rate a number of beverages according to how "typically German" they were. When this question was preceded by a question about the frequency with which Germans drink beer or vodka, contrast effects emerged in the typicality ratings. But when the preceding question pertained to the caloric content of beer or vodka, the typicality ratings were unaffected. The pattern of findings indicated that respondents only used the highly accessible drinks information in constructing a standard or scale anchor when the question that brought the drinks to mind addressed the underlying dimension of frequency of consumption that was relevant to a typicality judgment.

In sum, the inclusion/exclusion model holds that information that is excluded from the representation of the target category results in subtraction-based contrast effects if it has not been thought about with regard to the underlying dimension of judgment. If it has been thought about with regard to the relevant dimension, the excluded information is likely to be used in constructing a standard or scale anchor, resulting in comparison-based contrast effects. Whereas subtraction effects are limited to the evaluation of the target from which the information is excluded, comparison-based contrast effects generalize to the evaluation of every target to which the standard or scale anchor is relevant.

What Triggers the Exclusion of Information?

We assume that the default operation for most respondents is to include relevant information that comes to mind in the representation of the target. In other words, we should be more likely to see assimilation effects than contrast effects in survey research, an issue that should be addressed by meta-analyses. In contrast, the exclusion of information needs to be triggered by salient features of the question answering process. In principle, any variable that affects the categorization of information is likely to affect the emergence of assimilation and contrast effects, linking the present model to cognitive research on categorization processes in general (see Barsalou, 1989; Smith, 1990, for reviews). Schwarz and Bless (1992a) review a host of heterogeneous variables that have been shown to affect context effects in social judgment and trace their operation to inclusion/exclusion processes. Here we address the variables that are of particular relevance to survey research. The variables can be conceptualized as bearing on three decisions that respondents have to make with regard to the information that comes to mind, as shown in Figure 5.1.

Some of the information that comes to mind may simply be irrelevant, pertaining to issues that are unrelated to the question asked. Other information may be relevant and respondents have to decide what to do with it. The first decision relates to *why* this information comes to mind. Information that seems to come to mind for the "wrong reason"—for example, respondents are aware of the potential influence of a preceding question—is likely to be excluded (Lombardi, Higgins, & Bargh, 1987; Ottati, Riggle, Wyer, Schwarz, & Kuklinski, 1989; Strack, Schwarz, Bless, Kübler, & Wänke, 1993). The second decision relates to whether the information that comes to mind *belongs to* the target category. The content of preceding questions (Schwarz & Bless, 1992a), the width of the target category (Schwarz & Bless, 1992b), the extremity of the information (Herr, 1986), or its representativeness for the target category (Strack, Schwarz, & Gschneidinger, 1985) are relevant at

FIGURE 5.1 Emergence of assimilation and contrast effects.

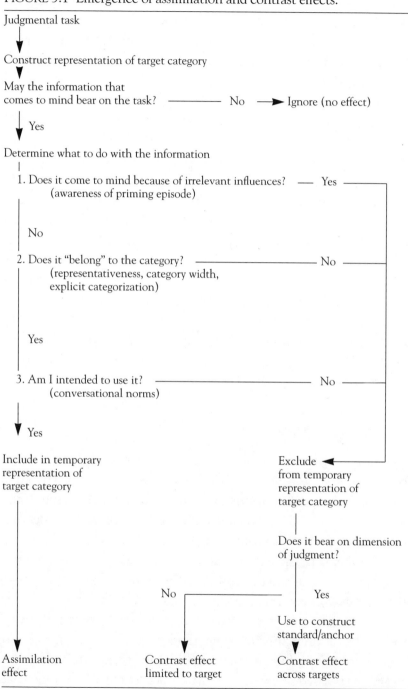

this stage. Finally, conversational norms may determine respondents' perception of what they are supposed to do with highly accessible information (Schwarz, Strack, & Mai, 1991; Strack, Martin, & Schwarz, 1988; Tourangeau, 1984; Tourangeau, Rasinski, & Bradburn, 1992).

Whenever any of these decisions results in the exclusion of information from the representation formed of the target, it will elicit a contrast effect, the size of which will depend on the variables discussed earlier. Whether the contrast effect is limited to the target or generalizes across related targets depends on whether the excluded information is merely subtracted from the representation of the target or used in constructing a standard or scale anchor. In contrast, when the information that comes to mind is included in the representation formed of the target, it results in an assimilation effect, the size of which also depends on the variables discussed earlier. Hence, the model predicts the emergence, the direction, the size, and the generalization of context effects in attitude measurement. In addition, it predicts the stability of attitude reports over time and offers some predictions about the dependence of these effects on the mode of data collection used.

Stability Over Time

The model's predictions about the stability of attitude judgments over time follow directly from the assumptions about the construction of representations of targets and standards (see Tourangeau et al., 1992, for a related discussion). Specifically, repeating the judgment process at different points in time will result in similar judgments to the extent that respondents form similar mental representations of the target and of the standard each time. Several variables determine how likely this is to be the case.

Obviously, no change is expected when the context of the attitude judgment remains the same, rendering the same information temporarily accessible. Similarly, no change is expected when the judgment is based solely on chronically accessible information that comes to mind at both points in time. Findings reported by Tourangeau et al. (1992) provide some support for this conclusion. They assessed respondents' attitudes toward abortion by asking them to report their thoughts in an open-ended format. When this procedure was repeated three weeks later, respondents' global attitude report was more strongly correlated with their previous attitude report when their open-ended responses at $t2$ showed overlap with their thoughts at $t1$ than when they did not. For example, when respondents reported two identical thoughts at both times, their judgments correlated $r = .84$ whereas this correlation was only $r = .35$ when their reported thoughts showed no overlap.

Even under conditions where the mental representations formed at both times include considerable amounts of different information, these differences in representation will only result in different judgments if the information used at $t1$ and $t2$ has different evaluative implications. Simply replacing one piece of information with a different one of similar valence will not change the evaluative judgment.

Our discussion of the size of context effects also bears directly on stability over time. As noted earlier, the size of assimilation effects decreases as the amount and evaluative consistency of other information included in the representation of the target increases. Hence, adding a piece of information at $t2$ to a representation of the target that is otherwise identical with that used at $t1$ will only result in change if the initial representation was based on a small amount of information or was evaluatively inconsistent. Support for the role of evaluative consistency is again provided by the Tourangeau et al. (1992) study. In their reinterview study, attitude measures assessed three weeks apart were correlated $r = .57$ for respondents who reported having mixed views on the topic, but $r = .81$ for respondents who reported being clearly on one side of the issue.

The same logic applies to changes in the representation of the target if a piece of information used at $t1$ is deleted at $t2$. Deleting a piece of previously used information will only result in different judgments if little other information was included in the first place or if the representation was evaluatively inconsistent.

Finally, similar considerations apply to changes in the representation of the standard, again paralleling our discussion of the size of comparison-based contrast effects. Accordingly, the variables that determine the size of context effects are also the variables that determine the stability of evaluative judgments over time.

Mode Effects

As already noted, the inclusion/exclusion model assumes that the default operation is to include information that comes to mind whereas the exclusion of information needs to be triggered by salient features of the question answering process. Moreover, exclusion processes require additional cognitive work. Accordingly, we should only see them when respondents are motivated and able to engage in this extra work. Consistent with this assumption, Martin, Seta, and Crelia (1990) observed that a lack of motivation—or distracting subjects from engaging in cognitive work—eliminated the emergence of contrast effects that were otherwise obtained. This suggests that we should be more likely to see contrast effects if respondents have a greater chance to engage in the necessary cognitive work. For example, such effects should be more likely under the leisurely conditions of a self-administered questionnaire (provided that respondents do not read all questions before answering them, thus eliminating question order; for example, Schwarz & Hippler, 1995) than under the time pressure of a telephone interview. However, data bearing on this assumed impact of the differential pace of different modes of data collection are not yet available.

Implications for Questionnaire Construction

How do the model's assumptions bear on the emergence of assimilation and contrast effects in survey research? In this section of the chapter, we review a number of different questionnaire variables, reporting empirical evidence where available. The most important variables are the content and number of preceding questions, the generality of the target question, the spacing of related questions in the questionnaire, introductions or the lack of introductions to a block of questions, and the graphical presentation of questions in self-administered questionnaires.

The Content of Preceding Questions

The content of preceding questions determines the information that becomes temporarily accessible in memory. In addition, it may determine respondents' decisions about whether the information brought to mind belongs or does not belong to the target category to be evaluated (see Schwarz & Bless, 1992a; Tourangeau, Rasinski, & D'Andrade, 1991).

In one of their studies, Schwarz and Bless (1992a) asked a sample of German college students to evaluate the Christian Democratic Party (CDU) in power in Germany. To do so, respondents presumably recalled chronically accessible information from memory, which may have included that the CDU was a conservative party, that Chancellor Kohl was a member of it, and so on. For some respondents, the party evaluation question was preceded by one of two political knowledge questions, each of which pertained to a specific politician, namely Richard von Weizsäcker. This politician, who was a member of the CDU, was highly respected by Germans no matter their party preference. To elicit the inclusion of Richard von Weizsäcker in respondents' representation of the Christian Democrats, Schwarz and Bless asked some respondents, "Do you happen to know which party Richard von Weizsäcker has been a member of for more than twenty years?" (See Table 5.1.)

As shown in the first row of Table 5.1, answering this question resulted in more favorable evaluations of CDU politicians than a control condition in which no question about Richard von Weizsäcker was asked. This assimilation effect reflects the inclusion of Richard von Weizsäcker in the representation formed of the CDU.

TABLE 5.1 Evaluation of political parties with and without inclusion of a respected politician.

Target	Preceding question about Richard von Weizsäcker:		
	Relating to his party membership	No question	Relating to his presidency
Christian Democrats	6.5	5.2	3.4
Social Democrats	6.3	6.3	6.2

Source: Adapted from Schwarz and Bless, 1992a.

Note: N = 19 to 25 per condition; 1 = unfavorable and 11 = very favorable opinion about politicians of the respective party.

However, Richard von Weizsäcker had not only been a member of the CDU for several decades. At the time of the study, he was also serving as president of the Federal Republic of Germany, and the office of president required him to refrain from active participation in party politics. As a representative of the Federal Republic, the president is supposed to take a neutral stand on party issues, much like the Queen in the United Kingdom. This position rendered him particularly suitable for the present experiment because it allowed the authors to ask other respondents, "Do you happen to know which office Richard von Weizsäcker holds, setting him aside from party politics?" Answering this question was expected to *exclude* Richard von Weizsäcker from the representation that respondents formed of CDU politicians, resulting in a contrast effect. As shown in the first row of Table 5.1, this prediction was again confirmed in comparison to the control condition.

Since neither the party membership question nor the presidency question tapped the evaluative dimension, the model predicts that the observed contrast effect would reflect a mere subtraction process. According to this assumption, Richard von Weizsäcker was chronically accessible to some respondents in the control condition. Answering the party membership question, however, rendered him accessible for all respondents, resulting in a more positive average evaluation of the party. In contrast, answering the presidency question induced all respondents, including those for whom he was chronically accessible, to exclude him from the representation formed of his party. As a result, the party membership question increased and the presidency question decreased the number of respondents who included this highly respected politician in their representation of the CDU. The result was the observed differences in judgment. The obtained contrast effect, however, should have been limited to evaluations of the Christian Democrats and not have generalized to evaluations of related targets. And indeed, evaluations of the Social Democrats, shown in the second row of Table 5.1, were not affected by the context questions about Richard von Weizsäcker. But had the context questions tapped the evaluative dimension, the model would predict that the contrast effects would have generalized across targets because Weizsäcker would be used in constructing a standard.

In summary, this study illustrates that the same information (in the present case, information about a highly respected politician) may result in assimilation or contrast effects in judgment depending on whether it is included in or excluded from the representation that respondents form of the target category. In the present case, these operations were a function of the specific content of the knowledge questions asked.

However, context effects can only be detected if the majority of the sample shares the same evaluation of the information that comes to mind. Suppose, for example, that only half the respondents thought highly of Richard von Weizsäcker. In that case, his inclusion in the representation of the CDU would have resulted in more favorable judgments for some respondents but less favorable judgments for others. Whereas each of these effects would reflect an assimilation of the general judgment to the evaluation of Richard von Weizsäcker at the theoretical level, these effects could have canceled one another, resulting in the apparent absence of context effects in the sample as a whole. Schwarz, Strack, and Mai (1991) observed such a finding in another study. In this study, thinking about one's marriage increased life satisfaction for happily married respondents but decreased life satisfaction for unhappily married ones, resulting in the absence of a context effect in the sample as a whole. It is therefore important to keep in mind that context effects are conditional (see Smith, 1992). For each respondent, the impact of the same general cognitive process depends on the implications of the specific information that is brought to the particular respondent's mind. Unless the conditional character of context effects is acknowledged in analyses, we may erroneously conclude that none were observed.

The implications of the conditionality of context effects for data analysis are often overlooked. Most important, the conditionality implies that any analysis of the impact of Question 1 on the answers given to Question 2 has to take respondents' substantive answers to Question 1 into account. Simply assessing the answers to Question 2 as a function of whether Question 1 preceded it or not is insufficient. Rather, we have to analyze the answers to Question 2 as a function of the placement of Question 1 and the answers given to it. This may be done by appropriate cross-tabulations or by a comparison of the correlation between both questions under both order conditions. In many cases, such a conditionality analysis reveals context effects where none are observed if only the overall means are compared.

The Number of Preceding Questions

According to the inclusion/exclusion model, the impact of a given piece of information depends on the amount and extremity of competing information used in constructing a representation. Accordingly, adding a piece of information to the representation of the target results in a larger assimilation effect when the representation contains little rather than a lot of other information.

Consistent with this assumption, Schwarz, Strack, and Mai (1991) observed that answering a marital satisfaction question before answering a question about one's general life satisfaction significantly increased the correlation of both measures from $r = .32$ (in the general-specific order) to $r = .67$ (in the specific-general order) when the marital satisfaction question was the only domain satisfaction question asked. However, the increase in correlation was less pronounced—and not significant—when three specific life domains (work, leisure, and marriage) were addressed prior to the general life satisfaction question, resulting in a correlation of $r = .42$ for marital and general satisfaction. Thus, the impact of information bearing on respondents' marriages was less pronounced as other information relevant to their lives became more accessible.

These effects, however, can be quite sensitive to what appear to be small changes in the number or content of previous questions. For example, Tourangeau, Rasinski, and Bradburn (1992) found what appeared on the surface to be a nonreplication of the results of Schwarz, Strack, and Mai (1991). Upon closer examination of the experimental conditions in the two studies, however, it was found that Tourangeau, Rasinski, and Bradburn (1992) asked about marital status before asking either the general or marital happiness question whereas Schwarz, Strack, and Mai asked about marriage and dating relationships without assessing respondents' marital status first. The question on marital status appears to have temporarily heightened the accessibility of the respondents' marriage in the Tourangeau, Rasinski, and Bradburn (1992) study and, as a result, explicitly asking the marital satisfaction question first did not further increase the impact of marriage-related information on general life satisfaction. In both studies, however, when the items were explicitly linked by a joint introduction, making it clear that they were related to one another, the results were similar: there was a lower correlation when the marital happiness question came before the general happiness question. This is a classic contrast effect, which we will discuss in more detail below.

The Generality of the Target Question

One of the most important determinants of assimilation versus contrast effects in survey practice is probably the generality of the target question. A question about the trustworthiness of politicians, for example, could refer to all politicians in the United States, to politicians of one party, or to a specific politician. In psychological terms, these questions would address target categories of different widths. The first question pertains to a wide category whereas the second question pertains to a narrower one. The last question, pertaining to one politician alone, is the narrowest and would not allow the inclusion of any other politician; the given person would make up a category by himself or herself. How would this differential category width affect the emergence of context effects?

Let us suppose, for example, that a preceding question asks respondents to recall some politicians who were involved in a scandal, rendering these politicians highly accessible. According to the model, the politicians involved in the scandal are members of the general category "politicians" and are therefore likely to be included in the temporary representation that respondents form of that category. If so, their evaluation of the trustworthiness of politicians in general should decrease, reflecting an assimilation effect. But the politicians who were involved in the scandal could not be included in the representation formed of the narrow category of one politician. Hence, the scandal-ridden politicians might now serve as a standard of comparison or scale anchor, resulting in a contrast effect.

A laboratory experiment with German respondents (Schwarz & Bless, 1992b) confirmed this prediction. (See Table 5.2.) Respondents who were asked to name two politicians involved in a well-known scandal subsequently reported less trust in German politicians in general. However, the same context question increased the reported trustworthiness of each of three specific politicians, although these exemplars were not perceived as particularly trustworthy to begin with. This pattern of findings suggests that the scandal-ridden politicians could be included in the representation formed of "German politicians" in general but not in the representation of any specific person. Since a question about "scandals" did tap the trustworthiness dimension to which the subsequent ratings

TABLE 5.2 Evaluation of trustworthiness of politicians.

	Scandal question	
	Not asked	Asked
Target		
Politicians in general	5.0	3.4
Specific exemplars	4.9	5.6

Source: Adapted from Schwarz and Bless, 1992b.

Note: N = 8 per condition; 1 = not at all trustworthy and 11 = very trustworthy.

pertained, the scandal-ridden politicians were used to construct the standard, creating a contrast effect.

In general, the inclusion/exclusion model predicts that assimilation effects are more likely to emerge when the target category is more inclusive. Accordingly, *general questions*, which assess respondents' opinions about a wide target category and allow for the inclusion of a variety of information, should be most likely to show assimilation effects. But *specific questions*, which assess respondents' opinions about a narrowly defined target, should be more likely to show contrast effects. The reason for this is that it is more likely that information that comes to mind can be included in a representation of a global target than of a specific target.

This assumption accounts for a variety of different observations. For example, Americans typically report low trust in congressmen in general but high trust in their own representative (see Erikson, Luttberg, & Tedin, 1988). Similarly, Americans are likely to endorse capital punishment in general but less likely to endorse it in any specific case (Ellsworth & Gross, 1994). Findings of this type suggest that extreme exemplars are likely to come to mind when respondents are asked a general question, presumably because extreme exemplars receive more attention in public discourse. These exemplars are included in the representation formed of a wide target category, resulting in assimilation effects on the general question. However, they cannot be included in the representation of the narrower target category, resulting in contrast effects on the specific question. As a result, the recalled examples of untrustworthy congressmen, for example, reduce trust in congressmen in general but increase trust in one's own Representative. Hence, apparent general-specific paradoxes of this type are actually a reflection of the impact of category width on the operation of inclusion/exclusion processes.

The Spacing of Questionnaire Items

The impact of item spacing in a questionnaire is likely to differ depending on the stage at which the respective context effect arises. At the question comprehension stage, respondents may deliberately turn to preceding items to make sense of a subsequent ambiguous question, as we have seen in Chapters Three and Four (for example, Strack, Schwarz, & Wänke, 1991). Adjacent items are more likely to be considered relevant than items placed at further distance from one another, reflecting a natural assumption that blocks of questions bear on related issues, much as they would during ordinary conversations. Moreover, respondents may lose track of more distant items, reducing the likelihood of their use. As a result, the impact of a context item at the question comprehension stage is likely to decrease as the number of intervening items increases.

At the judgment stage, however, the relationship between item spacing and context effects is more complicated. On the one hand, a large number of intervening items may interfere with recall of the primed information, again eliminating the emergence of a context effect (for example, Tourangeau, Rasinski, Bradburn, & D'Andrade, 1989a, 1989b). If the primed information still comes to mind, however, the spacing of the items may determine the use of the information, that is, its inclusion in or exclusion from the representation of the target. This is likely to be the case for two related reasons. First, psychological experiments have shown that respondents exclude information that comes to mind for what they assume to be the "wrong" reason. For example, Lombardi, Higgins, and Bargh (1987) observed that priming effects in a person perception task were obtained only when respondents were not aware of the priming episode (see also Strack, Schwarz, Bless, Kübler, & Wänke, 1993). If respondents are aware that the information that comes to mind may do so only because it was triggered by a preceding question they may disregard (exclude) it for that reason (Martin, 1986). As a second possibility, conversational norms may induce respondents to ignore information they have already provided in response to a specific question when they are later asked a more general one because conversational norms request us to provide information that is "new" to the recipient rather than reiterate information already given, as we saw in Chapter Three. (See Schwarz, 1994; Strack & Schwarz, 1992; Tourangeau & Rasinski, 1988, for more detailed discussions.) Both of these processes may be influenced by the spacing of items and by introductions to blocks of related items (to be addressed in the following section).

A study by Ottati, Riggle, Wyer, Schwarz, and Kuklinski (1989) illustrates the impact of item spacing on inclusion/exclusion operations. They asked respondents to report their agreement with general and specific statements pertaining to civil liberties. For example, a general statement read, "Citizens should have the right to speak freely in public." In one condition, this general statement was preceded by a specific statement that pertained to a favorable or unfavorable group, that is, "The Parent-Teacher Association (or the Ku Klux Klan, respectively) should have the right to speak freely in public." As expected, respondents expressed a more favorable attitude toward the general statement if it was preceded by a specific one that pertained to a favorable group. However, this assimilation effect was only obtained when the items were separated by eight filler items. If the items were presented one after the other, a contrast effect emerged. The latter finding presumably reflects the exclusion of the primed information as a function of conversational norms or of awareness of the preceding item's possible influence.

Thus, assimilation effects are likely to emerge when questions are separated whereas contrast effects are likely to emerge when they are consecutive. However, as the number of filler items (often called "buffer items" by survey researchers) increases, they may interfere with the recall of previously activated information, eliminating the basis for either type of context effect (see Tourangeau, 1992; Tourangeau & Rasinski, 1988, for reviews). Hence, the number of intervening questions may determine the emergence of assimilation or of contrast effects as well as the absence of both.

Introductions to Item Blocks and Graphical Layout

As discussed in Chapter Three, in general conversation communicators are expected to avoid redundancy (Grice, 1975). In psycholinguistics this is known as the "given-new contract," which requires speakers to provide information that is "new" rather than to reiterate information already "given" (Haviland & Clark, 1974). Several studies indicate that this conversational norm of nonredundancy is evoked when related questions are perceived as belonging to the same conversational context (Schwarz, Strack, & Mai, 1991; Strack, Martin, & Schwarz, 1988; Strack, Schwarz, and Wänke, 1991). If the questions follow a part-whole format, using the information that has already been provided in response to a specific ("part") question in answer to a subsequent more general ("whole") question would violate this conversational norm. Variables that evoke the norm are introductions to a block of related items and the graphical presentation of self-administered questionnaires.

For example, in a study addressed earlier, Schwarz, Strack, and Mai (1991; see also Tourangeau, Rasinski, & Bradburn, 1992) asked respondents to report their marital satisfaction and their general life satisfaction. When the marital satisfaction question was asked as the last question on one page of the questionnaire and the general question as the first question on the next, happily married respondents reported higher general satisfaction and unhappily married respondents reported lower general satisfaction than when the general question came first, reflecting an assimilation effect. When both questions were introduced by a joint lead-in, thus assigning them to the same conversational context, respondents excluded the information that they reported in response to the specific question, resulting in contrast effects on the general one.

A related study (Schwarz & Hippler, unpublished data) pertaining to the graphical presentation of self-administered questionnaires provided a conceptual replication of this effect. Specifically, presenting marital satisfaction and life satisfaction as two separate questions, each framed by a black box, resulted in assimilation effects. Presenting the two questions in a single box—thus emphasizing their relatedness—elicited contrast effects.

These and similar findings (see Schwarz, 1994; Strack & Schwarz, 1992) demonstrate that conversational norms can trigger the exclusion of information that has already been provided from the cognitive representation formed for answering a subsequent question. Variables that can elicit the application of the conversational norm of nonredundancy include lead-ins to blocks of items as well as the graphical layout of self-administered questionnaires.

Implications for Attitude Theory

As the findings reviewed in this and the preceding chapter illustrate, attitude reports are subject to pronounced context effects. This fact is not surprising when we conceptualize attitude reports to reflect complex judgmental processes, as we do throughout this book. This judgmental perspective, however, is sometimes disputed.

The term *attitude* is usually used to refer to "a psychological tendency that is expressed by evaluating a particular entity with some degree of favor or disfavor" (Eagly & Chaiken, 1993, p. 1). Traditionally, attitudes were assumed to have a cognitive component, referring to beliefs about the attitude object; an affective component, referring to the evaluation of the object; and a conative component, referring to behavior toward the object (see Eagly & Chaiken, 1993, for a comprehensive review). This classic tripartite definition has been abandoned by most researchers primarily because the three components have been found to be only weakly related, rendering it difficult to think of them as part and parcel of the same thing. In fact, what is usually assessed in surveys is only the affective component of attitudes, as reflected in evaluative judgments. For this reason, we prefer the term *evaluative judgments* when we refer to attitude measures in the present book.

When we consider attitude measures to reflect evaluative judgments, their context dependency is not surprising: after all, human judgment is always context-dependent, no matter if it pertains to psychophysical stimuli or to complex social issues. This position, however, is not shared by all researchers. Rather, some have argued that people have well-formed attitudes with regard to some objects and that such well-formed attitudes are unlikely to be affected by the immediate context in which they are assessed. From this perspective, the emergence of context effects suggests that we are assessing "nonattitudes" (Converse, 1964), that is, responses to objects for which people do not have well-formed or "crystallized" attitudes.

In cognitive social psychology, these perspectives are often referred to as the "file-drawer" versus the "construal" model of attitudes (see Wilson & Hodges, 1992, for a recent discussion). According to the file-drawer model, well-formed attitudes pertaining to some objects are stored in memory and can be "looked up" when a person is asked to answer an attitude question. Only when this search is unsuccessful do we need to form a judgment on the spot. But according to the construal model, our mental file-drawer does not contain "attitudes" at all and we always need to form a judgment based on information that is chronically or temporarily accessible at the time. As an intermediate position, one may assume that the accessible information sometimes includes a previously formed judgment, which may enter the computation of a new judgment as another piece of information that simplifies the judgmental process.

In another take on the issue, Tourangeau and colleagues (see Tourangeau, 1992, for a comprehensive summary) suggested that we think of attitudes as memory structures that include valenced pieces of information. According to this theory, attitude reports usually require the computation of a judgment but the attitude concept is "saved" by redefining attitudes as memory structures. Thus, the information stored in memory constitutes a respondent's attitude but reports of this attitude may vary as a function of context, reflecting that the context influences which pieces of the memory structure are brought to mind at any given point. Hence, individuals "have" attitudes but their reports vary as a function of context. This theory essentially coincides with the construal model except that the term *attitude* is maintained by redefining the concept as pertaining to chronically accessible information.

Of course, these distinctions are only useful to the extent that they generate different predictions for observable phenomena. In this last section, we argue that deriving such crucial predictions is far more difficult than one might expect. To make this point, we adopt a strong version of a construal model, assuming for the sake of the argument that respondents always need to compute a judgment from scratch. Starting from this assumption, we apply the principles of the inclusion/exclusion model to findings that are usually supposed to support the assumption that individuals have attitudes on some topics, but perhaps not on others. Throughout, we will show that these findings are as compatible with a construal model as they are with the classic attitude model, rendering the debate futile for the purpose of attitude measurement in surveys.

The Stability of Attitude Reports over Time

An issue that we have already addressed is the stability of attitude reports over time. Presumably, obtaining similar reports at different points in time suggests that respondents have an attitude toward an object that they can report with some accuracy. As we discussed in considerable detail previously, however, construal models predict similar responses at different points in time under conditions that are likely to elicit only small context effects. Accordingly, construal models are compatible with the observation of stability in attitude reports and specify the conditions under which such stability should be observed, rendering the approach clearly testable. In contrast, the conclusion that individuals must have a well-formed attitude because their reports are stable over time is utterly circular in the absence of other evidence. One such set of evidence pertains to measures of attitude strength.

Attitude Strength

Several researchers have suggested that attitudes vary in their degree of "strength," "centrality," or "crystallization" (see Krosnick & Abelson, 1992, for a review). These concepts have been found to be difficult to operationalize (see Scott, 1966) and researchers have used a variety of indicators to assess attitude strength, including the intensity of respondents' feelings about the object, the certainty with which they report holding the attitude, and the importance they ascribe to it. Unfortunately, the various measures of attitude strength are only weakly related to one another. Moreover, the widely shared hypothesis that context effects in survey measurement "are greater in the case of weaker attitudes has clearly been disconfirmed" (Krosnick & Abelson, 1992, p. 193). In the most comprehensive test of this hypothesis, based on more than a dozen experiments and different measures of attitude strength, Krosnick and Schuman (1988) found no support for it except for the not-surprising finding that respondents with a weak attitude are more likely to choose a middle alternative. But given the high plausibility of the hypothesis and its long tradition in survey theorizing (dating back at least to Blankenship, 1943; Cantril, 1944; Katz, 1960), it is likely to remain popular.

However, attitude strength has proved to be important in other domains of research. Most important, strongly held attitudes have been found to be more stable over time and less likely to change in response to persuasive messages. Moreover, they are better predictors of behavior than weak attitudes (see Krosnick & Abelson, 1992, for a review). Once again, however, a construal model allows the same predictions. To the extent that we are likely to think more, and more often, about topics that are important to us, a larger amount of information would be chronically accessible. Increased chronic accessibility, in turn, would result in higher stability over time and would decrease the likelihood of arriving at a different judgment when a few new pieces of information are added to the representation of the target. Moreover, an individual would be likely to draw on a similar set of information when asked to report a judgment and when faced with a behavioral decision, resulting in a higher consistency between the judgment and the behavior. Accordingly, a construal model would arrive at the same predictions if we assume that people think more about issues that are important to them, thus rendering more information chronically accessible, a plausible assumption. As a result, the findings of the attitude strength literature do not necessarily reflect that the processes underlying reports of "strong" attitudes differ from the processes underlying reports of "weak" attitudes.

Attitude Accessibility

Another body of research (for reviews see Bassili, 1995; Dovidio & Fazio, 1992; Fazio, 1990) suggests that some attitudes are more accessible than others, as reflected in respondents' reaction times. Presumably, a quick response to an attitude question reflects that a previously formed evaluation was accessible in memory whereas a slow response reflects computation of an evaluation. Several studies have found that highly accessible attitudes, as inferred from quick answers, are more stable over time and are better predictors of behavior (see Fazio, 1990).

Unfortunately, reaction time measures do not tell us which stage of the judgment process produces a fast or a slow response. A fast reaction may reflect the retrieval of a highly accessible previous judgment or the high speed of a current computation. Let us suppose, for example, that all information that comes to mind is evaluatively consistent. It would be easier to arrive at an overall judgment with this information than with inconsistent information. In the latter case, we would need to determine which weight we want to give to positive or negative features to arrive at an overall judgment. This would presumably take time, resulting in a slower response. But differences in reaction time might reflect differences in the evaluative consistency of the accessible information rather than the accessibility of a previously formed judgment.

Making this assumption, which is amenable to empirical testing, construal models would again arrive at the same predictions. To the extent that different pieces of chronically accessible information have similar implications, retrieving different pieces at different times would not result in different judgments. Moreover, retrieving different pieces when one makes a judgment and when one makes a behavioral decision would still result in a high consistency between the judgment and the behavior. It is only when different pieces of information have opposite implications that we should see low stability over time and low attitude-behavior consistency. Integrating the implications of these different pieces of information, however, would take time, resulting in the observed relationship between response time and stability or attitude-behavior consistency. Hence, the observed relationship does not necessarily reflect differences in the accessibility of existing attitudes, but may reflect differences in a mental construal process.

Concluding Thoughts

Our conclusion from these conjectures is not that the literature on attitude strength or attitude accessibility is necessarily mistaken. At present, we are not aware of data that bear on our conjectures. We simply note that the available findings are potentially compatible with construal models if one makes some rather plausible additional assumptions. In our reading, this suggests that asking whether people "have" attitudes is futile as far as survey measurement is concerned. We do not necessarily need different models for the measurement of attitudes and nonattitudes to account for the available findings. Rather, we can use a construal model of the type described (Schwarz & Bless, 1992a) to conceptualize the processes underlying the measurement of evaluative judgments, no matter whether they pertain to "attitudes" or "nonattitudes." Such a model has several advantages: it can account for stability as well as change; it predicts the conditions under which context effects are or are not likely to emerge; it predicts their direction, size, and generalization across targets; and it allows for the conceptualization of differences between respondents (such as expertise, attitude strength, and so on) as well as of questionnaire variables within a single conceptual framework. For the time being, we consider such an approach to be most likely to advance our understanding of survey measurement, although future research may teach us otherwise.

Summary

The inclusion/exclusion model provides a conceptual framework that allows predictions regarding the emergence, direction, size, and generalization of context effects in attitude measurement. Most important, the model holds that any variable that influences the categorization of information that comes to mind is likely to moderate the emergence of assimilation or contrast effects. Schwarz and Bless (1992a) provide a comprehensive review of a host of different variables that have been studied in psychological research. Most relevant to questionnaire construction are the content and number of preceding questions, the width of the target category, the spacing of items in a questionnaire, the lead-in to blocks of related questions, and the graphical presentation of self-administered questionnaires. Moreover, the model allows for the conceptualization of respondent variables such as expertise, motivation, and cognitive ability within the same conceptual framework and offers a number of straightforward predictions about the impact of the data-collection mode. Although some of the key predictions of the model have received considerable experimental support, the evidence bearing on others is rather limited. In addition, future research is likely to uncover other variables that may elicit inclusion/exclusion operations. We hope, however, that the present conceptualization provides a fruitful heuristic framework for future work in this area.

6

Order Effects Within a Question

Presenting Categorical Response Alternatives

In this chapter we turn to the impact of the order in which different response alternatives are presented within a single question. As is the case for question order effects, survey researchers have long been aware that the order in which response alternatives are presented to respondents can profoundly affect the obtained results (see Blankenship, 1943; Cantril, 1944; Payne, 1951, for early discussions). Empirically, *primacy effects* (that is, higher endorsements of the same items if presented early in the list) and *recency effects* (higher endorsements of the same items if presented late in the list) have been obtained in numerous studies. The emergence of response order effects is apparently not restricted to one response format and has been observed on verbal rating scales (for example, Carp, 1974) as well as on forced-choice questions that present a small number (McClendon, 1986) or a large number (Becker, 1954) of discrete response alternatives. Moreover, response order effects have been obtained on opinion questions as well as on factual reports (Schwarz, Hippler, & Noelle-Neumann, 1992, 1994) and they are not limited to survey results. The order in which alternatives are presented has also been shown to influence decisions with potentially important consequences. For example, a political candidate may receive more votes when his or her name is presented early rather than late on the ballot sheet, reflecting a primacy effect (Brook & Upton, 1974; Mueller, 1970).

Despite the considerable empirical evidence for the emergence of response order effects, we know relatively little about the conditions that determine their emergence and direction, and the area is characterized by a large number of apparently inconsistent findings. These inconsistencies presumably indicate that different processes may contribute to the emergence of response order effects. Moreover, these processes are not mutually exclusive, resulting in a rich set of possible interaction effects. Unfortunately, the presumably systematic character of these interaction effects can hardly be detected in the available studies because they are usually restricted to a manipulation of only one or two factors.

Complicating things further, the most frequently used research designs show a surprising lack of sophistication, rendering it impossible to isolate even the impact of the key variable, namely, presentation order per se. Let us suppose that a researcher presents three response alternatives. To explore a possible order effect, he reverses the presentation order for half of the sample, resulting in a Form A (ABC) and a Form B (CBA). In this typical design, presentation order is confounded with the content of preceding response alternatives. As a result, it is impossible to decide if differences in the endorsement of A are due to A's serial position or to the possible influence of thinking about C or B before being exposed to A. To isolate the impact of presentation order alone, one would need to employ a Latin square design, in which each response alternative occurs once in each ordinal position. In this example, such a design would result in six (rather than two) forms: ABC, ACB, BAC, BCA, CAB, and CBA. Whereas the use of Latin square designs is a standard procedure in experimental psychology (see Lindquist, 1953, pp. 273–281, for an early textbook introduction), adequate designs have rarely been used in survey research on response order effects because they are complex to administer (see Becker, 1954, for a noteworthy exception).

Because of these shortcomings in the available data, it is currently impossible to draw strong conclusions about the processes that underlie response order effects in survey measurement. Therefore, our goal for the present chapter is to review different process assumptions in the light of current psychological theorizing, highlighting plausible hypotheses that need to be tested in future research. Not surprisingly, our own favorite account of response order effects relies on the conceptual framework that we developed in the two preceding chapters and focuses on the impact of response alternatives on the cognitive accessibility of relevant information and its use in the construction of mental representations of the target. The reader should keep in mind, however, that much of our discussion is speculative. Although we pay close attention to the compatibility of our theorizing with the available data, the nature of these data does not allow unequivocal conclusions.

What Mediates Response Order Effects?

Different explanations for the emergence of response order effects have been offered over the decades. Surprisingly, none of the early hypotheses has suffered in popularity, reflecting the limited progress made in this area. One explanation assumes that respondents "like to reach for the first thing that catches their eye" (Payne, 1951, p. 83), an assumption that is also at the heart of Krosnick's (1991) discussion of satisficing in survey measurement. Hence, any item "that catches the eye" should be more likely to be endorsed if presented early rather than late. Accordingly, this notion predicts primacy effects and cannot account for the emergence of recency effects, rendering it unsuitable as a general explanation. A second account attributes response order effects to respondents' memory limitations (for example, Blankenship, 1943). As we show in detail in the following section, this explanation predicts recency effects under conditions that are typical for survey interviews and cannot account for primacy effects unless one makes questionable additional assumptions.

A more recent line of theorizing suggests as a third possibility that the presentation order influences respondents' opportunities to think about a given response alternative, thus influencing the judgment stage of the question answering sequence (Krosnick, 1992; Krosnick & Alwin, 1987; Schwarz, Hippler, & Noelle-Neumann, 1992, 1994). This cognitive elaboration account predicts a number of complex interactions of presentation order and presentation mode (that is, whether the response alternatives are presented in writing or are read to respondents) that are consistent with much of the available data.

Finally, some response order effects do not result from serial position per se but reflect an impact of the content of earlier items, as we discussed in the preceding chapters. We address each of these accounts in more detail in the following section.

Other hypotheses offered in the literature do not provide causal accounts of the emergence of response order effects but address limiting conditions. Many researchers assumed that response order effects are more likely to emerge when the questions are complex (Payne, 1949). This hypothesis is compatible with the memory limitation as well as the cognitive elaboration accounts. In addition, it has frequently been assumed that response order effects are not obtained when respondents' opinions are "crystallized" (Rugg & Cantril, 1942). This hypothesis is compatible with the cognitive elaboration account to be presented in this chapter, if we assume that "crystallization" implies that a considerable amount of relevant information is chronically accessible to respondents, limiting the impact of temporarily accessible information brought to mind by response alternatives. Similarly, the order of response alternatives should have little impact if respondents can recall a previously formed judgment, provided that this judgment matches one of the response alternatives offered. These considerations parallel our discussion of the emergence of question order effects in Chapter Five. In contrast, sheer familiarity with the subject matter is insufficient to eliminate order effects, as Becker (1954) observed in a study that assessed evaluations of well-known radio programs. In line with our previous discussion of the crystallization issue (see Chapter Five), Becker's findings indicate that having well-developed attitudes based on extensive experience with the subject matter is not sufficient to eliminate judgmental context effects unless a previous judgment is highly accessible.

We now turn to a detailed discussion of *memory limitations, cognitive elaboration,* and *contrast effects.* We focus on questions that present a number of discrete categorical response alternatives. Throughout, our emphasis is on the likely emergence of complex but systematic interaction effects. In the final section of the chapter, we address a special case, the emergence of order effects on verbal rating scales.

Memory Limitations

Response order effects have frequently been attributed to respondents' memory limitations. If respondents have forgotten a response alternative by the time they are supposed to report their answer, that alternative will not be endorsed. According to this theory, respondents' selection is restricted by their memory performance and a given response alternative is more likely to be endorsed if it is more likely to be recalled. Not surprisingly, psychological research into the learning of lists of verbal expressions indicates that recall is indeed influenced by the length of the list and by an item's serial position (see Baddeley, 1990; Smyth, Morris, Levy, & Ellis, 1987, for reviews). However, the direction of this influence is highly dependent on the time delay between learning and recall, a contingency that has frequently been overlooked in attempts to construct memory-based accounts of presentation order effects.

The left-hand panel of Figure 6.1 shows a typical serial position curve under conditions of immediate recall, that is, conditions under which recall follows learning without delay. Under these no-delay conditions, material presented at the end of the list is most likely to be recalled because the last few items are still accessible in working memory. However, the material presented at the beginning of the list is more likely to be recalled than material presented in the middle of the list even though more time has elapsed since it was learned. This reflects the fact that the first few items suffer "less competition for time and space" (Smyth et al., 1987, p. 123) in working memory than do later items. They are therefore more extensively processed and more likely to be committed to long-term memory. Recall is poorest for items presented in the middle of the list. These items are less likely to be committed to long-term memory, putting them at a disadvantage relative to the earliest items, and they are also no longer present in working memory, putting them at a disadvantage relative to the last few items. As a result, experimental research in the list learning tradition has typically obtained recency effects under conditions of immediate recall, indicating that recall is highest for the last few items.

Next, let us consider a typical serial position curve under conditions of delayed recall. An example is shown in the right-hand panel of Figure 6.1. Here, items presented at the beginning of the list are most likely to be recalled, indicating that these items are committed to long-term memory from where they can be recalled even after time has elapsed. The recall advantage of the last few items, however, can no longer be observed. Because of the delay, these items have been cleared from working memory, in particular if subjects had to work on a distractor task during the delay. Therefore, recall performance on the last items approaches the low level of the middle items, reflecting their disadvantaged status in long-term memory. Accordingly, list learning experiments have typically produced primacy effects under conditions of delayed recall.

What are the implications of this well-established interaction effect between serial position and time of recall for response order effects in survey measurement? These considerations suggest that we should typically observe the emergence of recency effects in long lists of response alternatives. Because survey respondents report their answer immediately after exposure to the response alternatives, there is no delay between "learning" and "recall." Accordingly, response alternatives presented at the end of the list should be easily accessible in working memory. Because under no-

FIGURE 6.1 Recall as a function of serial position and delay.

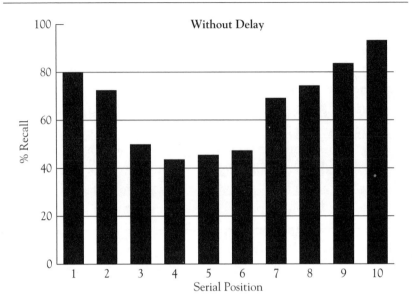

delay conditions recall of late items from working memory is better than recall of early items from long-term memory, the result should be pronounced recency effects, much as is shown in the left-hand panel of Figure 6.1. Primacy effects should only be obtained if a delay is introduced between exposure to the response alternatives and respondents' reports, which is not usually the case in survey interviews. Nevertheless, primacy rather than recency effects have usually been reported in survey experiments with long lists of response alternatives (Payne, 1951; Becker, 1954; Krosnick & Alwin, 1987; Mueller, 1970; Ring, 1975). We conclude from this inconsistency between the two literatures that, despite popular assumptions, sheer memory limitations are not the primary source of response order effects in survey measurement.

In fact, long lists of response alternatives are usually presented on show cards that remain visible until respondents report their answer, thus putting little burden on their memory to begin with. With telephone interviews the problem may be more acute because

FIGURE 6.1 Recall as a function of serial position and delay *(continued)*.

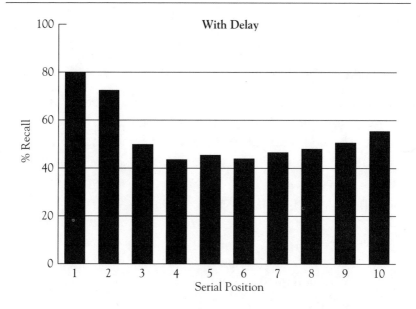

show cards cannot be used. However, response order effects have also been observed on questions that present only two or three response alternatives (Payne, 1951; McClendon, 1986; Schuman & Presser, 1981; Schwarz, Hippler, & Noelle-Neumann, 1992), and we will present some examples later in this chapter. Such a limited number of response alternatives should be easily accessible in working memory under the no-delay condition of survey interviews, thus rendering the emergence of order effects unlikely unless the alternatives are overly complex. Accordingly, it seems that we need to consider other processes if we want to explain response order effects in survey measurement.

In summary, memory limitations are most likely to play a role in the emergence of response order effects when numerous or complex response alternatives are presented without the help of show cards, thus taxing respondents' memory. Under this condition, psychological theorizing about memory limitations predicts the emergence of recency effects. Primacy effects would only be predicted under delayed recall conditions, which are atypical for survey interviews.

Cognitive Elaboration

If memory limitations do not provide a satisfactory explanation for most response order effects in survey measurement, what other processes should be considered? Following previous theorizing by Krosnick and Alwin (1987) and drawing on cognitive research in the area of persuasive communication (for example, Eagly & Chaiken, 1993; Petty & Cacioppo, 1986a, 1986b), one might expect that the order and mode in which response alternatives are presented affect respondents' opportunity to elaborate on their content. This effect, in turn, influences the thoughts they generate in response to opinion questions and the quality of retrieval cues they generate in response to behavioral questions. Such a model has been proposed by Schwarz, Hippler, and Noelle-Neumann (1992; 1994), and our current discussion draws on their theorizing. According to their model, the impact of an item's serial position is crucially dependent on whether it is presented in a visual or an auditory mode. Furthermore, the mediating process is the respondent's opportunity to think about the item's content. We first consider the implications of the cognitive elaboration approach for opinion questions and then turn to its implications for autobiographical reports.

Response Alternatives as Persuasive Arguments

Let us suppose that a respondent asked an opinion question is provided with several response alternatives that reflect different views. We may think of each response alternative as a short persuasive argument. Hence, the processes that are known to determine the impact of persuasive communications may also determine respondents' reactions to the items presented to them. As a large body of research has demonstrated, the impact of a persuasive argument is determined to a large degree by the recipient's cognitive responses, that is, by the thoughts that the recipient generates in response to the presented argument (see Eagly & Chaiken, 1993; Petty & Cacioppo, 1986a, 1986b, for reviews). The more positive, agreeing thoughts the argument elicits, the more the recipient is influenced by it, resulting in a positive attitude change. Conversely, if the argument elicits negative, disagreeing thoughts, the recipient is likely to exhibit a "boomerang" attitude change, moving away from the argument's implications.

These assumptions are compatible with Schwarz and Bless's (1992a) inclusion/exclusion model, which we reviewed in Chapter Five. Specifically, the agreeing or disagreeing thoughts that the response alternatives bring to mind are likely to become part of the mental representation that respondents form of the proposition offered in the response alternative. In general, the more agreeing thoughts a response alternative elicits, the more likely the respondents are to endorse it. Conversely, the more disagreeing thoughts a response alternative elicits, the less likely the respondents are to endorse it. The number of thoughts elicited by a given response alternative, however, is not only a function of the content of the response alternative. Thoughts are also influenced by the recipients' ability and motivation to process the content and by the opportunity that the situation provides them to do so. As research on persuasive communications has demonstrated (see Eagly & Chaiken, 1993; Petty & Cacioppo, 1986a, 1986b for reviews), a plausible argument is more likely to elicit agreement the more the respondent thinks about its implications whereas an implausible argument is more likely to elicit disagreement under these conditions. Thus, conditions that interfere with recipients' cognitive elaboration of the implications of a presented argument, such as distractions while they listen to the message, have been shown to eliminate the advantage of plausible over implausible arguments (Bless, Bohner, Schwarz, & Strack, 1990; Harkins & Petty, 1981; see Petty & Brock, 1981 for a review).

How do these considerations relate to response order effects? As Krosnick and Alwin (1987; see also Krosnick, 1992) have argued in a very persuasive paper that strongly influenced Schwarz et al.'s (1992) theorizing, the degree of cognitive elaboration that a given response alternative receives is likely to be influenced by the order and the mode in which the response alternatives are presented. Let us suppose that a long list of response alternatives is presented to respondents in a visual format, either on a show card as part of a face-to-face interview or in a self-administered questionnaire. Under these conditions, "Items presented early in a list are likely to be subjected to deeper cognitive processing," as Krosnick and Alwin (1987, p. 213) noted. "By the time a respondent considers the later alternatives, his or her mind is likely to be cluttered with thoughts about previous alternatives that inhibit extensive consideration of later ones." As a result, visual presentation formats facilitate the cognitive elaboration of items presented early in the list and inhibit the elaboration of those presented late in the list.

However, if the items are not presented visually but instead are read to respondents by the interviewer, either under face-to-face or telephone interview conditions, respondents have little opportunity to elaborate on the items presented early in the list. The time available for processing is restricted by the speed with which the interviewer moves on to the next item. "Under these circumstances, respondents are able to devote most processing time to the final item(s) read, since interviewers usually pause most after reading them" (Krosnick & Alwin, 1987, p. 203). In addition, respondents may find it difficult to keep all the response alternatives in mind without visual cues, as discussed earlier. Accordingly, auditory presentation formats facilitate the cognitive elaboration of items presented late in the list and inhibit the elaboration of items presented early in the list.

However, as we have seen, the impact of the opportunity to elaborate on the implications of a response alternative depends on the alternative's plausibility. In operational terms, a given item is "plausible" to a respondent if it elicits agreeing thoughts when the respondent thinks about it and "implausible" if it elicits disagreeing thoughts, paralleling the conceptualization of agreeing or dis-agreeing "cognitive responses" in persuasion research (see Eagly & Chaiken, 1993; Petty & Cacioppo, 1986a, 1986b). In combination with the impact of the visual and auditory presentation formats on a respondent's opportunity to think about items presented early or late in a list, these considerations predict a complex pattern of interaction effects.

If a visual presentation format is used, respondents are more likely to elaborate on the items presented early in the list, for the reasons already discussed. Accordingly, a given plausible item should elicit more agreeing thoughts and be more likely to be endorsed when it is presented early rather than late in the list, resulting in a primacy effect. Conversely, a given implausible item should elicit more disagreeing thoughts and be less likely to be endorsed when presented early rather than late in the list, resulting in a recency effect.

The opposite predictions hold for auditory presentation formats. As noted, in an auditory format items presented late in the list are likely to receive more elaborate processing than items presented early. Hence, a plausible item is likely to elicit more agreeing thoughts and is more likely to be endorsed if presented late in the list, resulting in a recency effect. Conversely, an implausible item is likely to elicit more disagreeing thoughts and is less likely to be endorsed if presented late in the list, resulting in a primacy effect.

Altogether, these considerations predict a triple interaction of serial position, presentation mode, and item plausibility. Assum-ing that an item is plausible, thus eliciting agreeing thoughts, pri-macy effects should emerge under a visual presentation mode and recency effects under an auditory presentation mode. On the other hand, if the item is implausible the opposite predictions hold. In the latter case, recency effects should emerge under a visual presentation mode and primacy effects under an auditory presentation mode.

As complex as these predictions are, an additional factor needs to be considered. As Krosnick (1992) noted, respondents' thoughts about a response alternative may exhibit a confirmatory bias. For example, a respondent who is asked which of a list of problems is more important may be more likely to search for reasons that make a given problem important than unimportant. In fact, the task of identifying important problems offers a directed search hypothesis, and numerous studies have shown that such directed searches favor the retrieval of confirmatory material (see Wyer & Srull, 1989, for a review). This confirmation bias should facilitate the generation of agreeing thoughts in response to plausible items and inhibit the generation of disagreeing thoughts in response to implausible items. As a result, the predicted response order effects should be more pronounced in the former than in the latter case. In other words, we should be more likely to find support for our predictions concerning plausible rather than implausible items. In addition, the impact of cognitive elaboration differences is most likely to be observed under conditions that do not tax respondents' memory, thus limiting the possible impact of the recall processes discussed, which may dilute elaboration effects.

In the next section we review the limited experimental evidence available.

Opinion Questions: Experimental Evidence

Unfortunately, well-controlled experimental studies that test the theoretically crucial triple interaction of serial position, presentation mode, and item plausibility are not yet available. With few exceptions, the available evidence is limited to studies that were not originally intended to test cognitive elaboration assumptions. Moreover, each of the available studies bears only on some of the variables, and none of the studies contains direct manipulations of item plausibility or measures of the assumed underlying cognitive processes. Given these limitations, however, it is encouraging to note that archival data, reviewed by Schwarz, Hippler, and Noelle-Neumann (1992, 1994), are largely consistent with predictions.

Presentation Order and Mode. Most studies that obtained primacy effects in long lists of response alternatives were presented in a visual format (for example, Becker, 1954; Krosnick & Alwin, 1987; Schwarz, Hippler, and Noelle-Neumann, 1992). This is consistent with the model's prediction of primacy effects under visual presentation conditions (assuming plausibility of the items). However, data bearing on the auditory presentation of long lists are missing, because long lists are usually presented visually to avoid memory problems. Thus, the available archival data allow no evaluation of the predicted recency effects under auditory mode conditions.

More important, analyses of split-ballot experiments that used questions with only two or three response alternatives found support for the predicted serial position times mode interaction. Specifically, secondary analyses of split-ballot experiments originally conducted by Elisabeth Noelle-Neumann of the Allensbach Institute in Germany revealed a preponderance of primacy effects if the response alternatives were presented on show cards but a preponderance of recency effects if they were read to respondents (see Schwarz, Hippler, and Noelle-Neumann, 1992, for details). These effects were obtained with complex as well as relatively simple response alternatives. Table 6.1 shows some examples. Other researchers who explored order effects with two or three response alternatives also obtained recency effects (Krosnick, 1992; McClendon, 1986; Schuman & Presser, 1981) when using an auditory presentation mode. It should be noted that the presentation of only two or three simple alternatives is unlikely to tax respondents' memory, further supporting the notion that these effects are likely to reflect differences in cognitive elaboration rather than sheer memory limitations.

Judgment Formation. Another implication of the cognitive elaboration assumption is that response order effects should be obtained only when respondents need to form a judgment on the spot, as our discussion in the preceding chapters would suggest. In such cases, their judgment should be influenced by their opportunity to elaborate on the response alternatives. If respondents can recall a chronically accessible judgment from memory, however, the impact of order and mode should be largely reduced. Similarly, differences

TABLE 6.1 Response order effects in dichotomous questions.

	Response order	
Presentation mode	Presented first	Presented second
Visual		
Example 1:		
Responsibility for welfare		
State	64%	50%
Private charity	34%	28%
Auditory		
Example 2		
Form of government		
Authoritarian	15%	26%
Democratic	58%	67%
Example 3:		
Preferred novel		
Serious	31%	35%
Humorous	48%	53%
Question wordings and data sources		

Example 1: Responsibility for welfare
Presentation order of statements on show card is manipulated.
"Here are two men talking with one another. Would you please read what the two of them say?" (Interviewer gives respondent time to read show card.) "Which of the two would you rather agree with? With the upper one or with the lower one?"

Show card presents two individuals with the following statements in speech bubbles:
"I feel it is the responsibility of the state to make sure that there is no social misery. Retirement payments, social welfare, and sick leave compensation must be sufficient for one's living. That is the only adequate way to eliminate social misery."

"I feel that the state cannot ease all social misery. There are many individual cases where state payments are not all that is needed. One often needs to consider the individual circumstances. Therefore, each individual should help through donations and personal commitment to ease social misery."

Source: HB 1064, Institut für Demoskopie, Allensbach.

TABLE 6.1 Response order effects in dichotomous questions (*continued*).

Example 2: Form of government
Presentation order of statements manipulated; no show card used.
"Two men talk about how a country should be governed.

One says: I prefer that the people put its best politician at the top and delegates all power to him. Then he and selected experts can make clear and fast decisions. There isn't much talking and things are really going to happen.

The other says: I prefer that several people have some influence in the state. That results in some talking before anything gets done but it makes sure that power cannot be abused that easily.

Which of these two opinions is closer to your own—the first one or the second one?"
    Source: HB 1044, July 1960, Institut für Demoskopie, Allensbach.

Example 3: Preferred novel
Presentation order of "serious"/"humorous" manipulated.
"If you had the choice to read either a serious or a humorous novel, what would you rather read these days: the serious or the humorous novel?"
    Source: HB 445, March 1957, Institut für Demoskopie, Allensbach.

in the elaboration of the response alternatives should be less influential if respondents elaborate on the same content domain while answering preceding questions, increasing the temporary cognitive accessibility of relevant thoughts. In sum, response order effects should be less pronounced when respondents have already formed a judgment that they can recall from memory or when preceding questions bear on related issues. Experimental findings support these hypotheses.

Schwarz, Hippler, and Noelle-Neumann (1992) conducted a

modified replication of Payne's (1951) "oil supply" experiment (see also Schuman & Presser, 1981). In their study, ninety-one adult citizens of Mannheim, Germany, were read the question, "Some people say that we will still have plenty of oil twenty-five years from now. Others say that at the rate we are using our oil, it will all be used up in about fifteen years. Which of these ideas would you guess is most nearly right?" The order in which the two opinions were presented was reversed for half of the sample. (See Table 6.2.)

As shown in the first part of the table, a pronounced recency effect of 33 percentage points was obtained for both response alternatives when presented in an auditory format, replicating previous findings. For half of the sample, however, the question was preceded by two other questions that tapped the same content domain, which should have triggered cognitive elaborations bearing on the oil supply issue. These questions concerned the respondents' attitudes toward restrictions in the consumption of oil and the development of alternative sources of energy. As expected, introducing these context questions not only affected respondents' overall attitudes but completely eliminated the response order effect, as shown in the second part of Table 6.2.

This finding supports the general hypothesis that response order effects are in part a function of the cognitive elaboration of the response alternatives: if respondents are induced by preceding questions to elaborate on the issue before being exposed to the response alternatives, response order effects may be reduced or even eliminated. At the same time, the impact of the preceding questions on respondents' reports indicates that having respondents elaborate on the content domain may elicit pronounced shifts in reported attitudes, as discussed in Chapter Five. Although this finding bears on the theoretical rationale offered here it is not intended to imply that researchers should replace response order effects by question order effects.

Some archival data are also consistent with the assumption that response order effects occur at the judgment stage and are reduced or eliminated if respondents can recall a previously formed judg-

TABLE 6.2 The elimination of response order effects.

	Response order	
	Presented first	Presented second
Context		
Without preceding questions		
25 years	36%	69%
15 years	31%	64%
With preceding questions		
25 years	73%	71%
15 years	29%	27%

Note: The percentage of respondents who endorsed a given response alternative is reported. N = 91. Response alternatives were presented in an auditory format.

ment from memory. Table 6.3 shows one of the examples reported by Hippler, Schwarz, and Noelle-Neumann (1990), again taken from the archives of the Allensbach Institute.

In a split-ballot experiment conducted in February 1958, German respondents were asked to evaluate Chancellor Adenauer's performance on the issue of German reunification. The question was presented in a forced-choice form, offering two different opinions: (1) Adenauer had not done much on the issue, and (2) Adenauer could not do much because the Russians were not cooperative. As shown in the first part of Table 6.3, a recency effect of about 11 percentage points emerged on this dichotomous question, presented in an auditory format.

What should we expect if we break these data down by party preference? In the late 1950s, Adenauer was a highly respected political figure for conservative voters. Conservatives may not have needed to form a judgment when asked about Adenauer's performance on any issue, because the specific evaluation could easily be derived from their general evaluation of him, as we have discussed in preceding chapters. But respondents with a different party preference faced a more difficult task. As survey data from that time indicate, most Germans who held a different party preference still greatly respected Adenauer but disagreed with him on some issues. Accordingly, these respondents presumably needed to consider the specific issue in determining their answer. Their responses were more likely to have depended on the specific thoughts elicited by the response alternatives. Indeed, the data shown in the second part of Table 6.3 are consistent with this assumption. Whereas conservatives' responses were not significantly affected by response order, those provided by respondents with a different party preference did show a recency effect of 13.5 percentage points.

Additional analyses showed that the emergence of these effects was not moderated by education. An apparent impact of frequency of church attendance was also eliminated when party preference was controlled for. Thus, attitudinal variables proved more important than sociodemographic variables, as we have previously noted in the context of question order effects. From an applied point of view, these findings indicate that the order in which the response alternatives are presented may have a differential impact on subsamples, adding to the complexities in this area.

TABLE 6.3 Response order effects as a function of necessary elaboration.

	Position	
	First	*Second*
All respondents		
Adenauer has not done much	32.7%	44.3%
Russians are uncooperative	55.7%	67.3%
Party preference: CDU		
Adenauer has not done much	12.8%	14.8%
Russians are uncooperative	85.2%	87.2%
Party preference: Other		
Adenauer has not done much	47.7%	61.2%
Russians are uncooperative	38.8%	52.3%

Source: Data based on a quota sample of German adults (IfD 1018, February 1958); DK excluded.

Note: Respondents were randomly assigned to one of the two presentation order conditions and response alternatives were presented in an auditory format.

Respondent Variables. Although no effect of level of education was observed in the preceding example, other researchers report that response order effects increase with decreasing education (Cochrane & Rokeach, 1970; Krosnick & Alwin, 1987; McClendon, 1986) and decreasing cognitive sophistication, as measured by grade point average in a college sample (Krosnick, 1992). On theoretical grounds, however, we would not expect education per se to be a reliable moderating variable. Although respondents with high cognitive sophistication should find it easier to consider a variety of different arguments, this effect may be overridden by respondents' familiarity with the specific issue under study (which may determine the accessibility of relevant information) or by motivational variables. Depending on how these factors covary with education, the impact of education alone is likely to follow the familiar rule of "sometimes you see it, sometimes you don't."

Future Research. Most urgently needed in this domain are experiments that provide orthogonal manipulations of the three key variables (presentation order, presentation mode, and item plausibility) within the same study, using identical items in all order and mode conditions. Because the analysis of response order effects is necessarily based on frequency data and because the size of the largest of these effects rarely exceeds 10 percentage points, complex experiments with adequate power would require very large sample sizes; this explains the paucity of relevant studies. Although secondary analyses of archival data, as we have reviewed them in the preceding sections, support the general plausibility of the cognitive elaboration account, they cannot provide adequate tests of the underlying processes.

A Complication: Judgmental Contrast Effects

Response order effects are a function not only of respondents' memory limitations and the cognitive elaboration of the response alternatives provided but also of other judgmental processes elicited by the items. To introduce these processes, we first have to highlight an important distinction between two types of response alternatives.

Dimensional and Nondimensional Response Alternatives

One type of response alternative consists simply of a list of hetero-geneous possibilities. For example, respondents may be asked, "What did you do last Saturday?" and offered alternatives such as "sleeping in," "working," and "shopping," as in the example shown in Table 6.4. (The table appears later in this chapter.) The pre-sented possibilities are not clearly related to one another and do not bear on a single underlying dimension. For lack of a better term, Schwarz et al. (1992) called sets of this type *nondimensional*. We assume that response order effects in the endorsement of nondi-mensional response alternatives are primarily a function of their elaboration likelihood if only a few alternatives are presented. If a large number of response alternatives is offered, limitations of respondents' memory may add to the emergence of order effects, as discussed previously.

But other response alternatives bear on a single underlying dimension. For example, respondents are asked, "Which of the fol-lowing drinks do you consider to be typically German?" and are offered "vodka," "wine," "beer," and so on, as the alternatives. In this case, all response alternatives are to be evaluated along a single dimension. Accordingly, we call them *dimensional*. The dimension-ality is not determined by the content of the response alternatives alone but by the respondents' task. If respondents were to report if they ever bought the respective drinks, these drinks would make up a set of nondimensional response alternatives. Evaluating the typi-cality of these drinks, however, introduces a dimension along which these drinks have to be ordered and gives rise to other judgmental processes that may dilute the impact of cognitive elaboration. We now turn to the nature of these processes, which we already touched upon in Chapters Four and Five.

Asymmetric Contrast Effects

If a given item is preceded by an item that is more extreme on the dimension of judgment, a contrast effect may emerge. For example, respondents are presented a list of persons and are asked to select persons that they like (Ring 1974, 1975). An extremely well-liked person is presented in the middle of a list. In this case, moderately liked persons who are presented in the second part of the list will seem less likable by comparison. Therefore, they will be less frequently selected as "liked" under this order condition. If we compared two orders of this list, the judgmental contrast effect would lead us to conclude that a pronounced primacy effect had emerged. In contrast, if the person presented in the middle of the list were extremely unlikable, the same mechanism of judgmental contrast would increase the endorsement of moderately liked persons presented in the second half of the list. In this case, a comparison of both order conditions would lead us to conclude that a pronounced recency effect had emerged. It should be noted, however, that the underlying cognitive process of judgmental contrast or scale anchoring discussed in Chapter Four is quite different from the cognitive elaboration processes discussed earlier.

A classic example for such a contrast effect was reported by Noelle-Neumann (1970). Respondents were presented a list of food items and were asked to select those that were "typically German." Respondents were more likely to consider a number of food items, including noodles or potatoes, as "typically German" when they were preceded by rice than when they were not. Thus, introducing rice as the first item resulted in pronounced contrast effects in the perception of the other food items. The evaluation of rice itself was unaffected by order manipulations.

While primacy and recency effects in lists are presumably a function of the cognitive elaboration that a given item receives in different positions, contrast effects of the type observed by Noelle-Neumann (1970) are thought to be a function of the items' extremity on the underlying dimension of judgment. Introducing a more extreme item results in a wider "perspective" regarding the set of stimuli, thus affecting their evaluation as described in Ostrom and Upshaw's (1968) perspective theory, which we reviewed in more detail in Chapter Four. Accordingly, contrast effects should also emerge under conditions where each item is likely to receive about the same degree of attention and elaboration.

To explore this possibility, Schwarz and Münkel (1988) used a rating rather than a selection task in a laboratory experiment. They asked subjects to rate each of a number of drinks according to how "typically German" they were. As expected, all drinks were rated as more "typically German" if an atypical drink, namely vodka, was presented as the first rather than the last item. In contrast, the rating of vodka was not affected by the order manipulations. Thus, an asymmetric contrast effect emerged, as predicted by Ostrom and Upshaw's (1968) perspective theory. According to that model, respondents use the most extreme stimuli that come to mind to anchor the response scale. In this case, presenting vodka as the first item resulted in a shift of the moderate stimuli away from the anchor. Vodka as the most extreme stimulus in the set, however, is itself unaffected by the order manipulation because the most extreme stimulus is assigned the extreme scores under any order condition except if preceded by a more extreme stimulus.

Moreover, contrast effects of this type do not require that the items be presented on the same list. They have also been shown to emerge if the extreme item is presented as part of a preceding question, provided that this question taps the same dimension of judgment. As an example of this phenomenon, we previously reviewed a study by Schwarz, Münkel, and Hippler (1990), who asked some respondents to estimate the percentage of Germans who drink vodka and others the percentage who drink beer. Subsequently, all were asked to rate the typicality of various drinks. As expected, respondents who estimated the percentage of Germans who drink vodka rated subsequent drinks as more typically German than subjects who estimated how many Germans drink beer. This replicates the contrast effects obtained when all stimuli were presented on the same list. But when other subjects were asked as part of the preceding questions to estimate the caloric content rather than the consumption rate of vodka or beer, subsequent typicality ratings were not influenced. Although this question also served to render these drinks highly salient in the interview context, it did not tap the typicality dimension behind the consumption estimates. This finding indicates that contrast effects can emerge as a function of preceding questions if they tap the same underlying dimension of judgment, as we discussed in more detail in Chapter Five.

This emergence of contrast effects bears in important ways on the emergence of primacy and recency effects in general. Specifically, it provides an interesting account for data sets that do not follow our predictions of primacy and recency effects as a function of elaboration and memory processes. If an extremely positive item is presented as part of the stimulus set, it will decrease the endorsement of subsequent moderate items. But if an extremely negative item is presented, it will increase the endorsement of subsequent moderate items. These judgmental effects may lead the researcher to conclude that the data show pronounced recency or primacy effects. Accordingly, the phenomenon of judgmental contrast may dilute the emergence of elaboration phenomena, thus contributing to the mixed findings that characterize this area.

Behavioral Questions

In the preceding discussion, the response alternatives presented as part of an opinion question were portrayed as persuasive arguments. Moreover, it was suggested that the order and mode in which response alternatives are presented influences respondents' opportunity to generate agreeing or disagreeing thoughts. Does this imply that elaboration-based response order effects are limited to opinion questions? We do not believe so. As we shall discuss in Chapter Seven, successful retrieval of information from autobiographical memory (memory about one's behavior) involves several processes that may be affected by the order in which different behaviors are presented on a list, as Schwarz, Hippler, and Noelle-Neumann (1994) suggested.

First, successful retrieval takes time. Recalling specific events may take up to several seconds (Reiser, Black, & Abelson, 1985) and repeated attempts to recall may result in the retrieval of additional material, even after a considerable number of previous trials (for example, Means, Mingay, Nigam, & Zarrow, 1988; Williams & Hollan, 1981). It is conceivable that respondents' motivation to engage in this effort declines over the course of the list, resulting in more successful retrieval attempts at the beginning than at the end. If so, responses to the first few items should be more accurate than responses to later items, a possibility that would deserve systematic investigation in future research.

Moreover, numerous studies indicate that recall increases as the retrieval cues better match the representation stored in memory (see Strube, 1987, for a review). Most notably, Wagenaar (1986) observed in a study of his own memory that he could retrieve many apparently forgotten events as more specific retrieval cues became available. The retrieval cues presented in standardized lists of daily activities, however, are not very specific. They are most likely to result in successful retrieval when respondents take time to think about them, thus constructing more specific personal retrieval cues from the generic material presented. The likelihood that respondents do this, however, may decrease as a function of motivational deficits. In addition, the respondents' idiosyncratic elaboration of the presented cues may be impaired by the elaborations that they generated in response to preceding cues.

For reasons discussed in the context of opinion questions, the degree of elaboration given to a response alternative is likely to depend on its serial position and its presentation mode (Krosnick & Alwin, 1987). Under visual presentation conditions the first few response alternatives receive more elaboration than the later ones, whereas under auditory presentation conditions the last few receive more elaboration. Therefore, the quality of self-generated retrieval cues may show an interaction effect of serial position and presentation mode, paralleling the interaction effect discussed for opinion questions. When the list is presented in a visual mode, items presented early in the list should receive more processing, resulting in primacy effects. When the items are read to respondents, however, items presented at the end of the list should receive more processing, resulting in recency effects. To the extent that more elaborate retrieval cues increase the accuracy of recall, we may also expect that retrospective reports are more accurate for early rather than late items in a visual presentation mode. For the same reason, they may be more accurate for late rather than early items in an auditory presentation mode.

To date, none of these hypotheses has been systematically tested. However, they indicate that order- and mode-induced differences in the elaboration of a given response alternative are not limited to opinion question but may affect recall from autobiographical memory as well. Table 6.4 shows an example, taken from Schwarz, Hippler, & Noelle-Neumann, (1994).

In two German surveys conducted by the Allensbach Institute under the direction of Elisabeth Noelle-Neumann (IfD 1008, May 1957; IfD 1022, September 1958), respondents were asked, "Could you please tell me, with the help of this list, what you happened to do last Saturday?" Respondents were provided a list of twenty-eight activities. The order in which the activities were presented was reversed for half of the respondents. Whereas 34 percent of the respondents of the 1957 survey, shown in the first two columns of Table 6.4, reported that they worked at their job when this item was presented first on the list, only 25 percent did so when the item was presented last. Conversely, 15 percent reported that they slept in when this item was presented first, whereas 10 percent reported doing so when the item was presented last. The 1958 data, shown in the second and third columns, replicate this pattern nicely. Primacy effects of up to 9 percentage points emerged when respondents were asked to recall activities they had engaged in last Saturday, that is, a maximum of six days earlier.

These data contradict Carp's (1974) frequently cited conclusion

TABLE 6.4 Reported activities as a function of presentation order.

	Presentation order			
	1957		1958	
	First	Last	First	Last
Activity				
Working	34%	25%	26%	22%
Sleeping in	15%	10%	17%	12%
N	347	317	318	309

Source: Data based on quota samples of German adults (IfD 1008, May 1957; IfD 1022, September 1958).

Note: Respondents were randomly assigned to one of the two presentation order conditions.

that response order effects are unlikely to emerge for factual reports. In her study, respondents were asked to report the frequency of local trips for various purposes. They were presented with a list of eight frequency alternatives, ranging from "never" to "every day" and the order in which the frequencies were presented was reversed for half of the sample. No effect of response order was obtained. Based on recent research on the impact of frequency scales on retrospective reports (see Schwarz, 1990a, for a review), we assume that frequency scales present a special case. In contrast to categorical response alternatives, where each alternative presents a different substantive option, frequency scales of the type used by Carp present a continuum. As numerous studies have shown (for example, Schwarz, Hippler, Deutsch, & Strack, 1985), respondents use the range of the frequency alternatives as a frame of reference in estimating their own behavioral frequency. Whereas this results in different reports along scales that offer different ranges, the order in which the same range is introduced (for example, "never" to "daily" as opposed to "daily" to "never") has not been found to affect the results (Carp, 1974).

Based on the limited evidence available, we assume that response order effects may emerge on factual reports as well as on opinion questions. We assume that in both cases, they are largely attributable to differential cognitive elaboration. However, the specifics of the elaboration processes involved are clearly different, reflecting the differences in the nature of attitude judgments and recall tasks.

Verbal Rating Scales

We now turn to the special case of verbal rating scales. In a 1929 paper, Mathews reported the emergence of primacy effects on a verbal rating scale. In a self-administered questionnaire, his subjects were asked to rate different study habits (for example, "take notes during a talk") according to how much they liked them on a scale including "like greatly," "like," "indifferent," "dislike," and "dislike greatly." He observed that "like greatly" was marked 2.9 percent more frequently when it was printed at the extreme left than when printed at the extreme right, whereas "dislike greatly" was marked "2.4 percent more often when it was printed at the extreme left" (Mathews, 1929, p. 130). This basic finding has been replicated in several studies, based on self-administered questionnaires (Belson, 1966; Payne, 1971) and face-to-face interviews (Carp, 1974; Mingay & Greenwell, 1989; Quinn & Belson, 1969). In all cases, "both negative and positive ends of the scale pulled more responses when presented first, and both pulled fewer responses when presented last," as Carp (1974, p. 584) summarized her findings.

How do we account for these findings? On first glance, it seems that the consistent emergence of primacy effects in face-to-face interviews contradicts the implications of the cognitive elaboration hypothesis, which would predict a recency effect under auditory presentation conditions. However, verbal rating scales do not present different substantive options that respondents need to elaborate on. Rather, terms ranging from "like very much" to "dislike very much" constitute a response continuum where the different options require far less elaboration than is the case with opinion questions of the type shown in Table 6.1. The terms presented on a verbal rating scale can neither be portrayed as persuasive arguments nor as retrieval cues, in contrast to the material discussed earlier. Similar effects have been obtained on numerical rating scales with labeled endpoints. In general, it seems that ratings are somewhat displaced toward the starting point of the scale. Schwarz and Wyer (1985) suggested that this finding may reflect an anchoring effect of the type described by Tversky and Kahneman (1974). In their study, which we discussed in more detail in Chapter Four, responses were displaced toward the left end of the rating scale when a preceding task induced respondents to proceed from left to right and toward the right end of the rating scale when the preceding task induced respondents to proceed from right to left. Unfortunately, the specific conditions under which anchoring effects of this type are likely to emerge are not yet well understood. At present, we can only note that ratings along a scale are sometimes displaced toward the beginning of the scale, resulting in a primacy effect. Whereas this renders ratings along reversed scales noncomparable, the frequency and size of response order effects along rating scales seems more limited than the frequency and size of order effects that involve discrete response alternatives of the type shown in Table 6.1.

Summary

The considerations reviewed in this chapter suggest that order effects in nondimensional sets of response alternatives are a function of their cognitive elaboration and of the limitations of respondents' memory although memory limitations are likely to be less crucial than has often been assumed. The processes that underlie order effects in dimensional sets of response alternatives, however, are more complex and require a consideration of judgmental contrast in addition to a consideration of cognitive elaboration.

The variations of elaboration likelihood assumptions offered by Krosnick (1992) and Schwarz et al. (1992) provide a rich set of predictions that have only partially been tested. First, the elaboration hypothesis predicts an interaction of serial position and administration mode that is well supported by the available data although more controlled experiments using the same questions under visual and auditory presentation modes are urgently needed. Second, it predicts conditions under which response order effects should be more or less pronounced, and these predictions have been supported in at least some experiments. Third, it predicts a reversal of response order effects if the presented response alternatives are implausible rather than plausible. Although data bearing on this issue are not yet available, this consideration suggests that response order effects may go in different directions, depending on respondents' attitudes. Accordingly, primacy and recency effects may cancel one another in heterogeneous samples. Moreover, the elaboration likelihood assumption points to a host of other variables—such as respondents' ability and motivation to elaborate on the implications of the response alternatives—that have been explored in research on persuasive communications (see Petty & Cacioppo, 1986a, 1986b; Petty, Ostrom & Brock, 1981, for reviews) but have not been systematically addressed in the context of response order effects (with the exception of cognitive sophistication, see Krosnick, 1992). These predictions deserve more systematic testing, both in sample surveys and in the cognitive laboratory, with a careful assessment of the cognitive responses that are assumed to mediate the observed effects.

In addition, assumptions about the impact of respondents' memory limitations and the emergence of judgmental contrast effects point to conditions under which the impact of cognitive elaboration may be diluted. In respect to memory limitations, our analyses suggest that a straightforward application of findings from the psychological list learning literature cannot account for the pattern of response order effects observed in survey research. Most important, this literature predicts recency effects in the absence of a delay between learning and recall, which is typical for survey research, and provides no mechanism for the emergence of primacy effects under these conditions. Memory limitations, however, may contribute to the size of recency effects under auditory presentation conditions; for example, when the response alternatives are lengthy and complex. Moreover, they may dilute the size of primacy effects under visual presentation conditions if one assumes that time pressure prevents respondents from going back over the list before reporting their answer, thus introducing some memory burden into the task. Finally, judgmental contrast effects may further dilute the operation of the previously discussed processes if a dimensional set of response alternatives is presented and some response alternatives are considerably more extreme than others.

Accordingly, it comes as little surprise that the emergence of response order effects on opinion questions seems to follow the rule, "sometimes you see them, sometimes you don't." When we consider these predictions, it becomes obvious that there is no single main effect. Rather, the emergence and direction of response order effects seems to depend on a complex interaction of serial position; presentation mode; item plausibility, complexity, and extremity; and respondent ability and motivation. Finally, a word of caution. As we noted in the introduction to this chapter, much of the available research is based on flawed designs that confound presentation order with content of adjacent items. Moreover, tightly controlled experiments that provide insight into the assumed underlying cognitive processes are largely missing and our discussion has primarily been based on secondary analyses of archival data. Thus, the conceptualization offered in this chapter is compatible with the general theorizing developed in the context of our discussion of question order effects, which emphasizes the role of cognitive accessibility in the construction of mental representations of the target as a key element of the judgment process. But the empirical support for this conceptualization in the domain of response order is severely limited, requiring more direct tests in tightly controlled experiments.

Practical Implications for Questionnaire Designers

It is clear from the discussion in this and the last two chapters that context effects are ubiquitous and cause complex interactions in response to attitude questions depending on question and response category order, mode of administration, and information recalled by respondents. As a first step, we believe that researchers need to evaluate the likelihood of context effects when a questionnaire is being designed, so that as far as possible context effects are deliberate rather than unanticipated.

In some cases, context effects are desirable because they help the respondent understand what the researcher wants; they aid in the information retrieval process. In such cases, the researcher should attempt to induce them. This is the equivalent of providing cues for reports of autobiographical behavior.

In other cases, however, the researcher may find the context effect introduces undesirable distortions. The obvious first solution is to eliminate the context by omitting earlier questions or response categories entirely, that is, using open rather than closed questions. If this solution is possible it is clearly the easiest thing to do. But it may be impossible because the data from the earlier questions are required or because the response categories are necessary for the respondent to be able to understand the question.

In personal interviews, the introduction given by the interviewer to a question or series of questions can be used to increase, reduce, or eliminate context effects, as desired by the researcher. In self-administered questionnaires, the same results can be obtained by printing instructions, by putting the questions together in a box on one page, or by putting questions on separate pages.

Other ways of reducing context effects involve the question itself. The more general or ambiguous the question, the more likely context effects will occur. It usually makes sense to keep the question as specific and unambiguous as possible. As we have pointed out, context effects will be much smaller or may vanish completely if the respondent already has a judgment or substantial amounts of relevant information chronically accessible in memory. This is not something the researcher can manipulate, but it needs to be kept in mind, for example, when the data from news polls that ask for respondent reactions to newly developing political events are interpreted.

Within a question, if response alternatives are necessary, their order may be randomized unless there is some natural ordering. However, randomization "eliminates" order effects only in a rather mechanical sense. By averaging across the effects generated by different orders, randomization simply ensures that our conclusions do not reflect one specific order. Nevertheless, any given respondent's answer will be affected by the order in which the response alternatives or questions were presented and the numerous different orders generated by randomization will increase the variance in the sample, potentially affecting statistical analyses. Technically, the use of computer-assisted interviewing makes it far easier to randomize the order of alternatives. An added advantage of computer interviews, even if self-administered, is that the respondent is aware only of the questions that precede a given question and not those that follow. Similarly, within a section of related questions in a questionnaire, it may be possible to randomize the order of the questions using computer-assisted interviewing, again assuming there is no natural ordering.

Finally, it is best to avoid items or persons that achieve extremely positive or negative ratings when asking for judgments about a series of items because those that follow will be strongly affected. Thus, if Adolf Hitler or Mother Teresa are included among a list of political personages, the ratings of a current president or prime minister will be strongly influenced based on their position in the list.

7

Autobiographical Memory

Survey researchers frequently ask respondents questions about their past behavior. In so doing, researchers are asking respondents to search a particular part of their memory that has come to be called *autobiographical memory*. Brewer (1986, 1994) distinguishes three types of memories that can properly be called autobiographical— *personal memories* (for example, having mental images of doing a particular thing, such as visiting the Taj Mahal), *autobiographical fact* (remembering that one visited an elderly aunt in St. Louis when one was ten years old but having no mental image of the event), and *generic personal memory* (having a mental image of what it is like in general to drive from Boston to New York but having a generic view rather than an image of any specific point in the drive). Generic personal memory is distinguished from semantic memory, which is knowledge of facts that are not experienced in time or place (for example, that Columbus discovered America in 1492) and from generic perceptual memory (for example, having a visual image of the shape of the state of California).

Autobiographical memory has become the subject of much recent work in cognitive psychology. (For a textbook introduction see Conway, 1990; for reviews see Bradburn, Rips, & Shevell, 1987; Neisser & Winograd, 1988; Rubin, 1986; Schwarz, 1990a.) In this chapter, we consider some of the approaches to the study of autobiographical memory and examine their implications for survey research. Many of these implications are discussed in some detail in the contributions to Jobe and Loftus (1991) and Schwarz and Sudman (1994).

Let us begin by considering the following questions, which were taken from several important national surveys:

1. During the two-week [reference] period, on the days when you drank liquor, about how many drinks did you have? (Health Interview Survey Supplement)

2. During the past twelve months, about how many visits did you make to a dentist? (Health Interview Survey Supplement)

3. How many weeks has [name of family member] been looking for work? (Current Population Survey, U.S. Bureau of the Census)

4. When you were growing up, how frequently did your father attend religious services? (General Social Survey)

5. About how much did heat, electricity, and water cost you last year? (Study of Family Economics)

6. What was the usual monthly expense for purchased dinners and other meals and snacks in restaurants, cafeterias, cafes, drive-ins, or other such places? (Asked of those reporting such purchases within the last three months; Consumer Expenditure Survey)

7. During a typical week in your principal job, what percent of working time do you devote to management and administration? (Survey of Science and Engineering Graduates)

These questions require not only the simple retrieval from memory of a number of experiences over a considerable period of time but also in many cases the manipulation of the retrieved information to produce summary quantitative measures. Clearly these questions make considerable cognitive demands on respondents.

Models of Memory

It is useful to think of memory as a large storehouse of information of various sorts. In the literature on memory, distinctions are sometimes made between different memory systems, such as short-term memory (sometimes called primary memory) and long-term memory. Although there is no agreement among psychologists that these memory types have fundamental differences or that they form systems that operate according to different principles (Crowder, 1976), the terms are useful distinctions and correspond to a commonsense view of memory. Short-term memory generally refers to information that is conscious or immediately active in our thought processes whereas long-term memory refers to information that we can recall, with more or less clarity and accuracy, only after some effort. Long-term memory is what we commonly refer to as "our memory," and retrieval from long-term memory is what we usually think of as "remembering."

A commonsense view regards remembering as a process by which the memory storehouse is searched to retrieve a particular item that is being sought, as in the example, "Where did I leave the book I was reading last night?" If we think of memory as a big storehouse, it is clear that it must be organized in some way in order for us to be able to retrieve things from it. Just as we must label files when we put them in file drawers, so we must attach some kind of labels to information in the memory storehouse. The labeling process, often called "encoding," refers to various aspects of the information or the experience attached to the item when we stored it in memory so that we can retrieve it.

Barsalou (1988) has recently proposed a theory that provides a good heuristic framework for discussing autobiographical memory. Drawing on the work of others (Kolodner, 1984; Reiser, 1983; Reiser, Black, & Abelson, 1985; Reiser, Black, & Kalamarides, 1987; Shank & Kolodner, 1979) as well as on his own he notes that information about activities or event types in autobiographical

memory includes not only specific events but also extensive idiosyncratic, generic knowledge about the events, that is, it includes
Brewer's generic personal memory. For activities to be stored in
memory, they must be comprehended. In other words, they must be
understood within some meaning system, usually linguistic, that
brings to bear knowledge of past activities and generic knowledge
about similar event types as well as the specifics of the event itself
and the context within which it occurred. This complex set of
information that goes into the comprehension of the event becomes integrated into the memory of the event. Thus, the comprehension process determines how the memories are encoded.

For example, a memory about a specific visit to a pediatrician
would become integrated with knowledge about visits to doctors in
general and to pediatricians in particular. Because people think
about doctor visits in different ways and have differing amounts of
knowledge about doctors and pediatricians, there are idiosyncratic
representations of the events in memory, although people from the
same culture are likely to have a fair amount of commonality in
their comprehension of common events.

Recalling an event is similar to answering a question. It involves the same four processes that we have described in answering
a survey question. When asked to recall an event one has to comprehend the question in such a way as to provoke a search among
memories that have been encoded in the same way. For example, if
respondents are asked about the last visit to a pediatrician, they
must comprehend what is meant by pediatrician visit and then be
able to find the answer among memory event types that are coded
as pediatrician visits. If a doctor visit has not been coded as a pediatrician visit it will fail to be retrieved, leading to an underreporting of events. Similarly, if a visit to a general practitioner in which
a child's health was discussed has been coded as a visit to a pediatrician, it may be incorrectly retrieved and lead to overreporting of
events.

Information, such as the wording of the question and any
explanatory material available to respondents at the time they are

asked to recall an event, acts as retrieval cues. Retrieval cues are any words, images, emotions, and so on that activate or direct the memory search process. If retrieval cues do not specify the event type (pediatrician visit) then the event type must be inferred before the search can begin. This inference can come from the wording of the question or from the larger context in which the question is asked, including the preceding questions or the introductory material to the survey. Once an event is retrieved, a judgment must be made about whether it is the "correct" memory before a response, even if it is an internal one, is made.

Organization of Autobiographical Memory

Understanding how autobiographical memories are organized should help us improve recall and make the recall task easier for respondents. In addition to activities, participants, locations, and times have been suggested as possible principles of organization for autobiographical memory. Reiser et al. (1985) have suggested that activities are the primary focus of organization and that activity cues will result in faster retrieval of memories than other types of cues. Further work by Barsalou (1988) and Wagenaar (1986), however, has failed to show consistent superiority of any kinds of cues, including location, participants, time, or activities, suggesting that no one type of information is more important than any other in organizing memory.

Wagenaar's study, however, did suggest that the types of cues that were important at the time of encoding are more effective that those generated later when thinking about the past. Such findings support Tulving's (1972) hypothesis of "encoding specificity," which states that events are encoded in specific ways when stored in memory and can be recovered only through cues matching those specific codes.

It is somewhat discouraging to those who hope for a simple principle around which to organize memory questions that studies of cued recall have failed to demonstrate the superiority of any particular type of cue. The studies suggest that individuals organize their memories in different ways and possibly even that the same persons organize their memories for different events in different ways with little or no consistency. Such a state of affairs would suggest that we give up trying to find clues about how best to ask questions so as to improve recall in surveys. Fortunately, studies of free recall in which cues are generated internally by subjects do suggest that things are less chaotic than they might seem.

Barsalou (1988) studied free recall by asking subjects to describe events from their summer vacation in whatever order they came to mind. Each subject recalled events for five minutes, and responses were recorded verbatim. When Barsalou looked at the protocols generated through this free recall method, he found that memories were hierarchically organized. The highest level of organization was chronological order. However, what was ordered was not specific events but event sequences—what Barsalou called "extended events," such as a trip, going to summer school, or working at a job. This finding suggests that people do not store in memory a stream of isolated events but rather bundle them into temporal-causal sequences. For example, a person might remember a stay in the hospital as beginning with a pain and a visit to a doctor, followed by admittance to the hospital and various treatments while there, followed by discharge and return home, and finally by follow-up doctor visits. Recall of specific events, such as an X ray or particular tests, would take place within the sequence rather than be treated as isolated incidents. Giving cues to remind the respondent about the sequence would be more effective than attempting to get directly at the specific events.

In addition to being chronologically organized, event sequences are hierarchically organized along meaningfully clustered lines— such as cause-effect relationships, goal attainment, or primary socially defined roles such as work, school, family, or social relationships—which Barsalou called *partonomies*. The clusters themselves may be subdivided into smaller sequences, also often chronologically organized. For example, events during college may be organized by freshman, sophomore, junior, and senior years. Specific events themselves are nested within larger categories of event sequences. Thus, health might be the superordinate category that is subdivided into chronologically organized health history—childhood diseases, episodes of acute illnesses, important encounters with health providers, onset of chronic illnesses, and so on. Within each of these categories further subdivisions are likely, down to the most recent illnesses and doctor visits.

It is tempting to think of memory as a continuous record that can be dipped into at any point. Conceiving of memory as event sequences, however, suggests that there is a more discrete temporal structure that may help or hinder recall. Some studies suggest that socially organized time periods, either generally shared periods such as those given by the calendar or more narrowly shared periods such as a school term or work cycle affect our memories of events. Calendars, both personal and socially shared, impose patterns on an individual's activities and influence the distribution of memories over the course of a time period. Studies of college students (Pillemer, Rhinehart, & White, 1986; Robinson, 1987) have shown that their memories for events during a year exhibit scallops with peaks near the beginnings and ends of school terms and vacation periods. (See Figure 7.1.) Although the study authors could not validate the correct dates of the experiences and thus are not sure whether the events were displaced from other months or subjects were actually recalling more events from the periods near the boundaries of school-defined time periods, it is clear that the respondents were recalling events as clustered in socially defined time.

Just as the calendar can provide a framework for recalling events, autobiographical sequences can provide reference points for locating other events in time (Brown, Shevell & Rips, 1986; Lieury, Aiello, Lepreux, & Mellet, 1980). When asked to give the dates for well-publicized events such as the first landing on the moon or the Chernobyl nuclear reactor accident, respondents may rely on personal sequences that can be easily dated, offering such typical responses as "When I was living in Chicago" or "Just after my visit to Kiev."

FIGURE 7.1 College student reported memories by time in school year.

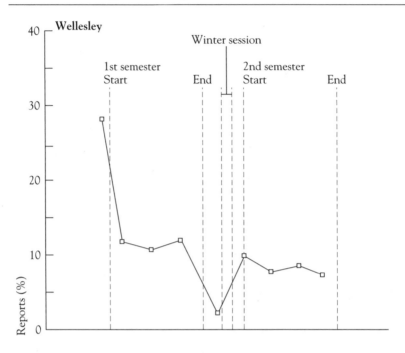

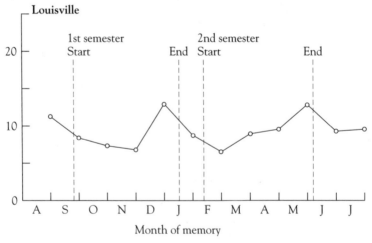

Month of memory

We noted earlier that the way events are comprehended and coded influences the effectiveness of different cues for recall. Similarly, not all autobiographical sequences are useful as temporal reference points. In one fortuitously timed experiment (Brown, Shevell, & Rips, 1986), the reaction time of college students was recorded as they decided for each of a series of news events (for example, the first space shuttle launch), whether the event took place during an earlier period (1978–1980) or a later period (1981–1983). The intervals were described in different ways. For half of the subjects, the earlier period was described as "Carter's term of office" and the later period was described as "Reagan's term of office." For the other half, the earlier period was described as "the time you were in high school" and the later period "the time you were in college." Because the subjects were seniors in college at the time of the experiment, the two sets of descriptions covered the same time periods. The events to be dated also were of two types: either obviously political events, such as Mitterrand's election in France or Andrew Young's resignation as ambassador to the United Nations, or nonpolitical but still public events such as the Mount Saint Helens eruption or the Three Mile Island nuclear reactor accident. On average the subjects were able to date political events more quickly within presidential terms but nonpolitical events more quickly within autobiographical periods. (See Figure 7.2.)

Forgetting or Failure to Retrieve?

One of the most intriguing and frustrating aspects of memory is its incompleteness. Some people have "good memories" and can remember many things in great detail; others have "poor memories" and may feel that they are constantly forgetting things. Although a few people may possess eidetic imagery or have what is called a photographic memory, they are rare to the point of being oddities. Many details of the past experiences of most people, even of relatively recent past experiences, are not easily retrievable and perhaps even forgotten entirely.

FIGURE 7.2 College student reported memories related to political and autobiographical events.

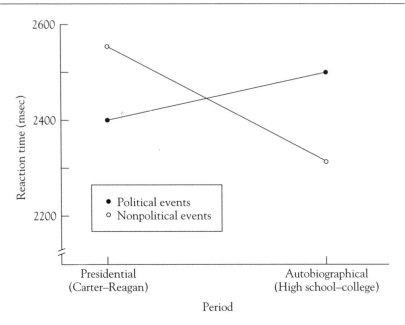

What we ordinarily call "forgetting" can occur in three ways. First, some details of an experience may never be noticed or stored in memory. Our minds have limited processing capacity and we must constantly pick and choose what we pay attention to. Not everything that is immediately perceived is actually processed beyond consciousness, that is, comprehended, encoded, and stored in memory. It is forgotten almost as soon as it is experienced because it is never transferred to long-term memory.

Second, as we noted earlier, memory is organized in a hierarchical fashion with memories for specific events embedded in an array of other information, some of it generic, some idiosyncratic, which is attached to it when it is first stored in memory. Information may also be added later if we "rehearse" memories, that is, recall events, think or talk about them, and then restore them in memory. Rehearsal increases the ease with which we can recall memories, and failure to rehearse or recall a memory for a long time can make it difficult or impossible to retrieve it when it is wanted. Even though it may still exist someplace in memory, it is effectively forgotten. It is as if we had not consulted a file for long time and when we go to look for it find we have lost the name of the folder that contains it and cannot locate it. In such cases, there is retrieval failure.

Psychologists distinguish among three methods of recall: *free recall, cued recall,* and *recognition.* Free recall, as the term suggests, involves the respondent trying to remember the information asked for with minimal information to direct the search. In surveys, open-ended questions are the primary example of free recall tasks. An example is "What did you eat for dinner last night?"

Cued recall resembles free recall in that respondents report in their own terms but they are given more or less detailed cues that can make the recall task easier and direct it to information desired. Sometimes these cues are contained in the question wording. An example is "People often are involved in sports activities such as playing golf, tennis, or softball, or going swimming or bowling. What sports do you participate in?" Sometimes the cue may come from information given to the respondent as part of the introduction to the interview or to a particular section of the interview.

Both free and cued recall require respondents to recall types of facts or attitudes that are relevant to the question as well as those that are true for them. In recognition, particular types of facts or attitudes that are being asked about are listed and respondents are only asked to answer about their own experience with them. Thus, instead of asking about which sports a person has engaged in as in a recall task, a recognition question is worded, "Now I have some questions about sports. Think about what sports you engage in. Do you play badminton? Do you play basketball? Do you go bowling?" and so on, until the entire list of sports that one is interested in has been presented.

As one might expect because of the differences in the difficulty of the tasks, in most situations retrieval failure occurs least in recognition tasks and less frequently in cued recall tasks than in free recall tasks.

The third way "forgetting" can occur is through alterations of memory. As was pointed out by Bartlett (1932) in some of the earliest studies of memory, remembering is a reconstructive process. We do not recall directly and completely a memory for a complex event but rather reconstruct the memory of the event through a process of remembering parts of a whole, filling in missing parts by inferring what logically would have gone with the parts we do remember and using things we remember first as cues to recover other parts that are harder to remember. As Loftus (1975) has shown, when the memory of an event is recalled to consciousness, other new "facts" about the event, even ones that are not true, may get added. When the memory is again stored in long-term memory, it may be stored in an altered fashion that includes the new information. It is unclear whether the altered memory "overwrites" the original memory so that what is stored is permanently altered and the original memory is permanently "forgotten" because it has been erased or whether the altered memory is stored alongside the original one and can be retrieved instead of the original. If the altered memory is the one that is most rehearsed then it is likely to become the "real" memory.

Thus, things may be forgotten because they were never stored in memory in the first place, because they have not been recalled in so long that the cues to activate them have become weak or cannot be located, or because they have been altered or erased in subsequent moments of recall and restorage.

Memory and Time

It is generally observed that there is a relationship between how long ago something happened and how hard it is to remember it. This is not a simple relationship, however, and it depends on many factors not fully understood. Figure 7.3 presents some different "forgetting curves." Ebbinghaus's ([1894] 1964) famous negatively accelerating curve describes the forgetting of a variety of material, ranging from nonsense syllables in his studies to alumni memory for the streets of a college town (Bahrick, 1983) and critical details of personal events selected at the time of occurrence to be "certainly" remembered if the events were recognized (Wagenaar, 1986). Although the curves show a similar form, it should be noted that the time scale for the nonsense syllables was days whereas that for personal events and street names was years. Thus, more meaningful material is forgotten at a slower speed, but the form of the forgetting curve is similar.

FIGURE 7.3 Forgetting curves for various topics.

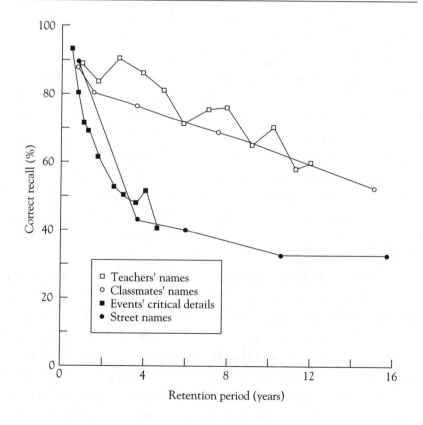

For other things, the long-term forgetting curve appears to be linear and quite small over a long period of years. We include among these other things names of grade and high school teachers (Whitten & Leonard, 1981) or high school classmates names (Bahrick, Bahrick, & Whittlinger, 1975). Unfortunately, we know little about what determines the form of forgetting curves.

When people experience many similar incidents, such as repeated visits to a doctor or shopping trips, recalling each event is more difficult. Initially distinguishable events may become confused or blended with later similar events into a schematic memory. For example, Linton (1975) observed that she could remember well the names of those who attended a seminar at the beginning of the semester but as the seminar continued to meet, she began to confuse the people who attended different sessions of the seminar. Neisser (1982) reports a particularly vivid example. In John Dean's testimony at the Watergate hearings, he gave a detailed description of his meeting with President Nixon on March 21, 1973, during which Dean said he told Nixon of the "cancer" growing on the presidency. The subsequent discovery of the tape recordings made of the president's conferences made it possible to compare Dean's testimony with what actually occurred. The March 21 recording contained deliberations about blackmail demands from Watergate defendants that Dean, in his testimony, placed eight days earlier. The gist of the conversation was accurate, but despite the intensive preparation for his Senate appearance and the significance of the March 21 meeting, Dean confused the March 13 meeting and the March 21 meeting.

Of course, sometimes people cannot recall an event even when they have numerous cues and the event itself is readily distinguishable from others. In a prodigious study, Linton (1975) kept a daily record of things that happened in her life over a six-year period and reviewed them every month. At the end of her study, she found that fewer than one percent of the items were forgotten during the calendar year in which they were written and that after that events were forgotten at about an even rate of 5 percent to 6 percent every year. Wagenaar (1986) found that after five years, 60 percent of the "critical details" of events described by subjects as being "certainly" remembered if the event were recalled at all were irretrievable even though the event itself was recalled.

Recall usually improves when a respondent has access to appropriate cues, although it is often difficult to determine what is an appropriate cue. As mentioned earlier, Wagenaar found that cues related to what happened on a particular occasion, who was involved, and where it took place improved memory for other aspects of events but that the date of the event was generally a poorer cue. Bradburn, Sudman, and Associates (1979) found that cues about location and social occasion of events successfully increased reports of alcohol and drug consumption.

Surveys that focus on the retrieval of complex information like medical expenditures, energy expenditures, or financial assets, often ask respondents to use records to refresh their memories for such data. Using records, however, does not ensure that the reports will be entirely accurate. A study in the Netherlands (Horn, 1960) found that only 47 percent of respondents who consulted records gave the precise amount in their saving account, an increase over the 31 percent accuracy rate for respondents who did not consult their records but still far from perfect. Other surveys, on topics such as magazine readership or organizational membership, use recall aids such as lists of publications or organizations to enable respondents to use recognition rather than recall as the strategy for reporting their activities.

Effort is important to successful recall, particularly for information that is not highly salient to the respondent. Williams and Hollan (1981) have shown that repeated attempts to recall names can bring to light relevant new material, even after nine retrieval sessions of an hour each. Even when events seem to a respondent to be entirely forgotten, additional information can produce new recall. Wagenaar (1986) took some events that his subjects had given up trying to recall and interviewed other participants about them to get additional information that could be used as cues.

When these cues were used with his subjects, additional events were recalled. These studies suggest that even if events do not disappear entirely from memory, the effort to recall them may exceed the willingness of even well-motivated respondents to engage in the necessary effort.

Searching memory to retrieve specific information asked for in a survey question takes time. Reiser, Black, and Abelson (1985) conducted experiments that suggest it takes several seconds to retrieve a specific event in response to instructions to recall participation in some common activity such as getting a haircut or going out for a drink. The more difficult the retrieval task, the longer it takes. Thus, survey accuracy may decline if too many questions are asked within the allotted survey time and respondents are not given enough time to consider those questions that demand difficult recall efforts.

Giving respondents more time for response can affect the strategy they use as well as the accuracy of the responses (Blair & Burton, 1987; Lessler, Tourangeau, & Salter, 1989). Increasing the length of the question also increases the accuracy of responses, perhaps because it gives respondents more time to think about the answer before responding (Bradburn et al., 1979; Cannell, Oksenberg, & Converse, 1977).

The amount of effort required for accurate recall is a particular problem for surveys. A personal interview of an hour to an hour and a half typically includes at least 150 questions, rarely allowing more than a minute for a well-considered answer. Telephone interviews, which are the predominant mode in use today, are usually shorter in total length than personal interviews and cannot use recall aids. In addition, the telephone implicitly demands responses more rapidly than face-to-face interviewing because both interviewers and respondents are uncomfortable with silence on the phone in the absence of the visual cues evident in face-to-face interviewing. Groves and Kahn (1979) have also shown that respondents' answers to open-ended questions on the telephone are on average shorter than in face-to-face interviews.

A Retrieval Model

Williams and Hollan (1981) view remembering as a reconstructive retrieval process in which information about the target item is used to construct a description of an aspect of the item. The description is then used to recover fragments of information about the item, which are added to what is already remembered to form a new description. The new description is used to retrieve still more information until the item being sought is finally recalled. This process takes place in three stages. First, the context in which to conduct the search must be found. Contexts are concepts such as locations, participants, times, activities, or extended event time lines, which Barsalou (1988) found to be the most common sources of cues that people use in free recall. Williams and Hollan used pictures (images) and name generation and general association (by sound or other cues) as other strategies in their task, which was to remember names of high school classmates.

Using the contexts, respondents search their memories for bits and pieces of information appropriate to the context until enough information is recovered to provide a satisfactory answer to the question. This process may take a number of iterations of the search process and involve several changes of contexts before enough information is retrieved.

Of course, sometimes false information is recovered, so the final step in the process is verifying that the information retrieved is correct. Because objective checks are rare, for example, checks against external sources like records, verification is usually a subjective process that relies heavily on consistency with other known (or remembered) facts or on a subjective feeling that the memory is correct. Subjective certainty is, in turn, often influenced by the vividness and clarity of the memory. When respondents feel that they have come up with as much information about the question as they can (or are willing to), they are in a position to answer.

When Memory Partially Fails

In discussing the retrieval process, we have assumed that the task is terminated when sufficient information is retrieved from memory to provide a satisfactory answer to the question asked. In simple memory models, there is the implicit assumption that all that one does is search the memory for the desired information and either finds it or not. If retrieval processes were all that happened when respondents answer a question such as "How many times have you been to the doctor in the past three months?" they would simply retrieve all the visits they could remember and count them. But two types of errors can occur. Errors of omission occur because people forget. Errors of commission occur when people report visits that occurred outside the reference period because they do not remember when the visit actually took place. (We deal with this second type of error more extensively in Chapter Eight.)

Furthermore, we know that people do not rely simply on their memories of specific events. We have already mentioned that people integrate generic information about types of events into their memories of specific events. They summarize and group classes of events and fill in information that is logically consistent with what they remember. (We elaborate on when and how respondents make these kinds of estimates in Chapter Nine.)

Thus, respondents appear to use all the information they have and not to rely on recall alone. Several strategies are commonly used to supplement recall. Difficult questions ("How many times did you eat out at a restaurant during the past month?") may be made easier by decomposing them. One decomposition technique is to divide the question into separate, mutually exclusive parts, such as going to a restaurant for breakfast, lunch, dinner, in-between meals, and so on, using one's memory of visits to establish probable weekly rates for each subpart, and then multiply by the number of weeks.

Because many survey questions deal with frequencies of activities within a period that are larger than can be recalled individually, decomposition can be an effective strategy to facilitate answering frequency questions and may well lead to more accurate answers than attempting to recall and enumerate.

A second strategy relies on the experienced ease with which information comes to mind. This strategy has been called the "availability heuristic" (Tversky & Kahneman, 1973). It is based on the usually correct assumption that it is easier to recall an example when there are many rather than only a few examples. Thus, the more easily a relevant memory can be brought to mind, the more frequent, likely, or recent the recalled event will seem to be. Sometimes, however, this heuristic leads us astray. Such is the case when an instance is easy to recall because it was particularly vivid or otherwise memorable although the respective class of events is not frequent. Accordingly, use of the availability heuristic may result in systematic errors when rare events come to mind easily (incorrectly suggesting, for example, that they are frequent) or when frequent events are difficult to recall (incorrectly suggesting that they are rare). (For more extended discussions, see Brown, Rips, & Shevell, 1985; Lichtenstein, Slovic, Fischoff, & Combs, 1978; Ross & Sicoly, 1979; Tversky & Kahneman, 1973.) In contrast, the previously discussed decomposition strategy often leads to increased accuracy (Armstrong, Denniston & Gordon, 1975; MacGregor, Lichtenstein, & Slovic, 1988).

Another strategy that appears to be commonly used was identified by Michael Ross and his collaborators (Ross, 1989; Ross & Conway, 1986). They found that respondents answer questions about the past by using their present status as a benchmark against which to estimate their previous status. With regard to many variables, people hold implicit theories of stability and change often related to naive conceptions of life span development, on which considerable interpersonal agreement has been documented (Ross, 1989). These implicit theories of self provide the basis for inferring previous attitudes and behaviors. In adopting this strategy, respondents use their current attitude or behavior as an initial estimate, which they adjust according to their implicit theory. The resulting reports of previous attitudes and behaviors are correct to the extent that the implicit theory is accurate (see also Nisbett & Wilson, 1977).

Research on this approach has primarily focused on reports of attitudes and opinions (Markus, 1986; Ross & Conway, 1986), but it is equally applicable to retrospective reports of behaviors. Frequently, individuals assume a high degree of stability, which results in an underestimate of the amount of change that has occurred over the reference period. Retrospective reports of income (Withey, 1954) and of tobacco, marijuana, and alcohol consumption (Collins, Graham, Hansen, & Johnson, 1985) were found to be heavily influenced by respondents' income or consumption habits at the time of the interview. In contrast, when respondents have reason to believe that things have changed they will report change even though none has occurred. For example, respondents who engaged in a study skills program that did not actually improve their tested skills reported change even though none had occurred. Presumably they used their belief in the efficacy of the training program to infer that the skills they had before had improved (Conway & Ross, 1984). Similarly, participants in a pain management program were found to remember more pain than they had recorded during the baseline period, again reflecting their belief that the program produced change in their perceived level of pain (Linton & Gotestam, 1983; Linton & Melin, 1982). Similarly, McFarland, Ross, and DeCourville (1988) found that women's retrospective reports of menstrual distress were a function of their theory of the menstrual cycle. The more respondents believed that their cycle affected their well-being, the more their retrospective reports deviated from diary data obtained during the cycle.

Another aspect of stability bias has been studied by Menon (1994), who found that respondents who are asked to report on a rate of behavior (for example, "How many times in the last month did you use an ATM machine?") retrieve a rate that may not reflect the activities in the reference period. Sometimes respondents recognize that the reference period is unusual and make an adjustment for special circumstances such as a holiday, illness, and so on, but the usual rate, when there is one, appears to be used at least as a starting point for an estimate. Strategies for estimating behavior are discussed in Chapter Nine. Most survey questionnaire designers pay little attention to the strategies respondents use to answer difficult information questions, such as questions about doctor visits, crimes, or periods of unemployment. For example, people prefer to recall a series of events by starting at the beginning of the sequence and moving forward in chronological order (Loftus & Fathi, 1985). But experimental laboratory studies by Loftus and Fathi (1985) indicated that backward recall—using reverse chronological order—was usually more accurate. Jobe, White, Kelley, and Mingay (1990) tested these findings in a survey that asked about medical visits and used record checks. They found the results when respondents were allowed to recall medical provider visits in whatever order they chose was superior to those when respondents were instructed to recall either in backward or forward temporal order. Further work by Means and Loftus (1991) suggests that manipulating recall order may be best for recall of a small number of visits while other strategies, for example, decomposition, may be better for a large number of visits.

Although the evidence to date suggests that the search strategies respondents use are varied, a small number of strategies are most common. More research on the recall of particular subject matters might reveal that there is even some correlation between certain strategies and certain subject matters. For example, periods of unemployment might be linked to previous periods of employment, and doctor visits might be remembered by location of the doctor's office. If such correlations were known, they could be incorporated into the questions to make the recall task easier. Even if there turns out to be no consistent relation between strategies and subject matters, instructing respondents in some of the commonly used strategies might improve reporting.

Summary

In this chapter we have presented a brief overview of some current thinking about autobiographical memory. Although much remains to be learned, certain themes seem to attract general agreement. Understanding the way memory is organized is key to understanding the retrieval process. There is strong evidence that memory is hierarchically organized and that coding schemes, particularly those used at the time of storage, provide important guideposts to retrieval. Events are not stored as discrete, isolated bits of information but rather are clustered in event sequences that have meaning to the individual. These event sequences have a strong chronological dimension, although they have many other dimensions as well. "Forgetting" is an imprecise term, and there is some debate about whether events that are stored in memory are ever totally "forgotten" even if the probability of retrieval is very low. There does not seem to be a single "forgetting curve." Rather, different types of things appear to be forgotten at different rates, and for some things, forgetting may be a simple linear function of time.

Remembering is not a simple retrieval of memory traces but a complicated process that may be influenced by both habitual behavior and the emotions, attitudes, and events happening at the time of retrieval, including the wording and context of the question that initiate the retrieval process. There are many reconstructive elements in the retrieval process. Some of the elements may reflect events that occurred or information that was obtained after the original event but was incorporated into the memory of it during earlier recall and memory rehearsals at some earlier time.

Understanding these aspects of memory should enable the survey researcher to construct better questionnaires. We present some specific suggestions for doing so at the end of Chapter Nine.

8

Event Dating

Many survey questions involve a request to date events. Explicitly, respondents are asked about when they graduated from high school or college or when they began a particular job; implicitly, they are asked about the frequency of events within a time period, for example, the number of doctor visits in the last six months. In longitudinal surveys, event dating is particularly important because the researcher is interested in events as they occur to particular individuals over time, often in the form of continuous histories of employment, schooling, or marital and family status. Some examples are the following:

> Please tell me each period between (DATE IN Q.6) and (now/DATE IN Q.7B), during which you didn't work for this employer for a full week or more. [ANSWERS GIVEN IN EXACT DATES.] (National Longitudinal Study of Labor Market Behavior/Youth)
>
> Now, we would like to ask you a few questions about the training that you were receiving on (DATE OF LAST INTERVIEW) at (TYPE OF TRAINING AGENCY CODED IN Q.6B). First, when did you finish or leave this training program? [RECORD MONTH AND YEAR.]
>
> Altogether, for how many weeks did you attend this training? [RECORD NUMBER OF WEEKS.] (NLS/Y)

In recent years, there have been important advances in our understanding of the cognitive processes used for temporal memory, stimulated in part by the problem of telescoping. Telescoping, a puzzling phenomenon, was first reported by Neter and Waksberg (1964) in a study of response errors in the Consumer Expenditure Survey. When respondents were asked about events occurring in reference periods at various distances from the present—for example, one month versus six months—the frequency of events reported for the most recent month was greater in the one-month reference period than in the six-month reference period. Other studies that investigated event dating found that more events were reported in the more recent past (Bachman & O'Malley, 1991; Sudman & Bradburn, 1974; Uhlenhuth, Haberman, Balter, & Lipman, 1977).

The evidence for telescoping is based largely on reports of the frequencies of events reported in reference periods of differing lengths, rather than on direct study of errors in the dating of events. As we will discuss in Chapter Nine, counting events is one method for determining frequency. If there are systematic errors in the dating of events, the number counted within the reference period will also be wrong. When estimation procedures are used, it is not clear why telescoping occurs unless there is some relationship between the estimation procedure and the memory of dates for events. If the availability heuristic (see Chapter Nine) is used in the estimation process then there may be systematic biases in the estimated frequencies if events are differentially accessible in memory.

Models of Event Dating

In order for respondents to answer questions about when events occurred or about the frequency of events over an interval, events must be associated in memory with some representation of time. A central question in the explanation of telescoping is whether the bias is the result of a bias in temporal memory (that is, whether there is a lack of correspondence between the subjective experience of time and its objective measurement) or whether the bias is the result of something in the process of retrieval and reporting. If the bias is the result of errors in the storage of information, there is probably little that can be done about. But if it is the result of the retrieval process, we may be able to devise strategies to improve the retrieval process and reduce the bias.

An event may be represented in memory by its place in a commonly shared calendar, such as a day, a month, a year, and so on, or in approximate calendarlike units, such as a season (for example, "in summer"), a socially defined time period ("during the spring semester"), or an idiosyncratic reference point ("two days after my birthday"). Events may also be represented by reference to the present in the form of elapsed time ("ten days ago"). Rubin and Baddeley (1989) have proposed a model to account for telescoping based on the dating of autobiographical events in calendar time. Huttenlocher, Hedges, and Bradburn (1990) have proposed a model to account for telescoping based on the dating of autobiographical events in terms of elapsed time from the present. The two models share the same general approach but differ in details because of their focus on how the events are represented in temporal memory.

Both models assume that there are no systematic errors in dating events (that is, dates associated with events are stored in memory correctly) but rather that observed errors in reporting are the result of errors in the retrieval process. The observed telescoping errors that result in overreporting are caused by the combination of three independent factors. The first of these is the normal forgetting process, that is, retention is greater for recent events. The second is that, even when events are remembered, errors in dating occur randomly and, furthermore, increase linearly with time. The third is that intrusions often occur from events outside the reference period but cannot occur from events that have not yet occurred. In other words, intrusions occur in only one direction, that is, from the past forward.

The second and third factors are particularly important for telescoping. Our common experience tells us that accuracy for temporal information lessens with time. Individuals are less certain about when things happened as they get further away from them in time. Baddeley, Lewis, and Nimmo-Smith (1978) studied memory for dates of laboratory visits. They showed that the variance of reported dates for visits increased markedly with the length of time since the last visit for subjects who participated in experiments in their laboratory. Because of the increasing uncertainty about dates as events became more remote in time, an imbalance in reports of events falling within a bounded time period, such as is typically asked about in surveys, occurs.

To see this effect more clearly, let us consider an example. Often in surveys we ask about the frequency with which respondents did something within a particular time period, such as, "How many times did you visit a doctor in the past three months?" Even if visits are spread evenly across the reference period and there is no bias in storing the dates in memory, we will still get more reports of visits within the period than actually occurred. The reason is that there will be greater uncertainty about events that occurred around the beginning of the period (sixty to ninety days earlier) than about those that happened near the end of it (within the previous thirty to sixty days). There will be even more uncertainty about the dates of visits that took place more than ninety days ago, or outside the reference period altogether. Because of this greater uncertainty, more events that occurred outside of the time period will be remembered as having occurred within it than the reverse.

This asymmetric consequence of increasing uncertainty results in the third element of the models: intrusions of events from outside the period. Furthermore, the intrusions will serve to increase reporting because the reference period is bounded by the present and intrusions cannot occur from events that have not yet occurred. Events cannot be incorrectly remembered as having occurred in the future, so intrusions into the period can come only from earlier events. These are also susceptible to greater error in dating because they are more distant in time. Although some visits that occurred within the period will be incorrectly remembered as having occurred before the beginning of it and will not be reported, the bounding by the present does not allow events from within the period to be pushed into the future. The result is telescoping and an overreporting of events.

Bradburn, Huttenlocher, and Hedges (1994) present a mathematical model for estimating the magnitude of forward telescoping effects on the number of reports of events within a reference period. In this model, the proportion of overreporting or underreporting depends only on the probabilities of reporting events that occurred on each day in the reference period and on the length of the reporting period. Using reasonable assumptions about the actual distribution of the timing of events, the model indicates that for a reference period of fifty days an expected overreporting on the order of 32 percent would not be unreasonable.

The general model applies whether the ending boundary of the reference period is the present or not. If the reference period both begins and ends in the past, it is possible for respondents to recall events as having occurred more recently than the near boundary and thus not report them, something that is impossible when the near boundary is the day of the interview. In such situations, events in the reference period are, on average, further back in time and thus have a somewhat higher degree of uncertainty attached to them. The model predicts a greater degree of backward telescoping than when the boundary is the present, although there should still be net forward telescoping. The model deals only with telescoping and does not take into account omissions because of failure to recall.

Both the Rubin and Baddeley and the Huttenlocher, Hedges, and Bradburn models assume that no other factors operate to produce telescoping. Sudman and Bradburn (1974) hypothesized earlier that at least some part of telescoping comes from the desire of respondents to be "good respondents" and report fully on events being asked about. In cases of doubt about whether an event belongs in or out of the reference period, respondents therefore decide to err of the side of too much rather than too little. Rubin and Baddeley (1989) note that their model could be extended to include such a tendency by assigning a probability of less than one to the rejection of events whose recollected dates fall outside the reference period.

Huttenlocher, Hedges, and Bradburn (1990) noted another phenomenon when respondents were asked to remember the date of a particular event, that is, when a previous interview took place. Respondents preferred to answer in terms of elapsed time rather than with exact dates, such as "six days ago" rather than "on September 8." As the elapsed time between the interview and the present became greater, reports became less exact, as one would expect if memory for dates became less certain (even though still unbiased), and respondents began to round their answers to estimated values. When respondents were asked about a recent interview they reported in terms of "days ago," and when the interview was somewhat further back in time they responded in terms of "weeks ago" or some prototypical number of days such as "ten days ago." When the interview was even further back in time they moved to reporting "months ago."

As memory became less certain, respondents rounded their answers to prototypical values, either based on the calendar (days, weeks, months) or on the decimal system (five, ten, fifteen, and so on) as shown in Figure 8.1. The two algorithms sometimes coincide, as in "thirty days" for a month or "sixty days" for two months.

Rounding to prototypical values also contributes to telescoping. As the elapsed time between the present and the reported events increases, the distance in reported time will also increase because the distance between adjacent rounded values increases. In this case telescoping will occur even if there is no bounded reference period.

To see why the increasing distance between adjacent rounded values will produce telescoping, let us consider the prototypic values, 10, 14, and 21 days. Let us assume that respondents do not remember exactly when something happened and choose the prototypic value nearest their remembered value. If they use the midpoint of the distance between the prototypic values, they will report an event as having occurred 14 days ago if they think it

FIGURE 8.1 Reported elapsed days since event occurred.

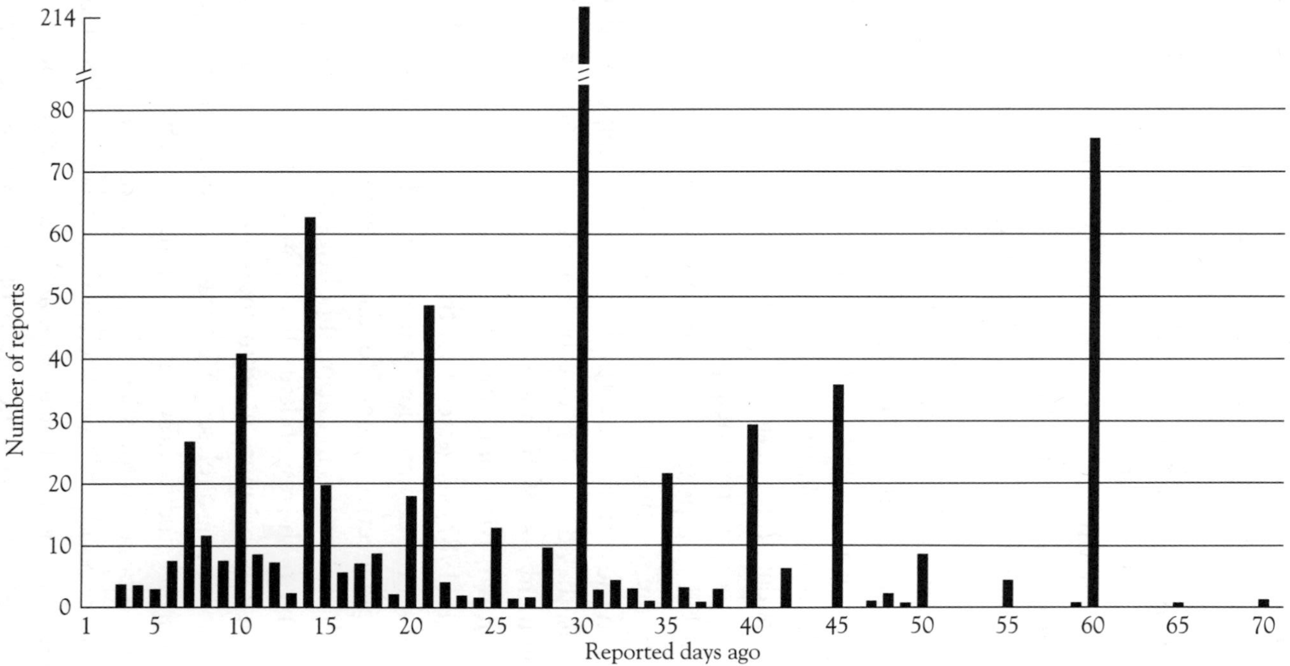

occurred anywhere from 12 (midway between 10 and 14) to 17.5 (midway between 14 and 21) days ago. It should be noted that the distance between 12 and 14 is smaller than that between 14 and 17.5. Because the range of remembered values to which a particular rounded value is assigned is smaller in a forward than in a backward direction, a smaller range of values is rounded up to 14 than is rounded down. This asymmetry in the size of the rounding distance produces a net forward bias in reporting. A similar forward bias will occur if rounding occurs by decimals, assuming that respondents first round to the nearest 5 value and then, as the elapsed time is greater, round by 10s and then by 25s and so on. Figure 8.2 shows the bias in reporting the dates of an interview as a function of the number of actual elapsed days between it and the report on it.

Another explanation for telescoping suggests that many events are not dated in relation to calendar time at all; rather, aspects of the memory of them help people infer when they occurred. In this view, because people understand that events that happened recently are remembered more clearly than those that happened further in the past, they use this knowledge to help them date events; that is, they date the events by how vivid, detailed, and accessible their memories of them are.

Brown, Rips, and Shevell (1987) and Bradburn, Rips, and Shevell (1987) suggested that the accessibility principle could account for the compression of temporal judgments and showed that it was an effective strategy for dating public events not clearly tied to political events in national politics or to the ongoing personal narrative of the respondents' lives (Brown, Shevell, & Rips, 1986). For such events more vivid memories lead to more recent datings, thus indicating a telescoping because of time compression.

Further studies, however, have failed to show that this is a powerful explanation for telescoping of events that are more directly tied to respondents' lives, such as those that are asked about in surveys. Thompson, Skowronski, and Lee (1988) failed to find any relationship between the clarity of memories as rated by their subjects and dating errors. Even for recent public events, Kemp (1988)

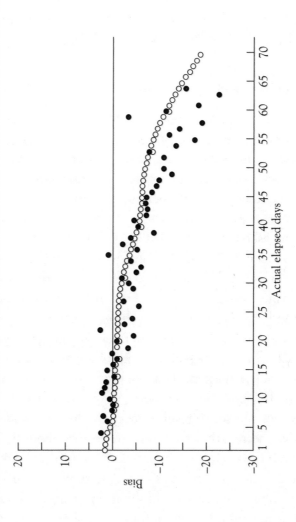

FIGURE 8.2 Bias in reporting of dates by actual elapsed days.

found no difference in signed error between little-known and well-known events, and for historical events he found the reverse of what was predicted by the accessibility hypothesis, namely, that the size of the signed error was greater for little-known than for well-known events. Thus, although accessibility may be used as an aid in dating some events, it does not offer an adequate basis for explaining the pervasive and well-documented phenomenon of telescoping.

Reduction of Telescoping

Because telescoping occurs as a natural part of the retrieval process, reductions in telescoping may be made by using techniques to reduce the uncertainty of temporal memory. Neter and Waksberg (1964) used a technique, which they called "bounded recall," that reduced forward telescoping. The technique requires asking the same questions on successive interviews with the same individuals. Respondents are asked about their behavior in a reference period, that is, in "the last six months." In the subsequent interview, they are asked to report on their behavior during the preceding reference period, that is, the time between the end of the first interview and the present time, and they are reminded of the events they reported in the first interview. Although the first interview suffers from considerable forward telescoping, the second (and subsequent interviews if the survey is a multiwave panel) has greatly reduced telescoping.

The reduction in telescoping in the second and all subsequent interviews appears to result from reminding respondents of events already reported, thus reducing uncertainty about the date of some events. If respondents remember an event that took place in the previous period but are unsure about it, they can check on the accuracy of their memory with information the interviewer gained during the previous interview. If they remember events that took place within the present period but recall them as having occurred in the previous period, this too can be checked. Thus, the misdating of events both forward and backward is discouraged by the provision of data to reduce the respondents' uncertainty.

Sudman, Finn, and Lannom (1984) have also shown that "bounding" can occur in one interview. In this format, respondents are first asked about events that occurred thirty to sixty days ago and then about events that occurred within the last thirty days. In this form of bounding, the events reported in the thirty- to sixty-day period are subject to telescoping and discarded. Only the events reported in the last thirty days are retained.

Calendars are also often used in surveys that attempt to get continuous histories to help respondents fix the dates of events. These can be effective especially when anchoring dates—such as those provided in a bounding process or especially memorable dates of personal history—are offered to help fix the times of less well-remembered events. If dated records can be used by the respondents, these may also help reduce uncertainty.

Summary

Event dating is a difficult cognitive task. When people try to recall distant events they become less certain of their dates, although the evidence suggests that there is no bias in the recall. Questions about past behavior frequently request reports of behavior that occurred within a bounded reference period, such as in the last six months. Surprisingly, studies that involve such reporting find that there is a tendency to overreport events that happened in the reference period rather than underreport them, as might be expected because of forgetting of events with time. This overreporting is called "telescoping."

Telescoping appears to be the result of processes that occur during the retrieval process. There is greater uncertainty about the date of events the further back in time they are. Respondents are asked to report only the events that occurred within the reference period. These two factors combine to produce an overreporting of events occurring in the reference period rather than an overreporting of events in the reference period occurring outside of it.

For questions about how long ago a particular event happened, the tendency to round reports of elapsed time to conventional time periods—such as a week ago, a month ago, three months ago, and so on—is a further source of telescoping because the rounding interval gets larger as time goes by. The inequality in the rounded time period has the consequence of rounding more things forward than backward in time.

Practical Implications for Questionnaire Designers

The obvious implications for questionnaire designers of the findings discussed in this chapter are to mistrust behavior reports that require respondents to remember dates accurately and to simplify respondents' memory task by making the time period in question as short as possible. Nevertheless, it should be recognized that short time periods increase the relative effects of telescoping. If respondents are asked only about yesterday or only about the last three days, then small absolute errors in dating lead to very large overstatements.

Telescoping can be reduced or eliminated with bounded recall methods. The questionnaire designer should be careful in using cues or bounded recall separately, because substantial overreporting or underreporting may result. These procedures are best used jointly and only when respondents are counting and not estimating.

9

Counting and Estimation

One of the most important contributions of cognitive science to date has been to broaden our understanding of the methods respondents use to answer questions about behavioral frequencies or other numerical quantities such as "How many times have you done [behavior] in the past two weeks?" or "How many aunts and uncles and cousins do you have?" One method respondents use is to recall individual instances of the phenomenon and count them. However, it is now well recognized that in many cases respondents make no attempt to count individual episodes or units but employ instead a second method: they estimate the number asked for based on rates that are either stored in memory as schema or computed on the spot from a sample of available data. A third method used by respondents is to draw on the response alternatives provided by the researcher to compute an estimate.

We begin this chapter with a brief overview of the research on this topic. We then describe the task variables that have been considered relevant to the use of estimation. Of greatest importance is the number of events or units to be remembered. In addition, the regularity and similarity of the events, the report basis (whether it refers to self or proxy), and the length of the time period in question have also been found to be important.

In the following sections of the chapter, we discuss the relative accuracy of estimation compared with counting. Both methods are subject to error for a variety of reasons. An important finding, however, is that for certain classes of activities estimation methods yield more accurate results than counting methods. After this discussion, we review procedures that have been used in attempts to reduce estimation errors, such as asking the respondent to try harder, increasing the length of time provided for answering, prompting the use of exceptions from the rule, decomposing events, and reducing the time period while controlling for number of events. Unfortunately, none of the methods has been shown to improve significantly the accuracy of reporting, although a few seem sufficiently promising to be worthy of additional research.

In the last section of the chapter, we turn to a special case of estimation: reliance on the response alternatives provided by the researcher. Respondents typically report higher behavioral frequencies when presented with high rather than low frequency response alternatives. We explore the processes underlying this estimation effect and address their theoretical and methodological implications.

Overview of the Research

Tulving (1972, 1983) was one of the earliest and most influential researchers to distinguish between episodic and semantic memory. However, Tulving points out that his ideas were shaped by Reiff and Scheever (1959) and had been anticipated by the philosophers Henri Bergson (1911) and Bertrand Russell (1921, 1948). Tulving's work was followed by that of several researchers. Linton (1975, 1978, 1982), Wagenaar (1986), and White (1982) kept records of their own activities over long time periods and then observed what they could remember and the memory errors they made. A general finding was that as the number of experiences of an event increased, the semantic knowledge about it also increased but individual episodes were harder and harder to distinguish (Thorndyke & Hayes-Roth, 1979; Watkins & Kerkar, 1985).

This work was followed by Blair and Burton's research (Blair &

Burton, 1987; Burton & Blair, 1991), which quantified the effects of number of events and time period on respondents' decision to use estimation or counting. Menon (1991) expanded on this work to look at the effects of regularity and similarity, factors that had already been discussed in the work of Linton and White. Recent research on proxy reporting (Bickart et al., 1989; Blair et al., 1991), where the investigators have examined differences between procedures used for self and proxy reporting, is also based on this earlier work.

When Is Estimation Used?

Several aspects of survey questions have an effect on a respondent's decision to estimate or count. We review these in the next sections.

Number of Events

Blair and Burton (1987) and Burton and Blair (1991) have shown that the most important factor determining whether respondents count or estimate is the actual number of items that they are trying to recall. There have been several replications of this finding (for example, Sudman & Schwarz, 1989). In their first study, Blair and Burton (1987) conducted telephone interviews with 384 general population respondents who reported their frequencies for six behaviors—dining at a restaurant, purchasing gasoline, attending movies, watching a favorite weekly television program, purchasing clothing, and making long-distance telephone calls. The time period was experimentally varied. A third of the sample reported on a two-week period, another third on a two-month period, and the final third on a six-month period. For the dining question, respondents were asked how they arrived at their answers. Table 9.1 indicates that nearly all respondents who reported three or fewer dining events said that they counted. For those reporting from four to ten events, the proportion who counted dropped sharply. No respondents reported counting more than ten events.

TABLE 9.1 Effect of reported frequency of restaurant dining on response formulation processes.

Frequency of dining at a restaurant[a]	N	Response formulation process			Total (percent)
		Enumeration (percent)	Rate	Other	
1	12	100	0	0	100
2	28	68	32	0	100
3	29	93	7	0	100
4–5	40	63	35	2	100
6–10	53	15	59	26	100
11–25	58	0	66	34	100
26–100	86	0	77	23	100
> 100[b]	26	0	100	0	100

[a]Chi-square = 231, df = 14, $p < 0.001$; with enumeration versus all other processes (i.e., rate and other categories combined) = 211, df = 7, $p < 0.001$.

[b]To 9 respondents at 183; 1 at 366.

In later work where 160 respondents were interviewed by telephone (Burton & Blair, 1991), the data showed a similar pattern for number of checks written and number of automatic teller machine (ATM) cash withdrawals. (See Table 9.2.) The same results were found in the study of proxy reporting and in network studies where respondents were asked how many aunts, uncles, and cousins they had.

In their first study, Blair and Burton did not obtain direct information on the cognitive processes used for behaviors other than dining. However, they did code whether respondents answered using absolute number of events or using a rate such as X times a week. These results are shown in Table 9.3. Again, the number reporting in absolute terms declined as the number of events increased. But when Tables 9.1 and 9.3 are compared, it is evident that this indirect measure is only a partial reflection of the cognitive

TABLE 9.2 Effects of task conditions on the use of episodic enumeration.

| Task condition | Percentage of respondents who used episodic enumeration | |
	Number of checks written	Number of ATM withdrawals
Overall	29	32
Number of events[a]		
1–2	86	88
3–10	40	21
More than 10	7	0
Time frame[b]		
1 week	51	—
6 weeks	9	—
Response time[c]		
Manipulated	36	37
Control	21	26
Question structure[d]		
Open	34	31
Closed	23	32

[a] x^2 pooled across behaviors = 89.5, df = 4, $p < .001$.

[b] x^2 = 30.5, df = 1, $p < .001$.

[c] Pooled x^2 = 5.0, df = 2, $p < .10$.

[d] Pooled x^2 = 1.5, df = 2, $p > .20$.

process used because many respondents who estimated gave their answer as a number and not as a rate.

It should be noted that the exact number of events where respondents switch from counting to estimating varies not only by respondent but also by characteristics of the event, such as its regularity and its similarity to other events. To date, no studies have attempted to relate individual characteristics such as intelligence, education, or preference for cognitive complexity to the choice of counting or estimation, controlling for the number of events.

TABLE 9.3 Effects of question form, time frame, and behavioral frequency on response format.

Experimental condition	Percent of respondents providing response in absolute format (number of events) for each behavior					
	Purchasing gasoline	Purchasing clothes	Calling long distance	Attending a movie	Viewing a favorite TV show	Dining at a restaurant
Total sample	53 ($\bar{x}$ = 19.1 events)[a]	86 ($\bar{x}$ = 5.6 events)	73 ($\bar{x}$ = 17.8 events)	90 ($\bar{x}$ = 3.6 events)	67 ($\bar{x}$ = 9.2 events)	78 ($\bar{x}$ = 29.4 events)
Frequency						
1–3	90	94	96	97	92	97
4–10	54	81	82	80	65	94
11 or more	28	55	44	53	36	61
p value[d]	<.001	<.001	<.001	<.001	<.001	~.001
Time frame						
Two weeks	86	100	93	100	92	97
Two months	47	89	79	93	66	79
Six months	26	77	52	80	46	59
p value[b]	<.001	<.001	<.001	<.001	<.001	~.001

[a] All results exclude respondents with zero frequency.
[b] χ^2 pooled across behaviors = 259.0, df = 12, $p < 0.001$.
[c] χ^2 pooled across behaviors = 28.8, df = 6, $p < 0.001$.
[d] χ^2 pooled across behaviors = 369.6, df = 12, $p < 0.001$.

Although such effects might exist, we would expect them to be relatively small compared with the effects of number of events and other task factors.

Regularity and Similarity of Events

Menon (1993, 1994) proposed a model that predicted how frequency data for common events would be retrieved based on the regularity and similarity of the events (see Figure 9.1). The model hypothesized that regular/similar events would be estimated, irregular/dissimilar events would be counted, and regular/dissimilar and irregular/similar events would use mixed strategies. Her model also predicted that estimation should be easiest for regular/similar behavior, which would merely require retrieval of a rate. Other kinds of behavior would require more cognitive effort.

The behaviors used in her experiments were derived from a series of pretests and are given as Figure 9.2. Two experiments were conducted. In the first, students at the University of Illinois, Urbana-Champaign reported frequencies of the twelve behaviors and gave verbal protocols on how they arrived at their answers. In the second experiment, students entered their estimates of event frequencies on a computer and response latencies were measured.

The data given in Table 9.4 confirm Menon's hypotheses. Almost 90 percent of respondents estimated for regular/similar events whereas only about a quarter estimated for irregular/dissimilar events. As hypothesized, mean response time and effort was lowest for regular/similar behavior.

Self and Proxy Reporting

Respondents may be asked to report on their own behavior or on the behavior of others. Others are referred to as proxies. A general discussion of the differences between self and proxy reports is given in Chapter Ten. In brief, as differences relate to use of counting and estimation, our own behaviors provide a rich set of experiences,

FIGURE 9.1 Model for the storage and retrieval of information about frequent behavior.

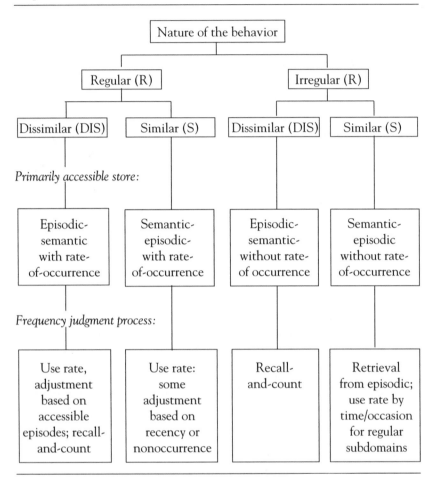

Note: Semantic-episodic implies a more accessible semantic store with few accessible episodes, whereas episodic-semantic implies more accessible episodes with or without accessible semantic stores within subdomains.

FIGURE 9.2 Behaviors used in experiments.

Regular/similar (R-S):	Regular/dissimilar (R-DIS):
Brushing teeth	Going out in the evenings
Washing hair	Having dinner
Attending class	Socializing with friends
Irregular/similar (IRR-S):	Irregular/dissimilar (IRR-DIS):
Leaving a message on someone's answering machine	Eating at a fast-food place
	Making unplanned stops to talk to friends during the day (more than "Hi!")
Drinking water from a public fountain	Snacking
Buying soft drinks from a vending machine	

including information about what we wanted to do, what we actually did, and how we felt while doing it as well as information on where the event took place and who else was present. Information about self should receive increased representation at encoding (Kuiper & Rogers, 1979; Rogers, Kuiper, & Kirker, 1977).

For these reasons, respondents should be more likely to use counting methods when reporting about themselves and estimation when reporting about other people. The results given in Table 9.5 confirm the hypothesis. It may also be seen in the table that the use of event cues and chronological sequences is higher in self than in proxy reporting, which was also predicted.

Length of Recall Period

In their research on the effect of number of events Blair and Burton (1987; Burton & Blair, 1991) also found similar effects for the length of the recall period. As shown in Table 9.6, the proportion counting dining at a restaurant dropped from 56 percent for a two-week period to only 4 percent for a six-month period. These results

TABLE 9.4 Usage of rates in formulating frequency judgments by regularity and similarity of the behavior.

Experiment/dependent measure/regularity of the behavior		Similarity of the behavior	
		Similar	Dissimilar
Experiment 1: (N = 29)			
Percent using estimation strategies			
	Regular	89.5	62.5
	Irregular	44.7	24.1
Mean usage of event cues			
	Regular	1.20	2.17
	Irregular	2.45	2.90
Experiment 2: (N = 28)			
Mean response time (seconds)			
	Regular	4.1	6.5
	Irregular	6.8	7.1
Mean effort ratings (1 = none; 7 = a lot)			
	Regular	1.5	3.2
	Irregular	3.5	4.0

are confirmed by the results shown in Table 9.3. It is evident, of course, that the number of events and length of the recall period are highly correlated. The question is whether or not length of the recall period has an effect over and above the number of events reported.

The evidence on this is weak. For the check-writing variable (see Table 9.2) Burton and Blair (1991) ran a hierarchical logistic regression with counting versus estimation as the dependent variable, number of events as the first independent variable, and time as the second independent variable. The analysis showed a marginally significant ($p < .10$) incremental effect. More data are needed, but it would appear that, controlling for number of events, the length of the recall period does not have a very strong effect.

TABLE 9.5 Methods used for responding to behavioral questions.

	Average number of uses of each reporting strategy		
Methods	(1) Self	(2)	Ratio proxy
Estimation	2.98	3.42	.87
Counting	6.94	5.00	1.39
Chronological sequence	1.28	.78	1.64
Event cues	2.40	1.52	1.58
Specific reference period	1.00	.82	1.22
No event report/no answer	3.12	3.84	.81
Total (without "no event" category)	16.22	14.88	1.09
Total (with "no event" category)	1.34	18.72	1.03

Such a finding, if confirmed, would make sense from a cognitive point of view. The key factor in making it difficult to distinguish events (and thus to be able to count them) is the emergence of a generic schema. It will take experience with several events of a similar type before the generic schema is established. Until the generic schema is established, individual episodes should be discriminable regardless of the length of the recall period and thus should be countable.

Open and Closed Questions

It might be argued that providing respondents with ranges of answers in a closed question would indicate to them that an exact answer is not needed and estimation is acceptable. Some indication of this effect is given in Table 9.2. Fewer respondents were seen to count checks for closed questions. But the differences are not statistically significant because of small sample sizes and because the direction of the differences is sometimes reversed. We discuss this effect in more detail later in the chapter.

TABLE 9.6 Effects of question form and time frame on response formulation processes.

Experimental condition	N	Response formulation process			Total (percent)
		Enumeration	Rate (percent)	Other	
Total sample	332	28	56	16	100
Time frame[a]					
Two weeks	108	56	36	8	100
Two months	108	25	54	21	100
Six months	116	4	76	20	100

[a]Chi-square = 76.1, df = 4, $p < 0.001$; with enumeration versus all other processes = 74.1 df = 2, $p < 0.001$.

Response Time and Effort

Burton and Blair (1991) manipulated response time and effort by making the following statement to half of their sample:

> The next question is very important. After I finish reading the question, I would like you to spend at least fifteen seconds thinking about it. I will let you know when the fifteen seconds are up. If you wish to take more time, just let me know. Okay?

As may be seen in Table 9.2, this manipulation increased the percentage of respondents who counted, although the results are only marginally significant.

Accuracy of Counting and Estimation Methods

We have understood for a long time (Sudman & Bradburn, 1974) that serious counting errors exist. These consist not only of errors of omission but also of telescoping or overstatements of behavior caused by incorrectly remembering dates (see Chapter Eight). Nevertheless, until recently, it has generally been believed that, even with its problems, counting is a more accurate method of obtaining information than estimation. Most of the early efforts using cognitive procedures have been devoted to getting respondents to use counting instead of estimation and to improve their counting ability.

The discussions in the previous sections, however, indicate that for certain kinds of regular/similar behavior one might well expect rate-based estimates to be superior to counting. In the following sections we discuss why estimates may be erroneous, give some limited empirical data on the accuracy of estimates, and contrast the errors of estimation to those of counting.

Why Errors in Estimation Occur

A primary reason for inaccuracies in estimated behavior is what Menon (1991) calls stability bias. That is, respondents in making an estimate retrieve a rate from memory and use it to answer a question about behavior in a given period. That rate may not reflect the activities in the current period for a variety of reasons such as seasonality, illnesses, and weather.

Some respondents may recognize that the stored rate needs adjustment and attempt to make such adjustments. These adjustments may overcorrect or undercorrect; the usual tendency is to undercorrect.

It is often the case that a rate will not be stored in memory but will be derived by counting over some period and then computing. This rate will then be used, with or without adjustment to answer the question. In addition to the problems of stability bias, additional errors are likely when the rate is computed. One possible error is incomplete retrieval so that the rate is underestimated. The error in the other direction may result from telescoping. (See Chapter Eight.)

Guessing and Other Strategies

We sometimes find that respondents report simply guessing or making a "wild guess" when asked a frequency question that taxes their cognitive processes or that they simply report that they have no idea of how they came up with their estimate. Further exploration usually suggests that they have developed a rate but not through the more usual way of counting for a short time period and then extrapolating.

It is sometimes the case that survey researchers ask questions that are so general and difficult that respondents can only answer using some vague general impression. This would be the case if respondents were asked questions about global categories, such as, "How many times have you read anything about crime in the past year?" An example of a general impression would be the use of the availability heuristic in which the estimate is based on the ease of retrieving information (Tversky & Kahneman, 1973). In such cases, respondents are usually unable to report how they retrieved information or made a judgment.

Survey researchers should generally avoid asking questions that require use of these general impression methods. Obvious ways to do so include asking about more specific behaviors over a shorter period of time. If respondents claim to guess, it may sometimes be useful to ask them about specific behaviors in a short time period and then to ask whether the frequency of such behaviors was higher, lower, or typical for the same behaviors over a longer time period.

Measuring Estimation Errors

The same methods available for measuring counting errors are available for measuring estimation errors. A reliable outside validation source must be used or responses must be compared to diaries to obtain previous estimates for the behaviors being measured. Of course, both of these validation methods are imperfect but they are the best available.

A relatively large number of studies have estimated measurement error on responses to behavioral questions but only a limited number have included information on whether respondents were counting or estimating. The following are two examples:

EXAMPLE 1

Menon (1991) had a group of twenty-four students keep
diaries for a week and then compared their recall and diary
responses. Although she did not obtain information on
whether the group counted or estimated, the twelve behaviors
were the same as those given in Figure 9.2. Thus, it is reasonable to assume that most respondents for this study, as in the
previous study, estimated regular/similar behaviors and tried to
count irregular/dissimilar behaviors. Table 9.7 gives the mean
absolute and actual error rates and the correlations between
reported and actual behavior. Absolute errors are those where
the plus or minus sign is ignored. Actual errors are net errors
where the sign is taken into account. It may be seen that the
estimates using rates for regular/similar behavior are significantly better than the counting estimates for dissimilar/irregu-
lar behavior. For example, the correlations between reported
and actual behavior are .93 for regular/similar and .24 for
irregular/dissimilar behavior. The primary error for those who
counted was overestimation of recalled behavior when compared with the diaries, probably the result of telescoping. The
telescoping process has often been found to affect recall of
fairly frequent and mundane behaviors for time periods of one
week.

EXAMPLE 2

Additional data from Burton and Blair (1991) are provided in
Table 9.8. Using the same measures of actual and relative
errors and correlations between actual and reported for check
writing and ATM withdrawals, they found counting was better than estimation for reported frequency of check writing, a
frequent/similar but irregular behavior, and for reporting ATM
withdrawals, a less frequent/similar but irregular behavior. The
data presented are for the control condition where respondents were free to select their method of recall. These data are
confounded with average number of events and a time length

TABLE 9.7 Relative actual and absolute error: correlations between reported and actual frequencies.

N = 24	Nature of the behavior			
	R-S	R-DIS	IRR-S	IRR-DIS
Actual error (reported-actual/actual) and standard deviations	.07[a]	.36[a,b]	.39[b]	1.13[c]
	(.22)	(1.52)	(.87)	(2.94)
Absolute error (reported-actual/actual) and standard deviations	.13[a]	.72[b]	.62[b]	1.30[b]
	(.18)	(1.38)	(.72)	(2.87)
Correlations between reported and actual frequencies	.93[a]	.59[b]	.85[a]	.24[b*]

Note: Indices with different letter superscripts are significantly different from each other, $p < .05$. Tests of significance were conducted separately for the two sets of indices. All correlations except the one marked with an asterisk are significantly different from zero, $p < .01$. Correlations with different letter superscripts are significantly different from each other, $p < .05$. All other pairs of correlations are significantly different, $p < .10$.

manipulation: for checks, half the sample was asked to recall for one week while the other half for six weeks; for ATM withdrawals, the time period was three weeks for all respondents.

It may be noted that although counting was better than estimation in terms of absolute relative error and correlations, the relative actual error for counting was larger for those who counted number of checks. This is not surprising given the six-week time period under consideration by some respondents. It has generally been found that as the time period lengthens omission effects are larger than telescoping effects and behavioral frequencies are underestimated.

It is difficult to generalize strongly from these two examples

TABLE 9.8 Effects of response processes on accuracy.

Process used	N	Mean number of events	Correlation Relative actual	Error absolute	Between reported and actual
Checks					
Counting	16	12.7	−.24	.41	.76
Estimation	49	17.1	−.01	.67	.30
ATM withdrawals					
Counting	19	2.3	.04	.30	.64
Estimation	39	5.2	.21	.44	.46

Source: Based on Burton and Blair (1987). Cognitive processes used by survey respondents to answer behavioral frequency questions. *Journal of Consumer Research, 14*, 280–288. Used by permission of The University of Chicago Press.

except to say that they make it clear that neither counting nor estimation is always better. Rather, it depends on the parameters of the required task. A tentative finding is that errors of estimation, even when larger than errors of counting, are often unbiased. That is, some respondents estimate too high and others too low so that measurement error may be large but the mean value over all respondents is reasonably close to actual behavior. In contrast, counting methods reduce variance but may be biased either upward, for short time periods, or downward for longer periods.

Improving Estimation

In an earlier work (Sudman & Bradburn, 1974), we described methods that can be used to improve counting by reducing omissions, reducing telescoping, or both. There have also been efforts to improve estimation. Burton and Blair (1991), in the study discussed earlier, attempted to influence the methods used by respondents and response accuracy with the manipulation of three variables: recall time period (as discussed), open and closed response categories, and response time. The results shown in Table 9.9 do not

TABLE 9.9 Effects of task conditions on response accuracy.

Task condition	Correlation			
	Mean (per 3-week period)	Relative actual	Error absolute	Of report and records
Time frame				
One week (checks)	17.1	.05	.67	.32
Six weeks (checks)	15.5	−.11	.48	.38
Question structure				
Checks				
Open	16.8	−.02	.57	.40
Closed	15.8	−.02	.59	.25
ATM withdrawals				
Open	4.3	.19	.44	.67
Closed	4.1	.07	.41	.68
Response time/effort				
Checks				
Manipulated	16.7	−.06	.57	.39
Control	15.9	.01	.59	.31
ATM withdrawals				
Manipulated	4.4	.11	.44	.70
Control	3.9	.18	.41	.62

indicate any significant improvement in reporting from any of these manipulations. For all three manipulations, the accuracy differences by treatment are mixed and not significant.

Some of the manipulations may have mixed effects. Burton and Blair speculate that manipulating the time allowed respondents and the resultant effort they use leads to greater use of counting but less accurate reporting by those who do. In other words, this treatment motivated respondents to use counting when they would have reported more accurately if they had estimated.

Similarly, Menon (1991) in the work discussed earlier attempted to encourage respondents to use either a stability bias reduction strategy or a decomposition strategy to improve estimation. In the stability bias reduction condition, respondents were asked specifically whether there might have been changes in their usual behavior during the time period in question. This strategy was intended for respondents who had a stored rate of behavior in memory.

In the decompositional strategy condition, mainly intended for respondents who were computing a rate in response to the question, frequencies were asked separately with several activity cues to improve retrieval and ensure that the respondent summed over these activities. The questions asked are shown in Figure 9.3.

The stability bias reduction strategy produced results in the expected direction but none of the results was significant because of the small sample sizes. The treatment reduced the relative absolute error for regular/dissimilar behaviors. It had no effect on regular/similar behaviors, probably because the error there was already minimal. However, the method appears to have increased the errors for irregular behaviors, possibly by encouraging the use of estimation when counting might have produced better responses. The results are not at all conclusive but are sufficiently suggestive to prompt additional testing of the method.

The decompositional strategy backfired in all situations, actually increasing the relative errors although the results are not significant. Although the effects were small for regular events, decomposition increased errors more for irregular events where, again, they may have encouraged estimation.

To sum up the results, we are still far from able to improve estimation accuracy through task manipulation. Of procedures tested to date, only the stability bias reduction method shows any promise at all and its use seems limited to regular behaviors. The main factor determining accuracy is still the difficulty of the cognitive task, which is not easy to manipulate. In general, the measurement errors that result from estimation are of the same order of magnitude as those that come from counting, sometimes moderately larger and sometimes smaller. These errors need to be measured and accounted for but do not rule out the use of estimation for many important purposes.

FIGURE 9.3 Question forms.

Control condition question:

1. How many times in the last one week did you snack? By snack we mean anything that you may have eaten between meals, excluding beverages.

    ___ times last week

Question form for the stability bias:

1. How many times, in a typical week, do you snack? By snack we mean anything that you may have eaten between meals, excluding beverages.

    ___ times a week

2. Would you say that last week was a typical week as far as your snacking behavior is concerned? Would you rate last week as (CIRCLE YOUR CHOICE AND FOLLOW THE INSTRUCTION):

Not at all typical:	1	ANSWER 3 AND 4
Somewhat typical:	2	ANSWER 3 AND 4
Extremely typical:	3	PLEASE TURN TO THE NEXT PAGE

3. Why was last week not a typical week for your snacking behavior? Please write down the difference(s) between last week and a typical week in *as much detail as possible*.

    _____

    _____

    _____

4. Keeping in mind these differences in the last week, how many times would you say you snacked in the *last one week?*

    ___ times a week

FIGURE 9.3 Question forms *(continued)*.

Question form for the decompositional strategy condition:

1. How many times in the last one week did you snack in any one of the following situations? By snack we mean anything that you may have eaten between meals, excluding beverages.

Number of times last week

Between classes _____

After exercising _____

After work/school before dinner _____

Before bed _____

At the movies _____

At a party _____

Watching TV _____

At bars _____

Others (PLEASE SPECIFY BELOW) _____

_____ _____

_____ _____

_____ _____

2. Overall, in the last one week, how many times did you snack?

_____ times a week

Using Response Alternatives in Estimation

So far, we have described estimation procedures that respondents use when asked an open-ended question. In many surveys, however, respondents are presented a set of frequency response alternatives and asked to check the one that applies. Although the selected alternative is assumed to inform the researcher about the respondent's behavior, researchers frequently overlook the possibility that a given set of response alternatives may be far more than a simple measurement device—it may also constitute an important source of information for the respondent. As we discussed in some detail in Chapter Three, respondents assume that every contribution to the survey interview, including formal features of the questionnaire, is relevant to their task. Reflecting the relevance principle that underlies the conduct of conversation in daily life (see Clark & Schober, 1992; Schwarz, 1994), respondents assume that the range of response alternatives reflects the researcher's knowledge of or expectations about the distribution of the behavior in the "real world." Thus, response alternatives in the middle range of the scale would reflect the "average" or "typical" behavioral frequency whereas the extremes of the scale would correspond to the extremes of the distribution. Such assumptions influence respondents' interpretation of the question (for example, Schwarz, Strack, Müller, & Chassein, 1988), as we saw in Chapter Three, as well as their behavioral frequency reports and related judgments.

Frequency Estimates

As already discussed, respondents turn to estimation strategies when the behavior in question is frequent or repetitive, rendering it difficult to recall and count relevant episodes. One estimation strategy that they may use is based on the response alternatives provided. Assuming that the response alternatives reflect the frequency distribution of the behavior, they may use the range of the response alternatives as a frame of reference in estimating their own behavioral frequency. This results in higher frequency estimates along scales that present high rather than low frequency response alternatives, as indicated in the following example.

EXAMPLE 3

Schwarz, Hippler, Deutsch, and Strack (1985) asked a sample of German adults to report how many hours a day they spent watching television. To test the impact of different response alternatives, half the sample received a scale ranging in half-hour increments from "up to a half hour" to "more than two and a half hours" whereas the other half received a scale ranging from "up to two and a half hours" to "more than four and a half hours." (See Table 9.10.)

Respondents' reports on these scales were coded to reflect estimates of either two and a half hours or less or more than two and a half hours. As expected, the range of the response alternatives had a pronounced impact on the reports. Specifically, only 16.2 percent of the respondents who were given the low frequency scale reported watching television for more than two and a half hours whereas 37.5 percent of the respondents who were given the high frequency scale did. Subsequent research indicated that the impact of the range of response alternatives on the obtained reports is robust and replicates over a wide range of content domains, including

TABLE 9.10 Reported daily television consumption as a function of response alternatives.

Reported daily TV consumption			
Low frequency alternatives		High frequency alternatives	
Hours	Percent reporting	Hours	Percent reporting
Up to ½	7.4	Up to 2½	62.5
½ to 1	17.7	2½ to 3	23.4
1 to 1½	26.5	3 to 3½	7.8
1½ to 2	14.7	3½ to 4	4.7
2 to 2½	17.7	4 to 4½	1.6
More than 2½	16.2	More than 4½	0.0

Source: Adapted from Schwarz, Hippler, Deutsch, & Strack (1985). Response scales: Effects of category range on reported behavior and comparative judgments. *Public Opinion Quarterly, 49,* 388–395. Reprinted by permission.

Note: N = 132.

media consumption, shopping behavior, sexual behavior, doctor visits, and medical complaints (Billiet, Loosveldt, & Waterplas, 1988; Schwarz & Bienias, 1990; Schwarz & Scheuring, 1988, 1991; see Schwarz, 1990a, for a review). In all domains, respondents report higher frequencies on scales with high rather than low frequency response alternatives.

It should be noted that the impact of response alternatives is likely to depend on respondents' knowledge about the behavior: the more respondents know about the frequency of the behavior the less they should be affected by the response alternatives. Several studies support this hypothesis.

Chassein, Strack, and Schwarz (1986) observed that the impact of scale range on reported television consumption was eliminated when respondents were given an opportunity to refresh their memories by browsing through last week's television program. Similarly, Menon, Raghubir, and Schwarz (in press) found that the impact of response alternatives depended on the regularity with which the respondents engaged in the behavior. When the behavior was an irregular one, respondents relied on the range of the response alternatives in computing an estimate. When the behavior was a regular one, however, respondents were able to recall relevant rate information from memory (as discussed earlier in this chapter) and the impact of the response alternatives was largely eliminated.

People know more about their own behavior than about the behavior of others. Schwarz and Bienias (1990) observed that proxy reports were more affected by scale range than were self-reports. Specifically, Schwarz and Bienias (Experiment 1) asked American college students to report their own television consumption, that of a close friend, and that of a "typical undergraduate" at their university along high or low frequency response scales. As expected, the impact of scale range was most pronounced for reports about the behavior of a typical undergraduate and least pronounced for self-reports. It should be noted that this finding is incompatible with a possible alternative explanation for response scale effects based on self-presentation concerns. It is conceivable that respondents remember their television consumption but hesitate to report it if they notice that doing so requires checking an extreme response category. But if respondents hesitate to present themselves as extreme, the range of the response alternatives would be expected to affect self-reports more than proxy reports. Yet the opposite was the case. Accordingly, the obtained pattern of results indicates that the impact of scale range reflects respondents' estimation strategies rather than concerns of self-presentation and social desirability. In line with this assumption, Schwarz and Bienias (Experiment 3) also observed that respondents' disposition to worry about the image they presented was unrelated to the impact of response alternatives, whereas individual differences in the cognitive accessibility of self-related information did moderate the impact of scale range. Respondents with a disposition to engage in extensive self-related thought were less affected by response alternatives than those who spent little time this way, suggesting that the former were more likely than the latter to retrieve relevant behavioral information from memory.

Finally, respondents' reliance on the frame of reference suggested by the response alternatives increases as the complexity of the judgmental task increases (Bless, Bohner, Hild, & Schwarz, 1992). More important, the impact of response alternatives is completely eliminated when the informational value of the response alternatives is called into question. Telling respondents that they were participating in a pretest designed to explore the adequacy of the response alternatives or informing student subjects that the scale had been taken from a survey of the elderly, for example, wiped out the impact of response alternatives (Schwarz & Hippler, unpublished data). Again, these findings illustrate that respondents assume the researcher to be a cooperative communicator whose contributions are relevant to the ongoing conversation unless the implicit guarantee of relevance is called into question, as we have discussed in Chapter Three.

Comparative Judgments

Although not directly relevant to the issue of estimation addressed in this chapter, it is important to note that the impact of response alternatives is not limited to respondents' behavioral reports. The information provided by the response alternatives may also affect their subsequent judgments. Assuming that the scale reflects the distribution of the behavior, checking a response alternative is the same as locating one's position in the distribution. For example, checking two hours on the low frequency scale shown in Table 9.10 implies that a respondent's television consumption is above average whereas checking the same value on the high frequency scale implies that his or her consumption is below average. In fact, when respondents are asked to estimate the typical behavioral frequency of an average respondent, their answers reflect these implications (Schwarz et al., 1985; Menon, Raghubir, and Schwarz, in press). As a result, respondents in Schwarz et al.'s study (Experiment 1) reported that television played a more important role in their leisure time when they had to report their television consumption on the low rather than on the high frequency scale, even though they had just reported a lower absolute television consumption to begin with. In a related experiment, respondents described themselves as less satisfied with the variety of things they did in their leisure time (Experiment 2) when the scale suggested that they watched more television than most people (see also Schwarz & Scheuring, 1988).

Finally, frame of reference effects of this type are not limited to respondents themselves. They influence the users of the reports as well. For example, Schwarz, Bless, Bohner, Harlacher, and Kellenbenz (1991, Experiment 2) observed that experienced medical doctors viewed having the same physical symptom twice a week to reflect a more severe medical condition when "twice a week" was a high rather than a low response alternative on the symptoms checklist presented to them.

Summary

In this chapter we discussed how respondents answer open and closed questions about frequency of behavior. Generally, we suggest that closed questions, either with numbers or vague quantifiers, be avoided. Closed questions may provide unintended information that causes respondents to distort their answers. Furthermore, there are no significant advantages in coding or analyzing closed questions when respondents give numeric answers.

When asked open questions about frequency of behavior, respondents either count or estimate, depending primarily on the number of events but also on other factors such as the regularity of the events, the length of the time period involved, and the subject of the report (themselves or others).

Neither counting nor estimating is always better. Estimating is better for regular events; counting is better for infrequent events. There are methods for improving both methods but they are not always effective, especially with more difficult memory tasks.

A variable under the researcher's control is the length of the time period respondents are asked to report on. Except for infrequent events that respondents count, shorter time periods for which respondents estimate provide as much information as do longer periods. If respondents, count, however, short time periods may lead to substantial overreporting because of telescoping.

Practical Implications for Questionnaire Designers

Respondents who are asked to retrieve information about the frequency of a specified behavior may either count or estimate, depending on the frequency of the behavior and its regularity; the likelihood that a number is readily stored in memory is small. There is little to suggest that the questionnaire designer can have much impact on which method the respondent chooses, except through the offer of an appropriate time period. Data users unfamiliar with cognitive processes often believe that they can obtain much more information by increasing the length of the time period that a question covers, but this belief is illusory.

If the behavior is frequent, irregular, and relatively unimportant, respondents asked about a short time period are likely simply to count and report the number of events retrieved. Respondents asked about a longer time period usually count for a short time period and then compute an answer based on this rate. The longer time period does not provide additional information but it may increase the possibility of a computation error because the respondent has to extrapolate.

If the behavior is regular, respondents will already have a rate stored in memory and will simply retrieve this rate and apply it to whatever time period is specified. It is obvious that increasing the time period for regular behaviors has no effect on the amount of data obtained. Only for infrequent/irregular behavior does increasing the length of the time period increase the amount of information retrieved.

The most common problem with respondents who remember a specified behavior as regular is that they may forget exceptions to the rule. Asking respondents about exceptions to regular behavior is useful for adjusting reported rates. Exceptions are difficult to remember, however, and should be asked about for only a limited and recent time period.

Respondents who count events are subject to forgetting errors of two kinds: omission and telescoping. It has long been recognized that omissions can be reduced by providing the respondent with additional cues in the question itself, in the answer categories, or in earlier related questions.

The problem is that behaviors that are not cued will be under-reported when compared with cued behaviors. This is not a critical issue if all the behaviors of interest are cued and if cued and non-cued behaviors are not compared.

We can give no general advice on which cues are most effective because this usually varies between respondents. It is evident, however, that the more specific the question the easier it is for the respondent to understand what the researcher wants and to retrieve information. Thus, a question about the number of times a person has gone swimming in the past week is easier to answer than a general question about exercise or leisure activities.

A factor that may be controlled by the researcher and interviewer is the amount of time allowed for a response. Cognitive processes take time, and the results suggest that respondents who try to remember individual events retrieve more information when given more time. Interviewers may be trained to slow the pace of the interview, but often it is better to build added time into the questionnaire by increasing the length of the question so respondents have more time to think or by specifically including instructions such as, "We know it may be hard to remember this, so take all the time you need before answering." It should be noted, however, that giving respondents more time will have little effect if they estimate, either by retrieving a rate or computing a rate based on readily accessible events.

Respondents use the range of numeric response alternatives as a frame of reference in estimating their own behavioral frequency, resulting in a systematic bias. To avoid such a bias, we recommend that researchers use open-question formats in assessing reports of behavioral frequencies. From a technical point of view, there is no difficulty in coding such responses because the data are numerical and can easily be processed without need for additional coding. For this reason, the primary technical disadvantages of the open-question format—time, cost, interviewer variability, coding, and analytical problems—are not of great concern in the assessment of frequencies. Of course, the reports provided in an open question format will not necessarily be valid, as we have seen in the preceding discussion of different recall and estimation strategies. However, the format avoids the systematic biases introduced by numerical response alternatives and is unlikely to influence responses to subsequent comparative questions.

Some researchers may be tempted to resort to vague quantifiers such as "sometimes," "frequently," and so on. Since behavioral frequency reports are error-prone anyway, why bother asking respondents for reports that suggest more precision than they can provide? Unfortunately, vague frequency expressions carry their own load of problems (see Bradburn & Miles, 1979; Moxey & Sanford, 1992; Pepper, 1981, for reviews). Most important, the same expression denotes different frequencies in different content domains. For example, "frequently" suffering from headaches reflects higher absolute frequencies than "frequently" suffering from heart attacks. Moreover, different respondents use the same term to mean different objective frequencies of the same behavior. For example, suffering from headaches "occasionally" denotes a higher frequency for respondents with a medical history of migraine headaches than for respondents without that medical history. Accordingly, the use of vague quantifiers reflects the objective frequency relative to respondents' (usually unknown) subjective expectations, making them inadequate for the assessment of objective frequencies. Instead, the most suitable strategy is an open-question format pertaining to a specific reference period. (See the questions in the last section of Figure 9.3.)

10

Proxy Reporting

In many surveys, respondents are asked questions not only about themselves but also about others: members of their households, relatives, and, sometimes, friends and co-workers. This practice is called *proxy reporting*. Survey organizations use proxy reporting for several reasons. By far the most important one is cost. Proxy reporting makes it possible to obtain information about all household members during a single visit, significantly reducing cost in government surveys and in many academic and commercial surveys.

There have been many studies about the quality of proxy reporting but until recently few have tried to explain the cognitive processes that underlie it. Much of the recent work on the cognitive aspects of proxy reporting has been done by the authors of this work and our colleagues.

In this chapter, we begin with a theoretical discussion of why and how proxy reporting would be expected to differ from self-reports. We then present data, based on the methods discussed in Chapter Two, that describe the processes proxy reporters say they use. Of special interest is how context effects influence proxy reporting. We close the chapter with a discussion of survey and experimental data that measure the accuracy of proxy reporting and of factors that lead to greater accuracy.

Although we will point out some differences in methods respondents use when giving self-reports and proxy reports, these are differences in degree rather than basic differences. All else being equal, people know more about themselves than about others but they are sometimes better able to report important information about close others than obscure information about themselves. Thus, studying proxy reporting helps provide a broader framework for understanding self-reporting.

Respondents are also sometimes asked to act as informants and provide data about organizations they are associated with, such as businesses, churches, governmental units, or the neighborhoods or communities in which they live. At present, we know very little about the cognitive processes used for such reporting. An understanding of proxy reporting may provide some clues.

Theoretical Differences Between Self-Reporting and Proxy Reporting

Using the framework developed in earlier chapters, it is possible to consider how self-reports and proxy reports differ during the various stages of the response process.

Behavioral Data

There is no reason for the understanding of the question to be affected whether the subject is self or proxy. But differences may be expected in the encoding, storage, and retrieval of information as well as in generating a response. Table 10.1 summarizes these differences.

At the encoding level, an individual's own behaviors provide a rich set of experiences, including information about what he or she wanted to do, what he or she actually did, how he or she felt while doing it, and so on. Thus, the episodic representation is likely to include information relevant to the event, such as the location and the emotional responses (Tulving, 1972, 1983). In contrast, proxy

TABLE 10.1 Information about self and other at states of information processing.

	Encoding	Storage	Retrieval	Response generation
Self:	1. Actually experience event: (a) Chronological (b) Experienced in entirety	1. If episodic, related to actual	1. Cues related to experience effects	1. Self-presentation
	2. Increased elaboration self	2. If semantic, related to chronological	2. Search likely to be 3. Event likely to be recently activated	
Other:	1. Learn about event through a. Observation b. Word-of-mouth direct (from target)	1. If episodic, related to reception situation unless joint participation in event	1. Cues related to encoding situation	1. Less sensitive to demand effects
	2. Not necessarily chronological	2. If semantic, related to "Other" knowledge structure, presumably not as well organized	2. Chronological retrieval is difficult	2. May not be aware of sensitive information
	3. Amount of elaboration depends on social distance		3. Less frequent activation	3. Social distance will influence both (1) and (2)

respondents usually answer questions about reported events, events that are learned at second hand. These events are likely to be represented as episodes that relate to the occasion of receiving, or learning about, the event. In line with this assumption, Larsen and Plunkett (1987) found that information about reported events was accessed through the memory of the context in which the respondents learned about it.

These considerations have several implications for the strategies used to answer behavioral frequency questions. First, cues related to the event itself should be more effective in enhancing recall in self-reports than in proxy reports. Second, reported events may not be encoded in chronological order, so proxy respondents should be less likely to use a chronological pattern (that is, forward or backward search of memory) when searching a reference period. Finally, the similarity between a respondent pair's episodic representation of an event should be related to their common participation in the behavior. Therefore, the similarity of reporting strategies should be directly related to joint participation in the event.

The organization of information stored about oneself rather than about others might differ for several other reasons as well. First, self-relevant information has been shown to receive increased elaboration at encoding (for example, Kuiper & Rogers, 1979; Rogers, Kuiper, & Kirker, 1977). This elaboration is thought to create a more significant memory trace for the event, resulting in enhanced recall. In other words, autobiographical events are likely to receive greater elaboration, and episodic representations of one's own behavior are likely to be more accessible. Self-reports should therefore be more likely to be based on the use of a recall and count strategy than proxy reports are. Moreover, the attention given to the behavior of others may be a function of the other people's importance. As several studies have shown, information that is relevant to important others (for example, one's spouse) also receives increased elaboration (Bower & Gilligan, 1979; Kuiper & Rogers, 1979). Therefore, it would be expected that the social distance between the self and the proxy would be a major factor in determining the similarity in reporting strategies, particularly when the behavioral frequency question involves reporting of relatively variant or infrequent behaviors.

The greatest difference between self-reporting and proxy reporting may occur when answering a question that requires the retrieval of a rate rather than a question about specific events. Recent research in social cognition has shown that recall of descriptive information, such as a rate, is facilitated when it pertains to the self (Klein & Kihlstrom, 1986; Klein, Loftus, & Burton, 1989). This is thought to be attributable to better organizational structure of this information in memory (Klein & Kihlstrom, 1986). Therefore, rate-based estimates should be more accurate when made about oneself.

Finally, the impact of social desirability and self-presentation concerns should be different for self-reports and proxy respondents. However, although proxy respondents may be more willing to report about socially undesirable behaviors of others, they may lack the knowledge to do so. Again, a primary factor is likely to be the social distance between the pair. This distance should affect both the information a proxy respondent has about the other and his or her willingness to report it. However, these effects may actually counteract one another and therefore be difficult to detect.

Attitudinal Data

As we have already seen, respondents asked about their own attitudes will sometimes retrieve them from memory and at other times construct an answer on the spot by retrieving information considered relevant. It is unlikely that respondents have the attitudes of others stored in their own memories. Yet they can often give very accurate information about their spouses' and close friends' thoughts. How do they do it?

Hoch (1987) suggests that people use three general inputs in answering a question about another's attitudes:

1. The individual's own attitude toward the topic
2. The perceived level of similarity between the person and the proxy
3. Other relevant general information, such as conversations or observed behavior

Supporting this model, Davis, Hoch, and Ragsdale (1986) found that when people predicted their spouses' preferences for a variety of consumer products they first anchored on their own preferences and then adjusted their judgment based on the spouse's perceived level of influence in the purchase decision for that product.

Cognitive Laboratory Results

Bickart et al. (1989) conducted cognitive interviews with fifty couples who were either married or living together. The data were coded using the scheme shown in Chapter Two. The behaviors covered in the study included a broad range of behaviors asked about in typical surveys; the attitudes related primarily to political parties and other political organizations.

Behavioral Data

Table 10.2 shows the methods that respondents reported using for self-reports and proxy reports for the behavioral items in the study. It also shows the number of respondents using chronological sequences, event cues, and a specific reference period.

As one would expect, the proxy reporters were more likely to use estimation than the self-reporters and the self-reporters were more likely to use counting than the proxies. Self-reporters were about 60 percent more likely to use chronological sequences and event cues than proxy respondents. There was limited use of specific reference periods, but self-reporters seemed slightly more likely to use them than proxies.

TABLE 10.2. Methods used for responding to behavioral questions
(average number of uses of each reporting strategy).

Method	(1) Self	(2) Proxy	Ratio (1)/(2)
Estimation	2.98	3.42	.87
Counting	6.94	5.00	1.39
Chronological sequence	1.28	.78	1.64
Event cues	2.40	1.52	1.58
Specific reference period	1.00	.82	1.22

Attitudinal Questions

Table 10.3 presents the processes used in reporting attitudes toward
political groups. In general, when respondents were reporting about
themselves, they relied primarily on their own general knowledge
or beliefs about the group or organization. For example, they used
beliefs such as "Environmental groups will preserve the earth for a
longer time" or "Women's groups make a big noise and do nothing."

When arriving at proxy reports respondents were more likely to
use general knowledge about the other person as a basis for their
judgment. For example, they used information such as "She always
supports women's causes so I would think she is favorable to
women's rights groups" to form a judgment about the other person's
attitude. Slightly less than a quarter of all respondents used anchoring on themselves as a strategy for reporting about others. This
result modifies some earlier work (Hoch, 1987; Davis et al., 1986)
that suggested that anchoring is the most commonly used strategy
in answering attitude questions about another household member.
Responses based on general knowledge of the proxy, however,
appear still more common.

The latter observation is consistent with a large body of
research in social psychology that suggests that people draw inferences about the behaviors and attitudes of others from assumptions
about their enduring personality traits (see Schwarz & Wellens,
1994, for an application of this literature to proxy responding).

TABLE 10.3 Processes used in reporting attitudes toward political groups.

Process	Self	Proxy
Anchor on self	—	23.7
Base on general knowledge about self/proxy	20.0	34.2
Base on general knowledge about political group	60.2	13.8
Base on discussions with other person	—	9.6
Base on specific behavior event	9.9	8.3
Don't know	9.9	10.4
	100.0	100.0
N	(94)	(94)

The Accuracy of Proxy Reporting

It has generally been found that proxy reporting is highly correlated with self-reports although the measurement error is higher for proxy reporting. The best review is by Moore (1988), who points out that most studies that use proxy reporters select on the basis of availability so that when differences are analyzed it is difficult to separate sampling and response effects.

In a study of proxy reporting Menon et al. (1995) controlled for sample differences by asking both members of the household to report about themselves and the other person. Thus, differences noted could not be caused by sample differences. There are two limitations to the results of that study:

1. There were no outside validation measures and only measured convergence between self-reports and proxy reports. That is, both sets of data may have contained common measurement error.

2. The sample consisted only of husbands and wives or couples living together and did not include other kinds of proxy reporters such as children or other relatives who might be less well informed.

Factors Related to Convergence Between Self-Reporters and Proxy Reporters

The literature review suggests that the greater the joint participation between the respondent and the person being reported about, the higher the convergence in reporting. Some activities such as watching television or eating in restaurants are naturally participated in jointly. For other activities, such as reading, or for attitude questions, it is not joint participation but joint discussion that should be related to greater convergence.

These expectations are confirmed in the data from the Menon et al. (1995) study presented in Table 10.4. These data consist of two samples. The first sample of fifty pairs of couples was the same one, described earlier, used to get data on cognitive processes. The second sample consisted of two hundred couples in Champaign County, Illinois, who were interviewed by telephone with a similar questionnaire. Respondents were dichotomized on the basis of their reported level of participation and discussion.

On fourteen of fifteen comparisons, the correlations were higher for partners who reported participating more. On thirteen of sixteen behavior comparisons and sixteen of twenty-three attitude comparisons, with one tie, correlations were higher for partners who discussed more. The effects of discussion were not quite as strong as those of direct participation.

For noncontinuous items where a correlation coefficient is not appropriate, Table 10.4 shows the percent agreement between self-reports and proxy reports. Partners who discussed or participated more were more accurate in fourteen of seventeen comparisons. To summarize, in 80 percent of seventy comparisons greater participation or discussion led to greater agreement between self-reports and proxy reports.

Menon et al. hypothesized that convergence between self-reports and proxy reports would also be related to the importance of the behavior or attitude, but this hypothesis was not confirmed. Importance was correlated with level of discussion between partners

TABLE 10.4. Agreement between self and proxy reports by level of participation and discussion.

	Telephone		Face-to-Face	
	Higher	Lower	Higher	Lower
Average correlations				
Participation	.62	.48	.78	.29
Discussion-behavior	.49	.41	.32	.20
Discussion-attitudes	.47	.38	.60	.49
Percent agreement				
Participation/discussion				
Behaviors	92.5	90.0	83.2	75.7
Attitudes	85.6	74.8	92.6	82.1

but there was no separate effect of importance after controlling for level of discussion.

Experiments to Measure Factors Related to the Accuracy of Proxy Reports

As indicated in the preceding section, in the absence of validation information the high convergence between self-reports and proxy reports may be caused by common error. Also, reports about level of participation are subject to possible measurement errors. One control for these problems is to conduct laboratory experiments where validation is possible and the level of participation between partners can be accounted for.

Such an experiment was designed to simulate a real-world situation (Bickart et al., 1991). Couples in Gainesville, Florida, searched for information about a vacation, and one couple selected at random won the vacation they chose. Subjects individually examined vacation options through an interactive computer program that recorded their search activities. Menus were presented describing four beach locations and three cities in Florida. Information was provided on activities, accommodations, and restaurants.

After the search phase, the thirty-one couples discussed the alternatives and made a selection. They then were asked questions about their own and their partner's search behavior, specifically, the number of options that they and their partners had examined. The computer program provided a count of the actual number.

The time allowed for discussion was manipulated. In the high discussion condition, the couples spent ten minutes discussing the vacation together. In the low discussion condition, they spent only five minutes.

The results are given in Tables 10.5 and 10.6. Table 10.5 gives the mean number of options actually examined and the self-reports and proxy reports. Table 10.6 gives the relative accuracy overall of the two reports. Not surprisingly, the accuracy of self-reports was greater than that of proxy reports for all items. Self-reports were about 90 percent accurate or greater for reports about all options except activities.

Table 10.6 indicates that proxies tended to underreport their partner's behavior. Several explanations for this are possible. Because of the limited time for discussion, knowledge about the partner's specific behavior was limited. Once the couple agreed on a vacation place, they often did not discuss restaurants and accommodations at places not considered. Thus, if respondents were using a counting strategy, they would not have complete information about their partner's behavior.

Furthermore, if respondents were using a counting strategy, they may have had difficulty retrieving specific information even when it was available in memory. Respondents who used estimation may have followed a conservative anchor and adjust strategy; they may have used their own behavior as an anchor and then adjusted down because they did not know exactly what their partners had done.

Table 10.7 shows the correlations between actual and reported behavior for self-reports and proxy reports. Again, self-reports were more highly correlated with actual behavior than were proxy reports. More important, in all cases convergence between self-reports and proxy reports was higher than accuracy of proxy reports. This indicates that there is shared error between the self-reports and

TABLE 10.5. Mean number of options examined: actual versus self-reports and proxy reports.

Option	Actual $\bar{x}$	(Std)	Self-report $\bar{x}$	(Std)	Proxy report $\bar{x}$	(Std)
Total places	3.90	(1.75)	3.64	(1.63)	3.42	(2.09)
Total accommodations	8.55	(4.34)	7.59	(4.20)	3.30	(4.21)
Total restaurants	7.16	(4.77)	7.35	(3.85)	2.71	(3.79)
Total activities	9.45	(6.97)	6.51	(4.15)	2.12	(3.02)

Note: Based on $N = 62$ respondents.

TABLE 10.6. Relative accuracy of self-reports and proxy reports.

Option	Self-report	Proxy report
Total places	.93	.88
Total accommodations	.89	.39
Total restaurants	1.03	.38
Total activities	.69	.22

Shown is the ratio of the reported behavior to the actual behavior.

the proxy reports. Couples are more similar in their reports about partners than they are accurate. Thus, convergence is an overestimate of accuracy.

Finally, Table 10.8 compares the mean absolute differences between self-reports and proxy reports by level of discussion. The absolute difference is smaller when there is more discussion, except for total places where there is no difference. Thus, these experimental results confirm the survey results given in the preceding section.

Validation of Self-Reports and Proxy Reports

An alternative to experiments is to ask respondents to keep diaries of their activities and then, at a later date, recall information about

TABLE 10.7 Accuracy and convergence of self-reports and proxy reports.

| | Accuracy[1] | | | | Convergence[2] | |
| | Self-report | | Proxy report | | | |
Option	r	(n)	r	(n)	r	(n)
Total places	.73*	(61)	.36*	(50)	.37*	(50)
Total accommodations	.59*	(61)	.05	(60)	.12	(60)
Total restaurants	.58*	(60)	−.08	(59)	−.06	(58)
Total activities	.05	(59)	.08	(59)	.21**	(57)

[1]Correlation between report and actual behavior.

[2]Correlation between self-report and proxy report.

*$r \neq 0, p < .05$.

**$r \neq 0, p < .10$.

Table 10.8 Mean absolute difference between proxy report and actual behavior, by discussion level.

| | Low discussion | | High discussion | |
Option	$\bar{x}$	(Std)	$\bar{x}$	(Std)
Total places	1.70	(1.29)	1.74	(1.45)
Total accommodations[1]	7.72	(3.81)	5.06	(4.46)
Total restaurants	6.68	(4.99)	5.52	(4.55)
Total activities[2]	9.11	(7.92)	6.97	(5.52)

[1]Low < High, $p \leq .05$.

[2]Low < High, $p \leq .10$.

themselves and proxies and compare this recall to diary records. Mingay and his colleagues (1994) conducted a study of twenty-six college student respondents who kept daily diaries for five weeks and reported on eighteen separate activities.

Respondents and their roommates were asked to recall the respondents' activities over the five-week diary period on the day after the period ended. The mean frequencies reported by diary, self-report, and proxy report are given in Table 10.9. The proportional errors of self-reporting and proxy reporting are given in Table 10.10. The explanatory variables used in this study were the relative frequencies, with events being characterized as low, medium, and high frequency, and a memorability rating which reflected how salient and unusual the respondents believed the event to be.

Mingay and his colleagues found significant underreporting by both self-respondents and proxy respondents, but self-respondents were better for fourteen of the eighteen items. When bias was measured, proxies were not significantly less accurate than self-respondents. In contrast, using absolute or squared error, self-respondents were considerably more accurate than proxies. This finding is in complete agreement with the finding related to household couples.

As one might expect, the mean reporting error increased with frequency but the relative error declined. However, the reporting error in Table 10.10 was lowest for both self-reports and proxy reports for the only behavior on the list that was highly regular—eating in the dorm. Respondents' ratings of memorability were only weakly associated with more accurate reporting by either self or proxy.

Mingay and colleagues did not ask roommates directly if they had observed their roommate's behavior, talked about it, or done neither. Without such information, it is difficult to determine how the roommates made their estimates.

Summary

This chapter discussed how the process of reporting about another's behavior and attitudes differs to some extent from self-reporting. A particular difference is the use of anchor and adjust methods. Proxy reports and self-reports converge with increased participation and discussion, although some of this simply reflects common measurement error. Findings were reviewed based on data about couples who knew each other well and some data about college roommates

TABLE 10.9. Mean frequencies of activities as recorded in daily diaries and reported (excluding activities never done).

	Mean[1] five-week frequencies		
	Diary records	Respondent reports	Proxy reports
Low frequency group			
Go to a music store	1.5	2.0	0.8
Go to a grocery store	2.8	2.2	1.7
Make a deposit in bank account	2.9	2.0	2.3
Go on a date	3.3	2.5	1.9
Do laundry	3.4	2.8	2.6
Doze in class	3.8	3.4	3.9
Medium frequency group			
Write a check	4.1	3.2	2.0
Go to a bookstore	4.5	3.9	2.6
Leave Hyde Park	5.9	4.5	2.6
Go to the Regenstein Library[2]	8.5	9.0	10.0
Write a letter	8.5	4.7	5.4
Drink alcohol	8.9	4.8	4.6
High frequency group			
Talk to parent on phone	10.7	8.9	6.8
Buy food at restaurant, fast-food place, or coffee shop	11.8	8.1	7.7
Nap, other than in class	12.6	10.0	16.9
Do a sport or physical activity	15.3	12.7	11.0
Watch TV	19.7	12.3	14.8
Eat evening meal in dorm	23.1	25.1	27.1

[1] 1 = Definitely remember one week from now, 2 = probably remember, 3 = might or might not remember, 4 = probably not remember, 5 = definitely not remember.

[2] The Regenstein Library is the main University of Chicago library.

TABLE 10.10. Mean proportional error of respondents and proxies (excluding activities never done).

| | Proportional error | | |
	Respondents	Proxies	Mean[1] memorability
Low frequency group			
Go to a music store	.33	−.47	2.38
Go to a grocery store	−.21	−.39	2.89
Make a deposit in a bank account	−.31	−.21	2.70
Go on a date	−.24	−.42	1.29
Do laundry	−.18	−.24	2.99
Doze in class	−.11	.03	3.62
Medium frequency group			
Write a check	−.22	−.51	2.94
Go to a bookstore	−.13	−.42	2.94
Leave Hyde Park	−.24	−.56	1.30
Go to the Regenstein Library[2]	.06	.18	2.99
Write a letter	−.45	−.37	2.28
Drink alcohol	−.46	−.48	2.3
High frequency group			
Talk to parent on phone	−.17	−.36	2.51
Buy food at restaurant, fast-food place, or coffee shop	−.31	.35	2.72
Nap, other than in class	−.21	.34	3.38
Do a sport or physical activity	−.17	−.28	2.76
Watch TV	−.38	−.25	3.19
Eat evening meal in dorm	.09	.17	3.30

[1] 1 = Definitely remember one week from now, 2 = probably remember, 3 = might or might not remember, 4 = probably not remember, 5 = definitely not remember.

[2] The Regenstein Library is the main University of Chicago library.

who were in close proximity but might know each other less well. Additional research is needed to study the cognitive methods used by respondents asked to report about others who are less well known—such as relatives, friends, and co-workers—or about their organizations or neighborhoods.

Practical Implications for Questionnaire Designers

The findings reviewed in this chapter encourage the use of proxy reports. For many behaviors and even for some attitudes, proxy reports are not significantly less accurate than self-reports. Obviously, accuracy depends on the proxy's observation of and discussion with others. Information about the behavior of another person in the home is usually better than information about that person at work or away from home, unless the behavior is shared or discussed extensively.

11

Implications for Questionnaire Design and the Conceptualization of the Survey Interview

In the previous chapters we presented an eclectic theoretical framework drawn from social and cognitive psychology and reviewed the growing literature on questionnaire design that uses such a framework for the study of response errors in surveys. In this chapter we summarize our key conclusions. In the first part we outline a social-cognitive framework for conceptualizing the survey interview that we hope will provide a useful integrative perspective for future research. In the second part we present some basic applied implications for questionnaire design. We conclude with some thoughts about the future.

A Social-Cognitive Framework for Studying Question Answering in Surveys

As we have noted throughout this book, the survey literature on response effects is full of seemingly inconsistent findings and a sense of "Here you see it, here you don't" with regard to these effects. In this final section of the book, we highlight what we believe to be the key theoretical principles that emerge from the discussions of the preceding chapters. We begin with a dual conception of a survey; on the one hand it is a social phenomenon and on the other it involves elaborate cognitive work by individuals. We view the survey process, in the first instance, as fundamentally a social encounter. By calling it a social encounter, even if it is conducted through a self-administered questionnaire, we call attention to the fact that those conducting the survey are asking questions of respondents in situations that are very similar to ordinary conversations and, as such, follow the linguistic and social rules that govern conversations. To be sure, this conversation has some special characteristics that set it apart from others, but the activity is still a conversation and needs to be understood as such. Similarly, the survey is a social—and usually voluntary—encounter between strangers and follows the rules that govern social relations between strangers. Thus, understanding the rules that govern both conversations and social encounters in general should help us understand how our questions are being understood and also offer insight into how to "get" the interview, that is, enlist the cooperation of the respondents in participating in the survey (see Groves, Cialdini, & Couper, 1992, for a discussion of the latter aspect).

Language is the medium of the survey questionnaire. Thus, understanding how people comprehend speech and written material is important for understanding response effects. Both formal structure (syntax) and pragmatic factors (that may affect meaning) must be clear. Much of the research we have discussed in the previous chapters centers on the factors that influence respondents' comprehension of the meaning of questions and how the inferred meaning may differ from the researcher's intended meaning. If different respondents answer what are, in effect, different questions, their answers cannot be compared. Indeed, they may answer a question the researcher never wanted to ask.

Explorations into how respondents understand questions lead inevitably to basic cognitive questions about the ways in which people understand the world around them and communicate with one another. Accordingly, the preceding chapters draw heavily on cognitive psychological research on memory and information processing as fundamental processes that underlie the answering of questions in a survey.

Surveys as Social Encounters

Our model of the survey interview is that of a social system with two roles, the interviewer and the respondent (see Sudman & Bradburn, 1974). The obligations of the interviewer are to ask the questions as intended by the researcher, to record the responses accurately, to hold the answers confidential, and to transmit the full set of answers back to the researcher. The interviewer is also obligated to treat the respondent with respect and not intrude any of his or her own opinions or views into the interview situation.

Once admitted into this social system, the interviewer also has some rights. The interviewer has the right to guide the conversation, not only to ask questions, some of which may be quite personal or require respondents to reveal potentially embarrassing or incriminating information, but also to ask respondents to provide information from records or even to look at documents or objects. The interviewer also has the right to set limits on what is relevant to the interview and to steer the conversation back to the questionnaire if it wanders off the track.

Respondents too have rights and obligations. They have the right to refuse to participate in the interview at all or to answer specific questions, and they have the right to terminate the interview at any time. They have the right to be treated with respect and to be asked questions that are appropriate for them. Once having agreed to become a respondent, however, they take on the obligation to answer questions as best they can, unless exercising their right to refuse to answer. They also have the obligation to treat the interviewer courteously and not waste time.

Interviews have similarities to other social encounters where there may be a conversation between strangers. When the interview takes place in the respondent's home, social norms about the treatment of strangers in the home are often brought into play. Interviewers have to be careful to ensure that a balance is maintained between the impersonal role of the interviewer and the role of a social visitor. Anyone with experience in personal interviewing knows that there is a tendency on the part of many respondents to try to convert the interview into a pleasant social event and to introduce conversational topics that are, at best, only tangentially relevant to the topic at hand. Good interviewers develop a fine sense of how far they can go in accommodating the respondent's desire to be a good host and still maintain their professional role. Although respondents have an obligation to answer questions truthfully, this obligation may conflict with other social norms, such as presenting oneself in a good light, not causing tension in a social encounter by contradicting the interviewer, and not appearing to be a "bad" respondent. Thus, factors of social desirability may intrude in the interview process and affect respondents' answers to survey questions (see DeMaio, 1984, for a review). Interviews conducted over the telephone have fewer problems of this kind because of the lack of physical presence, but telephone interviews are also subject to the general norms that affect telephone and other conversations.

Although there is some debate over the degree to which survey interviews should be considered conversations (see Suchman & Jordan, 1990), we believe that they are sufficiently similar to ordinary conversations that they share important structural features. Conversations between people, even strangers, are subject to a socially accepted set of rules that has been described by Grice (1975). These rules implicitly set expectations that influence the way in which respondents understand particular questions within the context of the overall interview. We believe that the tacit assumptions that govern the conduct of conversation in daily life are key to understanding a wide range of response effects, from the impact of response alternatives to wording and order effects (see Clark & Schober, 1992; Schwarz, 1994; Schwarz & Hippler, 1991; Strack & Schwarz, 1992, for extended discussions).

Grice argues that there are four principles that structure conversations. These principles are the following: (1) speakers should not say things that they believe to be false; (2) speakers should make comments that are relevant to the purposes of the conversation; (3)

speakers should make their contributions as informative as possible and not repeat themselves; and (4) speakers should express themselves as clearly as possible. In Chapter Three, we summarized these principles by saying that conversational norms require participants to be truthful, relevant, informative, and clear (see Clark & Clark, 1977). These norms may be thought of as a set of tacit rules that have their origin in the socialization processes by which people learn to communicate with others. They are learned as part of the process of learning a language and how to communicate and, thus, they are part of the social world in which people live.

Although interviews with structured questionnaires have special characteristics arising from the preset nature of the questions and (often) the response categories, respondents still bring the assumptions that govern the use of language in any other context to the survey interview. In fact, they even do so when the "conversation" does not involve the actual presence of another person, as Strack and Schwarz (1992) observed in their analysis of self-administered questionnaires. This fact has two wide-ranging implications for the survey interview.

The first implication reflects the "guarantee of relevance" (Sperber & Wilson, 1986) that characterizes conversations. Respondents assume that every contribution to the conversation is relevant to the conversation unless indicated otherwise. In the survey interview, the researcher's contributions include apparently formal features of the questionnaire, such as the nature of the response alternatives or the numeric values provided on a rating scale, as well as the content of related questions. Respondents use formal features in interpreting the meaning of questions, inferring, for example, that "not at all successful" refers to the absence of success when combined with the numeric value 0 on a rating scale but to the presence of failure when combined with the numeric value −5 (Schwarz, Knäuper, Hippler, Noelle-Neumann, & Clark, 1991). Far from reflecting "superficial responding," such findings indicate that respondents act as cooperative communicators who do their best to make sense of the questions asked. In doing so, they frequently draw on context features that the researcher considered irrelevant. This insensitivity of researchers to the conversational aspects of questionnaire construction is most obvious when they ask meaningless questions about fictitious issues, a conversational act that violates every norm of conversational conduct. Having no reason to assume that the researcher is not a cooperative communicator, respondents draw on the content of related questions to disambiguate meaning (for example, Strack, Schwarz, & Wänke, 1991). Having interpreted the ambiguous question, they draw on related knowledge to provide a meaningful answer to what they think they have been asked. Again, their responses reflect cooperative conversational behavior rather than meaningless utterances offered in an attempt to look knowledgeable. In fact, without drawing on the context of an utterance, we would be unable to carry on any meaningful conversation (see Clark & Clark, 1977).

A second implication of the relevance principle is that respondents try to provide answers that are relevant to the recipient. Hence, they do not reiterate information they provided earlier and they do not offer information that the researcher may take for granted. This process underlies the frequent differences between answers to open and closed questions (see Schwarz & Hippler, 1991, for a review) and related phenomena. Moreover, respondents' attempt to avoid redundancy may sometimes lead them to reinterpret the meaning of a question when a general question follows a more specific one. As discussed in Chapter Five, respondents are likely to interpret the general question as referring to aspects that have not yet been addressed by the specific question, resulting in pronounced context effects (for example, Schwarz, Strack, & Mai, 1991). Again, these influences reflect appropriate conversational conduct rather than superficial responding.

As these examples illustrate, we believe that many apparent "artifacts" of survey measurement are simply the result of respondents behaving as cooperative communicators and relying on tacit assumptions that are perfectly adequate for guiding conversations in most situations of everyday life. However, as researchers, we are often insensitive to the conversational implications of our questionnaires and tend to blame the respondents rather than the instrument for unanticipated influences (see Clark & Schober, 1992; Schwarz, 1994).

Any comprehensive theory of the survey interview has to incorporate these aspects of human communication. However, such a theory would be incomplete without a consideration of the cognitive processes that individuals engage in when responding to a survey question. These are the aspects to which we turn next.

Surveys as Cognitive Tasks

Much as we consider conversational rules to be the key ingredients for a conceptualization of the survey interview as a social encounter, we assume that the concepts of information accessibility and mental construal are the key ingredients for a conceptualization of respondents' cognitive processes.

In Chapter Three we outlined the tasks that respondents have to solve in order to answer a survey question (Strack & Martin, 1987; Tourangeau, 1984; Tourangeau & Rasinski, 1988). As a first step, they must interpret the question to know what we are asking about and what information is sought. The conversational processes discussed in the preceding section are of crucial relevance at this step. Next, respondents have to form a mental representation of the attitude object or the behavior addressed. To do so, they need to retrieve relevant information from memory. Based upon this information they must compute an appropriate response, which may require the application of inference rules or the comparison of the attitude object to some standard. Finally, respondents must format the answer to fit the response alternatives, and they may want to edit the answer before communicating it to the interviewer. Each of these processes takes time, although the amount of time varies widely depending on the difficulty of the question. Although we talk about the tasks as if they were discrete and occur in sequence, it is likely that in real interview situations multiple processing is going on, with residues from previous questions still active while later questions are asked. Indeed, the effect of processing information related to previous questions is the main explanation for many of the context effects discussed throughout this book.

Questions may be about attitudes or opinions or about behavior. Somewhat different cognitive processes are involved in answering different types of questions. But in all cases, respondents' answers depend on the information accessible to them at the time they answer the question and on the way in which they use the information to form a mental representation of the attitude object or behavior under study.

For information to be used, it must be available in memory, that is, it has to have been encoded and stored. However, not all information potentially available in memory can be retrieved at a given point in time, that is, it may not be accessible.

Attitude Questions

Attitude questions essentially ask respondents to convey an evaluative judgment. As shown in Chapter Five, evaluative judgments require mental representations of the target and of a standard against which the target is evaluated. If the topic of the attitude question is very familiar, respondents may be able to retrieve a judgment that they have formed at a previous time. In most cases, however, a previous judgment is not accessible or does not tap the specific aspect addressed in the question. Moreover, the specific context may lead respondents to consider or to disregard certain aspects. As a result, most respondents are likely to compute the answers to most attitude questions on the spot.

In doing so, they draw on the information that is most accessible at that time and truncate the search process as soon as enough information to form a judgment has come to mind. Hence, their judgment is based on the subset of potentially relevant information that comes to mind most easily. This information may be chronically or temporarily accessible. The chronic accessibility of information reflects respondent variables and contributes to the stability of answers over time. In contrast, the temporary accessibility of information reflects the influence of questionnaire variables and other fortuitous events, such as what happens to be in the news that day. We discussed issues of information accessibility in some detail in Chapters Three to Five. We emphasize here that the principle of information accessibility and truncated information search is a key component of any conceptualization of context effects in survey interviews.

Knowing what information comes to mind, however, is not sufficient to predict its impact. Rather, the ways in which accessible information influences judgment depends on the ways in which respondents use the information. Information that is included in the representation formed of the attitude object results in assimilation effects. Information that is excluded from the representation of the attitude object results in contrast effects. If the excluded information is merely "subtracted" from the representation of the attitude object, the emerging contrast effect is limited to this particular object. If it is used in forming a mental representation of a relevant standard, however, the emerging contrast effect generalizes to all attitude objects to which this standard is applicable (Schwarz & Bless, 1992a). In Chapter Five we reviewed the variables that determine the use of information in forming mental representations of attitude objects and standards and discussed the conditions that determine the emergence, direction, size, and generalization of context effects.

Finally, it is important to remember that the process of thinking about an attitude object may itself generate "experiential information" (see Strack, 1992) that respondents can use to form a judgment. As we discussed in Chapter Four, the feelings evoked when people think about an attitude object and experiences of ease or difficulty in recalling relevant information, may themselves serve as input into a judgment. For example, realizing that we find it difficult to recall anything that our congressional representative has done for the district (Bishop, 1987) may be as relevant for evaluating the work of our representative as what we do recall. The impact of such experiential information, however, follows the same logic as that of any other information (see Banaji, Blair, & Schwarz, 1995; Clore, 1992; Schwarz & Clore, in press, for a more detailed discussion).

In sum, we propose that context effects in attitude and opinion measurement can be understood by considering which information is accessible at the time of judgment and how it is used in forming mental representations of the attitude object and a relevant standard. Whereas these dual notions of information accessibility and mental construal have received considerable support in experimental research, we note that their application to a given set of questions is often difficult. Our theoretical notions specify variables that produce the predicted effects provided that these variables are clearly operationalized. It is often difficult, however, to determine to what extent a given question, written with some substantive rather than methodological interest in mind, reflects a certain theoretical variable. As a result, we can often predict that a given question would certainly produce an assimilation effect if changed a bit in this direction and a contrast effect if changed a bit in that direction, but we can't tell what the effect will be if the question is asked as is. Many questions are "mushy" with regard to the key theoretical variables that have been identified. Dissatisfying as this may be from an applied point of view, we doubt that this state of affairs is likely to change. As in any other area of research, understanding a theoretical principle allows the specification of some successful operationalizations. But whether other operationalizations are sufficient or insufficient to produce the expected effect can only be determined on an empirical basis. The best we can hope for in such cases is that the theoretical framework allows us to identify the questions that are likely to be affected by a given context and to specify the proper conditions for a parsimonious test.

Behavioral Questions

Much like attitude reports, behavioral reports depend on information accessibility and use. As we have emphasized throughout, answering a behavioral question may take a great deal of effort in retrieving information that is not easily accessible. Motivating respondents to make that effort is not easy and giving them the time to search their memories thoroughly, even if they are motivated to do so, goes against other requirements of the survey—to keep respondent burden to a minimum and to keep costs down.

In answering a behavioral question, respondents may draw on their episodic as well as their semantic memory. Episodic memory refers to memories about events that take place in time and space; it makes up what is sometimes called our autobiographical memory. Semantic memory refers to our knowledge base, including knowledge about language and its meaning, abstract knowledge, and other generic knowledge not tied to events that we have personally experienced; it is knowledge *about* rather than *of* events. This useful distinction, however, blurs when we experience many instances of similar events over a lifetime. We may find it difficult to recall any particular episode and the representation may come to resemble semantic knowledge about a class of events, lacking particular time and space markers. Such representations may be referred to as autobiographical knowledge.

To recall information about an event, it must have been encoded and stored in long-term memory in the first place. Encoding can be along multiple lines; for example, events may be encoded by type of activity, participants, locations, and time. No particular type of encoding appears to be superior as a cue to retrieve information from long-term memory although chronology seems to have a pervasive role. That is, events in autobiographical memory seem to get marked with some type of temporal code that places them in a chronological order. However, this temporal code is unlikely to resemble calendar dates, as we may conclude from the observation that calendar dates are very poor recall cues.

The chronological ordering of events plays an important role in the organization of autobiographical memory and probably represents the highest level of hierarchical organization (Barsalou, 1988). Specifically, events are not stored as discrete entities but rather as event sequences or extended events. These sequences are organized along meaningfully clustered lines such as cause-effect relationships, logically related to some sort of goal or socially defined role, such as work, family, school, and social relationships. Higher levels of organization can be further divided into lower levels, such as school year (for example, first grade) or particular job (when I worked at the XYZ Corporation). Specific events are nested within these different organizational levels.

In the following section we summarize the processes involved in recalling and dating specific past events and in reporting frequencies of classes of events.

Questions About a Specific Event. To get to the memory of a specific event, one has to activate pathways that run through the hierarchical organization. Obviously the ease and length of time it takes to find the memory depend on whether the search process uses the organization properly or is misled into exploring the wrong branch of the hierarchy. Accordingly, the formulation of questions about respondents' past behavior may make it easier or harder for them to retrieve the requested information.

Event dating has proved to be a particularly difficult problem in surveys. Increasingly the interest of survey researchers is in continuous event histories, that is, the record of employment, income, education, use of medical care services, and so on, over a defined time period. Even when respondents do not need to know the date of every event, many studies ask for the number of events within a particular period. To answer such questions, respondents must remember the relevant events that took place during the specified period.

Questions About Multiple Events. Although studies that ask for reports of number of events in a reference period might appear as if they are asking respondents to retrieve each of the events that occurred and count them, studies have shown that in practice people have a great deal of difficulty remembering discrete events of the same type when there are about five or more of them. Instead, they use various methods to estimate the number and then report the estimate. To make such estimates they rely on heuristics, such as taking the usual rate at which they do things and adjusting it for any unusual circumstances in the reference period ("anchor and adjust") or disaggregating the total, perhaps counting for a short period of time and then multiplying to get a total for the period ("decomposition"). If the question presents a set of numeric response alternatives, respondents may use the range of alternatives as a frame of reference, reflecting their assumption that the researcher constructed a meaningful scale. Accordingly, scales that present high frequency response alternatives yield higher frequency estimates than scales that present low frequency response alternatives.

Whereas researchers usually hope that respondents follow a recall and count strategy, estimation may actually produce better results than counting under certain circumstances. When rates are stable and the reference period fairly long, estimation may produce more accurate answers, particularly in proxy reporting, when respondents are reporting for other members of the family. Of course, it can lead to biased estimates if the estimation strategy has some built-in biases. In contrast, counting, particularly with a large number of instances, is prone to omissions because the separate instances become more difficult to differentiate as they grow in number. Counting may also be subject to a type of error called "telescoping," in which events are overcounted. The phenomenon refers to the observed tendency of respondents to report that more events happened in a reference period than actually occurred.

Telescoping can be accounted for by the fact that, as events grow more distant in time, there is greater uncertainty about when they occurred even though there is no bias in the temporal representation of the events in memory. Because questions about events usually relate to the number that occurred within a limited time period (usually bounded at the front end by the date of the interview), more past events, the dates of which respondents are uncertain about, are reported as having occurred within the period than events that actually occurred within the period are remembered as falling outside of it and not reported. This asymmetric reporting bias is what we call telescoping.

Estimation can also play a role in telescoping. When dates are estimated, they are usually reported in terms of elapsed time rather than exact dates. The amount of elapsed time gets rounded in increasingly larger time periods as they grow more distant, for example, a week ago, a month ago, three months ago, and so on. Because the rounding intervals are not of equal length, more dates will be rounded forward in time than backward, thus producing what appears to be a forward telescoping of time.

Practical Implications for Questionnaire Design

Groves (1989, p. 5) makes the useful distinction between those who attempt to measure and understand measurement errors and those who attempt to reduce them. As we have pointed out, the survey process, depending as it does on language, judgment, and communication, is enormously complex. The total elimination or even the substantial reduction of measurement error does not seem likely, at least at our current state of knowledge. Moreover, the concept of measurement "error" is itself only useful for factual reports about events or behaviors, where respondents may err about the facts. As we noted in Chapter Four, the concept makes less sense in the domain of attitude measurement. Attitude reports reflect evaluative judgments, and human judgment is always context-dependent in surveys as in daily life. Depending on which aspect of a complex issue we are evaluating against which standard, our evaluations will indeed differ without one being more "accurate" or "valid" than the other. Hence, our questionnaire may introduce a context that we find undesirable in light of the goal of the research, but in contrast to factual questions this does not mean that respondents give "erroneous" reports. It simply means that they arrive at different judgments on the basis of different accessible information or question interpretations.

What, then, are the recommendations that follow from the cognitive research reviewed in this book? Our first and most important recommendation is to distrust any general recipes. Questionnaire designers need an understanding of the cognitive and communicative processes that underlie question asking and answering to identify likely problems. Once a problem is identified, there is no alternative to thinking one's way through it. Accordingly, our recommendations do not take the form of "If X, do Y" but only point to possible solutions that need to be evaluated in light of the specifics of the question and the research goal. This said, we shall nevertheless attempt to give some practical advice to researchers faced with the task of designing a questionnaire. We assume that these questionnaire designers are already familiar with the basic principles discussed in *Asking Questions* (Sudman & Bradburn, 1982). Most of what we said there still remains useful. We offer additions and modifications to that earlier advice based on the findings reviewed in this book. Some of the recommendations are for things to do or not to do; others are for things to think about when designing a questionnaire. Because we don't want to duplicate the previous chapters in this discussion, our advice will be short. We encourage readers to refer back to the respective chapters for details and references.

A final word of warning on these recommendations: many of them increase the time and cost of the questionnaire development and the interview. This seems inevitable as one becomes more aware of the complexity of the response task. Given the purposes of their studies and the resources available, some researchers may deliberately accept less than optimal questionnaires. But such a decision should be deliberate, not accidental.

Use of Thinkaloud Interviews and Other Methods for Understanding Cognitive Processes Respondents Use and Determining Problems with Questions

We strongly recommend the use of thinkaloud interviews (reviewed in Chapter Two and in the contributions to Schwarz & Sudman,

1995) for determining what respondents think questions mean and how they retrieve information to form a judgment. This is already being done by federal data-collection agencies and other large survey organizations during the beginning stages of questionnaire development before pretesting in the field. Although such interviews increase the time required to develop a questionnaire, they are an efficient means for identifying questions that are difficult to understand or answer.

Thinkaloud questions and prompts range from totally nondirective to very specific. Although there can be no general rule, we believe that some directive probing is necessary for general population samples. But we would urge that the probes not be too directive because respondents would be unduly affected by the cognitive processes suggested.

Even after problem questions have been identified and modified, some respondents may still interpret a question differently than the researcher intended. For selected behavioral questions, it may be useful to ask respondents what the question means, even during the main interview. If the respondent interprets the question in a way other than intended, a well-trained interviewer, in his or her own words, should be able to explain it. The interviewer variability introduced in this manner may well be less serious than the variability resulting from misinterpretations. We hesitate, however, to offer the same advice for attitude questions. In this case, giving the interviewer flexibility to elaborate on the meaning of a question is likely to introduce context effects that are unmeasurable because the information provided by the interviewer remains unknown. Although the context effects introduced by the interviewer's elaborations follow the same logic as the context effects introduced by any standardized content of the questionnaire, the latter effects can at least be tracked.

Before the thinkaloud interviews, several of the methods described in Chapter Two may be useful. Focus groups are an efficient first step in determining how some of the key concepts being studied are understood and retrieved by potential respondents. Because they are conducted in group settings, they are less expensive to carry out than thinkaloud interviews. However, they also provide less detailed information. We think that focus groups and thinkaloud interviews are most effective when used jointly, but if time and cost do not permit both, we recommend thinkaloud interviews. Nonverbal techniques such as sorting may also be useful in special situations.

Having a cognitive expert examine a questionnaire before interviewing is a low-cost, efficient way of identifying potential problems. Obviously, this is a more practical option if an expert is available locally or is known by the researcher.

Tape-recording pretest interviews and analyzing respondents' difficulties with a questionnaire are useful additional step after the thinkaloud interviews. It is important to remember that this is not a single-stage process. When problems are discovered with a questionnaire, either from thinkaloud interviews or analysis of pretests, the questionnaire designer will usually modify it. The redesigned questionnaire must then be reevaluated. Otherwise, revision may introduce new problems that are as serious as or more serious than those in the original version.

Improving Autobiographical Reports

As discussed in Chapters Seven through Nine, respondents asked to retrieve information about the frequency of a specified behavior may either count or estimate, depending on the frequency of the behavior and its regularity. The likelihood that a number is already stored in memory is small. To date, there is little to suggest that the questionnaire designer can have much impact on this decision except through the selection of an appropriate time period. Data users unfamiliar with cognitive processes often believe they can obtain much more information by increasing the length of the time period that a question covers, but this belief is illusory, as we saw in our discussion of recall and estimation strategies.

If the behavior is frequent, irregular, and relatively unimportant, respondents asked about a short time period will simply count and report the number of events retrieved. Respondents asked about a longer time period usually count for a short time period and then compute an answer based on the rate obtained. Hence, the longer time period does not provide additional information but may increase the possibility of a computation error because the respondent will extrapolate. Moreover, facing the need to compute an estimate, respondents may rely on the frame of reference suggested by the response alternatives, resulting in systematic bias.

In contrast, if the behavior in question is regular, respondents may already have a rate stored in memory and simply retrieve it and apply it to the time period specified. In this case, the impact of response alternatives is likely to be minimal. However, it is obvious that increasing the time period for regular behaviors does not result in more informative responses because all that is needed is an extrapolation from the rate given. Only for infrequent, irregular behavior does increasing the length of the time period increase the amount of information retrieved. Fortunately, infrequent behaviors are the ones for which respondents are most likely to have episodic information stored in memory, at least if the behavior is sufficiently relevant.

The most common problem with respondents who remember a specified behavior as regular is that they may forget exceptions to the rule. Questions about exceptions to regular behavior may be useful for adjusting reported rates. Obviously, these questions must address exceptions that may result in frequencies that are higher as well as lower as the usual rate, a point that is sometimes overlooked. Exceptions are difficult to remember, however, and should therefore be asked about for only a limited and recent time period.

Respondents who count events are subject to forgetting errors of two kinds, omission and telescoping. It has long been recognized that omissions can be reduced by providing the respondent with additional cues within the question itself, in the answer categories or in earlier related questions. The problem is that behaviors that are not cued will be underreported compared with cued behaviors. This is not critical if all the behaviors of interest are cued and if cued and noncued behaviors are not compared.

We can give no general advice on which cues are most effective because they vary between respondents. It is evident, however, that the more specific the question the easier it will be for a respondent to understand what the researcher wants. Thus, a question about the number of times a person has gone swimming in the past week is easier to answer than a question about exercise or leisure activities. Asking about more specific activities both clarifies the intended meaning and provides more detailed recall cues.

One factor that may be controlled by the researcher and the interviewer is the amount of time given for response. Cognitive processes take time, and the results suggest that respondents who try to remember individual events retrieve more information when given more time. Although interviewers are often trained to slow the pace of the interview, it may be better to build added time into the questionnaire. This can be done by increasing the length of a question (so respondents have more time to think while it is being asked) or by specifically including instructions (such as, "We know it may be hard to remember this, so take all the time you need before answering"). Giving respondents more time is likely to improve recall if respondents can use recall and count strategies. But it will have little effect if respondents estimate, either by retrieving a rate, computing it based on readily accessible events, or relying on the range of the response alternatives. In fact, if the behavior under study is unlikely to be represented in a form that allows the use of a recall and count strategy, giving respondents more time may actually induce them to use this strategy under suboptimal conditions and result in poorer data than would be obtained otherwise.

Telescoping, which results in overreporting, can be reduced or eliminated by the use of the bounded recall methods discussed in Chapter Eight. The questionnaire designer should be careful in using either cues or bounded recall methods alone because substantial overreporting or underreporting may result. The two procedures are best used jointly and only when respondents are counting and not estimating.

Context Effects in Attitude Measurement

It is clear from the discussion in Chapters Four to Six that context effects are ubiquitous and cause complex interaction effects in attitude measurement, depending on the order of the questions and response categories, the mode of administration, and the information that respondents retrieve from memory. As we emphasized in Chapter Four, human judgment is always context-dependent, in surveys as in daily life. What renders this context-dependency problematical is the researcher's desire to generalize from a sample that provided answers in the context of a specific questionnaire to a population that was never exposed to this specific context. At first glance, one might believe the solution is to mirror in the questionnaire the context in which people are likely to form the judgment in daily life. Although correct in principle, any questionnaire reduces the myriad possible contexts in which people may think about an issue. Hence, the best we can do is avoid asking questions in a context that is likely to deviate strongly from the probable context in which an issue will be considered.

What should researchers do? As a first step, we believe that researchers should evaluate the likelihood of context effects when a questionnaire is being designed so that, as much as possible, these effects are deliberate and not unanticipated. More important, we urge researchers to use split-ballot designs, which allow the detection of context effects and their consideration in data interpretation. As we noted in Chapter Five, the deliberate introduction of context effects often provides a useful strategy for testing substantive hypotheses.

Moreover, context effects at the comprehension stage are desirable in some cases because they help the respondent understand which information the researcher wants. Similarly, early questions may facilitate the retrieval of information that the researcher wants respondents to consider. But in some cases a specific context effect is undesirable. The obvious first solution is to change the context by omitting questions that may have an undesirable impact or by putting the crucial question in the first position. Similarly, a researcher may want to eliminate response categories entirely to guard against response order effects, thus using open rather than closed questions.

In personal interviews, the introduction given by the interviewer to a question or a series of questions can be used to increase, reduce, or eliminate context effects, as desired by the researcher. In self-administered questionnaires, the same results can be obtained by including printed instructions, putting the questions together in a box on one page, or putting the questions on separate pages. The logic of the model presented in Chapter Five provides useful guidelines in this regard. Whether it is desirable to induce respondents to consider certain information or to exclude it from consideration, however, can only be answered on substantive grounds.

Context effects can also be reduced by the wording of the question itself. The more general or ambiguous the question, the more likely context effects are to emerge at the comprehension stage. Thus, it usually makes sense to keep questions as specific and unambiguous as possible. In contrast, context effects at the judgment stage are likely to arise for general as well as for specific questions. However, they are likely to take different forms, as noted in our discussion in Chapter Five. General questions are prone to assimilation effects and specific questions to contrast effects. In either case, context effects will be much smaller or may vanish altogether if a previously formed judgment or substantial amounts of relevant information are chronically accessible in memory. This is not something the researcher can easily manipulate but it needs to be kept in mind, for example, when interpreting data from news polls that ask respondents to react to developing events.

If response alternatives to a question are necessary, their order may be randomized unless there is a natural ordering. The use of computer-assisted interviewing makes it far easier to randomize the order of alternatives than is possible using paper questionnaires. Computer interviews, even if self-administered, have the added advantage that the respondent is aware only of the questions that precede a given item and not those that follow. Similarly, within a section of related questions it may be possible to randomize the order of the questions using computer-assisted interviewing, again assuming there is no natural ordering. However, randomization is a "mechanical" solution that does not reduce the impact of context at the level of individual respondents. It simply ensures that these influences result in random noise rather than systematic bias in the sample as a whole. In contrast, the use of split-ballot designs allows the identification of context effects and their consideration in the substantive interpretation of the collected data. For this reason, split-ballot designs often provide the most sensible solution.

Moreover, it is advisable to avoid items or stimuli that receive either extremely positive or extremely negative ratings when asking for judgments about a series of items, because items that follow will be strongly affected. Thus, if Enrico Caruso or Maria Callas are included in a list of opera singers, the ratings of a current tenor or soprano will be strongly affected by their position on the list. Finally, the material reviewed in Chapter Six suggests that it is very difficult to make comparisons of responses across modes. Even when the wording of the question and the ordering of the response alternatives are identical, a visual presentation mode (such as response alternatives presented on a show card or in a self-administered questionnaire) is likely to result in a different pattern of response order effects than will an auditory presentation mode. Hence, any emerging differences may reflect an interaction effect of mode and response order rather than substantive change.

Proxy Informants

In Chapter Ten we encourage the use of proxy informants. For many behaviors and even for some attitudes, proxies are not significantly less accurate than are respondents answering for themselves. Obviously, accuracy depends on the proxy's observation of others in the household or on levels of discussion with others. Information about another's behavior in the home is usually better than information about that person at work or away from home, unless the behavior is shared or discussed extensively.

Conclusions

We suppose that many readers would like to see more specific recommendations for questionnaire design. But such recommendations would be unlikely to capture the complexity of the processes we examined in this book. Unwelcome a task as it may be, questionnaire design problems require analysis of the design issue at hand in light of the theoretical principles highlighted in the preceding chapters.

Into the Future

Given the range of topics that surveys ask about, it is not surprising that respondents are often uncertain about their answers and use all the information available to them in coming up with an answer. In addition to the private information available from their own memories, the format of the question and the response categories offered may produce cues that are taken as information with a bearing on the question asked. "Good" respondents, that is, those who are fulfilling the role obligations of respondents, will use all the information they can to answer the questions in what they believe to be the correct manner.

Our dual conception of the survey—that it is both a social encounter and a series of cognitive tasks—focuses attention on the information that comes not from respondents' own experiences and knowledge but from cues within the interview situation itself. These cues come from other questions in the questionnaire (particularly perceived to be related to the question being answered), from the response alternatives offered, from information contained in the respondents' previous answers, from interviewer cues about what kinds of answers might be wanted, and from other comments or material provided to respondents as part of the introduction.

When respondents comprehend questions, they do more than interpret the literal meaning. They try to interpret the researcher's intention by determining what the question might mean in the context presented.

Survey questionnaire designers need to be more aware of the tremendous complexity, both cognitive and social, that constitutes the survey interview. It is unlikely at the present state of the art that we will soon develop new techniques to alter radically our ability to reduce response effects. However, we can do a better job with what we do know. By increasing the questionnaire designer's sensitivity to the cognitive and social principles that underlie the response process, we can produce better questionnaires that obtain more valid and reliable behavioral reports and that render the context dependency of attitude reports less of a surprise.

As we noted in the Introduction, research on response effects in survey measurement has long been characterized by demonstrations of particular wording or order effects, some of which have proved robust and highly replicable. Many of these demonstrations, however, did not accumulate to a consistent body of knowledge that allowed generalization from one question to the next. Nor did these demonstrations allow for the derivation of rules that could alert investigators to the types of situations in which wording or order effects are apt to appear. We believe that the past decade of research into the cognitive and communicative processes underlying survey responding has changed this state of affairs. Although the empirical regularities and theoretical conceptualizations that we reviewed in this book fall far short of answering all the questions we'd like to answer, we are optimistic that they provide a coherent framework that will allow future research on response effects to proceed in a more cumulative fashion than it did in the past. We will judge our book a success if the conceptualizations offered here enable researchers to produce the respective effects reliably and to bring them under experimental control. We also hope that our theorizing is precise enough to draw clear conclusions from research that proves us wrong. In our reading, the development of falsifiable theoretical frameworks has been the most important contribution of a decade of interdisciplinary research on survey measurement, providing the basis for cumulative research programs. The actual execution of such programs is facilitated by the now widespread use of computer-assisted telephone (CATI) and computer-assisted personal (CAPI) interviewing, which enable researchers to conduct more easily experiments in question wording, response alternatives, and question order. We hope that this technological advance together with a theoretical framework will lead to rapid advances in the knowledge of response effects.

The purpose of this book has been to summarize what we know today. We fully expect that future research will modify some of the theoretical and practical conclusions reached in this book and uncover dimensions of the survey response process that have not yet even been considered. The complexity of the survey process makes it difficult to achieve perfection—but it also makes the research process exciting and challenging.

References

Aaker, David A., et al. (1980). On using response latency to measure preference. *Journal of Marketing Research*, *17*, 237–244.

Anderson, J. R. (1980). *Cognitive psychology and its implications*. New York: W. H. Freeman.

Armstrong, J. S., Denniston, W. B., & Gordon, M. M. (1975). The use of the decomposition principle in making judgments. *Organizational Behavior and Human Performance*, *14*(2), 257–263.

Bachman, G., & Alcser, K. (1993). Limitations of conventional polling methods in studying attitudes about health care in America: An example of question sequence effects. Unpublished manuscript, University of Michigan.

Bachman, J. G., & O'Malley, P. M. (1991). When four months equals a year: Inconsistencies in student reports of drug use. *Public Opinion Quarterly*, *45*, 536–548.

Baddeley, A. (1990). *Human memory: Theory and practice*. Hillsdale, NJ: Erlbaum.

Baddeley, A. D., Lewis, V., & Nimmo-Smith, I. (1978). When did you last . . . ? In M. M. Gruneberg, P. E. Morris, & R. N. Sykes (Eds.), *Practical aspects of memory*. New York: Academic Press.

Bahrick, H. P. (1983). The cognitive map of a city: Fifty years of learning and memory. In C. Bower (Ed.), *The psychology of learning and motivation: Advances in research and theory* (Vol. 17, pp. 125–163). New York: Academic Press.

Bahrick, H. P., Bahrick, P. O., & Whittlinger, R. P. (1975). Fifty years of memory for names and faces: A cross-sectional approach. *Journal of Experimental Psychology: General, 104*(1), 54–75.

Banaji, M., Blair, I., & Schwarz, N. (1995). Implicit memory, subjective experiences, and survey measurementt. In N. Schwarz & S. Sudman (Eds.), *Answering questions*. San Francisco: Jossey-Bass.

Barsalou, L. W. (1987). The instability of graded structure: Implications for the nature of concepts. In U. Neisser (Ed.), *Concepts and conceptual development: Ecological and intellectual factors in categorization* (pp. 101–140). Cambridge, England: Cambridge University Press.

Barsalou, L. W. (1988). The content and organization of autobiographical memories. In U. Neisser & E. Winograd (Eds.), *Remembering reconsidered: Ecological and traditional approaches to the study of memory*. Cambridge, England: Cambridge University Press.

Barsalou, L. W. (1989). Intraconcept similarity and its implications for interconcept similarity. In S. Vosniadou & A. Ortony (Eds.), *Similarity and analogical reasoning* (pp. 76–121). Cambridge, England: Cambridge University Press.

Bartlett, F. C. (1932). *Remembering: A study in experimental and social psychology*. Cambridge, England: Cambridge University Press.

Bassili, J. N. (1995). The how and why of response latency measurement in telephone surveys. In N. Schwarz & S. Sudman (Eds.), *Answering questions*. San Francisco: Jossey-Bass.

Bateson, N. (1984). *Data construction in social surveys*. London: Allen & Unwin.

Becker, S. L. (1954). Why an order effect? *Public Opinion Quarterly, 18*, 271–278.

Belson, W. A. (1966). The effects of reversing presentation order of verbal rating scales. *Journal of Advertising Research, 6*, 30–37.

Belson, W. A. (1968). Respondent understanding of survey questions. *Polls, 3*, 1–13.

Belson, W. A. (1981). *The design and understanding of survey questions*. Aldershot, England: Gower.

Belson, W. A. (1986). *Validity in survey research*. Brookfield, VT: Gower.

Bergson, H. (1911). *Matter and memory*. London: Allen and Ulwin.

Bickart, B. (1992). Question-order effects and brand evaluations: The moderating role of consumer knowledge. In N. Schwarz & S. Sudman

(Eds.), *Context effects in social and psychological research*. New York: Springer-Verlag.

Bickart, B., & Felcher, E. M. (1995). Expanding and enhancing the use of verbal protocols in survey research. In N. Schwarz & S. Sudman (Eds.), *Answering questions*. San Francisco: Jossey-Bass.

Bickart, B., et al. (1989, October). *Cognitive aspects of proxy reporting of behavior*. Paper presented at the annual conference of the Association for Consumer Research, Chicago, IL.

Bickart, B., et al. (1991). An experimental study of the effects of level of participation on proxy reports of vacation plans. *Proceedings, Survey Research Methods Section*. Alexandria, VA: American Statistical Association.

Biderman, A. (1980). *Report of a workshop on applying cognitive psychology to recall problems of the National Crime Survey*. Washington, DC: Bureau of Social Science Research.

Billiet, J., Loosveldt, G., & Waterplas, L. (1988). *Response-effecten bij survey-vragen in het Nederlands taalgebied*. Leuven, Belgium: Katholieke Universiteit.

Bingham, W. V. D., & Moore, B. V. (1934) *How to interview* (Rev. ed.). New York: HarperCollins.

Bishop, G. F. (1987). Context effects in self-perceptions of interest in government and public affairs. In H. J. Hippler, N. Schwarz, & S. Sudman (Eds.). (1987). *Social information processing and survey methodology* (pp. 179–199). New York: Springer-Verlag.

Bishop, G. F., Hippler, H. J., Schwarz, N., & Strack, F. (1988). A comparison of response effects in self-administered and telephone surveys. In R. M. Groves, P. Biemer, L. Lyberg, J. Massey, W. Nicholls, & J. Waksberg (Eds.), *Telephone survey methodology* (pp. 321–340). New York: Wiley.

Bishop, G. F., Oldendick, R. W., & Tuchfarber, R. J. (1986). Opinions on fictitious issues: The pressure to answer survey questions. *Public Opinion Quarterly, 50,* 240–250.

Blair, E. A., & Burton, S. (1987). Cognitive processes used by survey respondents to answer behavioral frequency questions. *Journal of Consumer Research, 14,* 280–288.

Blair, J., Menon, G., & Bickart, B. (1991). Measurement effects in self versus proxy response to survey questions: An information processing perspective. In P. P. Biemer et al. (Eds.), *Measurement errors in surveys* (pp. 145–166). New York: Wiley.

Blair, J., et al. (1991, November). Information processing by proxy respondents: implications for survey design. Workshop on cognition and survey methodology, Utrecht, Netherlands.

Blankenship, A. B. (1940). The influence of the question form upon the response in a pubic opinion poll. *Psychological Record, 3,* 345–422.

Blankenship, A. B. (1943). *Consumer and opinion research.* New York: HarperCollins.

Bless, H., Bohner, G., Hild, T., & Schwarz, N. (1992). Asking difficult questions: Task complexity increases the impact of response alternatives. *European Journal of Social Psychology, 22,* 309–312.

Bless, H., Bohner, G., Schwarz, N., & Strack, F. (1990). Mood and persuasion: A cognitive response analysis. *Personality and Social Psychology Bulletin, 16,* 331–345.

Bodenhausen, G. V., & Wyer, R. S. (1987). Social cognition and social reality: Information acquisition and use in the laboratory and the real world. In H. J. Hippler, N. Schwarz, & S. Sudman (Eds.), *Social information processing and survey methodology* (pp. 6–41). New York: Springer.

Bolton, R. N. (1991). An exploratory investigation of questionnaire pretesting with verbal protocol analysis. *Advances in Consumer Research, 18,* 558–565.

Bolton, R. N., & Bronkhorst, T. M. (1995). Questionnaire pretesting: Computer-assisted coding of concurrent protocols. In N. Schwarz & S. Sudman (Eds.), *Answering questions.* San Francisco: Jossey-Bass.

Bower, G. H., & Gilligan, S. G. (1979). Remembering information related to one's self. *Journal Research in Personality, 13,* 420–432.

Bradburn, N. M. (1983). Response effects. In P. H. Rossi & J. D. Wright (Eds.), *The handbook of survey research.* New York: Academic Press.

Bradburn, N. M. (1992). What have we learned? In N. Schwarz & S. Sudman (Eds.), *Context effects in social and psychological research.* New York: Springer-Verlag.

Bradburn, N. M., Huttenlocher, J., & Hedges, L. V. (1994). Telescoping and temporal memory. In N. Schwarz & S. Sudman (Eds.), *Autobiographical memory and the validity of retrospective reports.* New York: Springer-Verlag.

Bradburn, N. M., & Miles, C. (1979). Vague qualifiers. *Public Opinion Quarterly, 43*, 92–101.

Bradburn, N. M., Rips, L. J., & Shevell, S. K. (1987). Answering autobiographical questions: The impact of memory and inference on surveys. *Science, 236*, 157–161.

Bradburn, N. M., Sudman, S., & Associates (1979). *Improving interview method and questionnaire design*. San Francisco: Jossey-Bass.

Brewer, M. B., Dull, V. T., & Jobe, J. B. (1989). Social cognition approach to reporting chronic conditions in health surveys. *Vital health statistics, 6*(3). Washington, DC: National Center for Health Statistics.

Brewer, M. B., & Lui, L. J. (1995). Use of sorting tasks to assess cognitive structures. In N. Schwarz & S. Sudman (Eds.), *Answering questions: Methodology for determining cognitive and communicative processes in survey research*. San Francisco: Jossey-Bass.

Brewer, W. F. (1986). What is autobiographical memory? In D. C. Rubin (Ed.), *Autobiographical memory*. Cambridge, England: Cambridge University Press.

Brewer, W. F. (1988). Memory for randomly sampled autobiographical events. In U. Neisser & E. Winograd (Eds.), *Remembering reconsidered: Ecological and traditional approaches to the study of memory*. Cambridge, England: Cambridge University Press.

Brewer, W. F. (1994). Autobiographical memory and survey research. In N. Schwarz & S. Sudman (Eds.), *Autobiographical memory and the validity of retrospective reports* (pp. 11–20). New York: Springer-Verlag.

Brook, D., & Upton, G. J. G. (1974). Bias in local government election due to position on the ballot paper. *Applied Statistics, 23*, 414–419.

Brown, D. R. (1953) Stimulus similarity and the anchoring of subjective scale. *American Journal of Psychology, 66*, 199–214.

Brown, N. R., Rips, L. J., & Shevell, S. K. (1985). The subjective dates of natural events in very long-term memory. *Cognitive psychology, 17*, 139–177.

Brown, N. R., Shevell, S. K., and Rips, L. J. (1986). Public memories and their personal context. In D. C. Rubin (Ed.), *Autobiographical memory*. Cambridge, England: Cambridge University Press.

Burton, S., & Blair, E. A. (1991). Task conditions, response formulation processes, and response accuracy for behavioral frequency questions in surveys. *Public Opinion Quarterly, 55*(1), 50–79.

Cannell, C. F., Fowler, F. J., & Marquis, K. H. (1968). The influence of interviewer and respondent psychological and behavioral variables on the reporting in household interviews. *Vital and health statistics, 2*(26). Washington, DC: Public Health Service.

Cannell, C. F., & Kahn, R. L. (1968). Interviewing. In G. Lindzey & E. Aronson (Eds.), *Handbook of social psychology* (2nd ed.). Reading, MA: Addison-Wesley.

Cannell, C. F., & Oksenberg, L. (1988). Observation of behavior in telephone interviews. In R. M. Groves et al. (Eds.), *Telephone survey methodology* (pp. 475–496). New York: Wiley.

Cannell, C. F., Oksenberg, L., & Converse, J. M. (1977). *Experiments in interviewing techniques: Field experiments in health reporting: 1971–1977.* Hyattsville, MD: National Center for Health Services Research.

Cantril, H. (1944). *Gauging public opinion.* Princeton, NJ: Princeton University Press.

Cantril, H., & Fried, E. (1944). The meaning of questions. In H. Cantril, (Ed.), *Gauging public opinion.* Princeton, NJ: Princeton University Press.

Carlston, D. E. (1980). The recall and use of traits and events in social inference processes. *Journal of Experimental Social Psychology, 16,* 303–328.

Carp, F. M. (1974). Position effects on interview responses. *Journal of Gerontology, 29,* 581–587.

Chassein, B., Strack, F., & Schwarz, N. (1986, March). *Befindlichkeitsurteile im sozialen Kontext: Die Rolle der Augenfälligkeit von Vergleichsinformation.* 28th Tagung Experimentell Arbeitender Psychologen, Saarbrücken, Germany.

Clark, H. H., & Clark, E. V. (1977). *Psychology and language.* Orlando, FL: Harcourt, Brace, Jovanovich.

Clark, H. H., & Schober, M. F. (1992). Asking questions and influencing answers. In J. M. Tanur (Ed.), *Questions about questions* (pp. 15–48). New York: Russell Sage Foundation.

Clore, G. L. (1992). Cognitive phenomenology: Feelings and the construction of judgment. In L. L. Martin & A. Tesser (Eds.), *The construction of social judgment,* 133–164. Hillsdale, NJ: Erlbaum.

Cochrane, R., & Rokeach, M. (1970). Rokeach's value survey: A methodological note. *Journal of Experimental Research in Personality, 4,* 159–161.

Collins, L. M., Graham, J. W., Hansen, W. B., & Johnson, C. A. (1985). Agreement between retrospective accounts of substance use and earlier reported substance use. *Applied Psychological Measurement, 9*(3), 301–309.

Converse, P. E. (1964). The nature of belief systems in the mass public. In D. E. Apter (Ed.), *Ideology and discontent* (pp. 206–261). New York: Free Press.

Conway, M. A. (1990). *Autobiographical memory: An introduction.* Milton Keynes, England: Open University Press.

Conway, M. A., & Ross, M. (1984). Getting what you want by revising what you had. *Journal of Personality and Social Psychology, 47,* 738–748.

Cook, R. L., & Stewart, T. R. (1975). A comparison of seven methods for obtaining subjective descriptions of judgment policy. *Organization Behavior and Human Performance, 13,* 31–45.

Crowder, R. G. (1976). *Principles of memory and learning.* Hillsdale, NJ: Erlbaum.

Daamen, D. D. L., & de Bie, S. E. (1992). Serial context effects in survey items. In N. Schwarz & S. Sudman (Eds.), *Context effects in social and psychological research* (pp. 97–114). New York: Springer-Verlag.

Davis, H. L., Hoch, S. J., & Ragsdale, E. K. E. (1986). An anchoring and adjustment model of spousal predictions. *Journal of Consumer Research, 13,* 25–37.

DeMaio, T. J. (1984). Social desirability and survey measurement: A review. In C. F. Turner & E. Martin (Eds.), *Surveying subjective phenomena* (Vol. 2, pp. 257–281). New York: Russell Sage Foundation.

Dovidio, J. F., & Fazio, R. H. (1992). New technologies for the direct and indirect assessment of attitudes. In J. M. Tanur (Ed.), *Questions about questions: Inquiries into the cognitive bases of surveys.* New York: Russell Sage Foundation.

Eagly, A. H., & Chaiken, S. (1993). *The psychology of attitudes.* Orlando, FL: Harcourt, Brace, Jovanovich.

Ebbinghaus, H. (1964). *Memory: A contribution to experimental psychology.* New York: Dover. (Original work published 1894)

Ellsworth, P. C., & Gross, S. R. (1994). Hardening of the attitudes: Americans' views on the death penalty. *Journal of Social Issues, 50,* 19–52.

Ericsson, K. A., & Simon, H. A. (1980). Verbal reports as data. *Psychological Review, 8,* 215–251.

Ericsson, K. A., & Simon, H. A. (1993). *Protocol analysis: Verbal reports as data*. Cambridge, MA: MIT Press.

Erikson, R. S., Luttbeg, N. R., & Tedin, K. L. (1988). *American public opinion*. New York: Macmillan.

Fazio, R. H. (1986). Self-monitoring and attitude accessibility. *Personality and Social Psychology Bulletin, 12*(4), 468–474.

Fazio, R. H. (1989). On the power and functionality of attitudes: The role of attitude accessibility. In A. R. Pratkanis, S. J. Breckler, & A. G. Greenwald (Eds.), *Attitude structure and function* (pp. 153–179). Hillsdale, NJ: Erlbaum.

Fazio, R. H. (1990). A practical guide to the use of response latency in social psychological research. In C. Hendrick & M. S. Clark (Eds.), *Research methods in personality and social psychology* (Vol. 11). Newbury Park, CA: Sage.

Fee, J. (1979). *Symbols and attitudes*. Unpublished doctoral dissertation, University of Chicago.

Feldman, J. M. (1992). Constructive processes in survey research: Explorations in self-generated validity. In N. Schwarz & S. Sudman (Eds.), *Context effects in social and psychological research* (pp. 49–61). New York: Springer-Verlag.

Feldman, J. M., & Lynch, J. G. (1988). Self-generated validity and other effects of measurement on belief, attitude, intention, and behavior. *Journal of Applied Psychology, 73*, 421–435.

Forgas, J. P. (1981). What is social about social cognition? In J. P. Forgas (Ed.), *Social cognition: Perspectives on everyday understanding* (pp. 1–26). New York: Academic Press.

Forgas, J. P. (1992). Affect in social judgments and decisions: A multiprocess model. In M. P. Zanna (Ed.), *Advances in experimental social psychology* (Vol. 26, pp. 123–162). San Diego: Academic Press.

Forsyth, B. H., & Lessler, J. T. (1991). Cognitive laboratory methods: A taxonomy. In P. P. Biemer et al. (Eds.), *Measurement errors in surveys* (pp. 393–418). New York: Wiley.

Forsyth, B. H., Lessler, J. L., and Hubbard, M. L. (1992). Cognitive evaluation of the questionnaire. In C. F. Turner, J. T. Lessler, & J. C. Gfroerer (Eds.), *Survey measurement of drug use: Methodological studies*. (DHHS Publication No. 92–1929). Washington, DC: U.S. Government Printing Office.

Fowler, F. J. (1989). The effect of unclear terms on survey-based estimates. In F. J. Fowler et al. (Eds.), *Conference proceedings, health survey research methods* (pp. 9–12). Washington, DC: National Center for Health Services Research.

Fowler, F. J., & Cannell, C. F. (1995). Using behavioral coding to identify cognitive problems with survey questions. In N. Schwarz & S. Sudman (Eds.), *Answering questions*. San Francisco: Jossey-Bass.

Glass, A. L., Holyoak, K. J., & Santa, J. L. (1979). *Cognition*. New York: Random House.

Grayson, C. E., Schwarz, N., & Hippler, H. J. (1995, May). *The numeric values of rating scales may affect scale meaning*. Paper presented at the meeting of the Midwestern Psychological Association, Chicago, IL.

Gregory, W. L., Cialdini, R. B., & Carpenter, K. M. (1982). Self-relevant scenarios as mediators of likelihood estimates and compliance: Does imagining make it so? *Journal of Personality and Social Psychology, 43*, 89–99.

Greenwald, A. G., Carnot, C. G., Beach, R., & Young, B. (1987). Increased voting behavior by asking people if they expect to vote. *Journal of Applied Social Psychology, 72*, 315–318.

Grice, H. P. (1975). Logic and conversation. In P. Cole & J. L. Morgan (Eds.), *Syntax and semantics: 3. Speech acts* (pp. 41–58). New York: Academic Press.

Groves, R. M. (1989). *Survey errors and survey costs*. New York: Wiley.

Groves, R. M., Cialdini, R. B., & Couper, M. P. (1992). Understanding the decision to participate in a survey. *Public Opinion Quarterly, 56*, 475–495.

Groves, R. M., & Kahn, R. L. (1979). *Surveys by telephone: A national comparison with personal interviews*. New York: Academic Press.

Harkins, S. G., & Petty, R. E. (1981). The multiple source effect in persuasion: The effects of distraction. *Personality and Social Psychology Bulletin, 7*, 627–635.

Hastie, R. (1987). Information processing theory for the survey researcher. In H. J. Hippler, N. Schwarz, & S. Sudman (Eds.), *Social information processing and survey methodology* (pp. 42–70). New York: Springer-Verlag.

Haviland, S. E., & Clark, H. H. (1974). What's new? Acquiring new information as a process of comprehension. *Journal of Verbal Learning and Verbal Behavior, 13*, 512–521.

Herr, P. M. (1986). Consequences of priming: Judgment and behavior. *Journal of Personality and Social Psychology, 51*, 1106–1115.

Herr, P. M. (1989). Priming price: Prior knowledge and context effects. *Journal of Consumer Research, 16*, 67–75.

Higgins, E. T. (1989). Knowledge accessibility and activation: subjectivity and suffering from unconscious sources. In J. S. Uleman & J. A. Bargh (Eds.), *Unintended thought* (pp. 75–123). New York: Guilford Press.

Higgins, E. T., & King, G. (1981). Accessibility of social constructs: Information processing consequences of individual and contextual variability. In N. Cantor & J. F. Kihlstrom (Eds.), *Personality, cognition, and social interaction*. Hillsdale, NJ: Erlbaum.

Hippler, H. J., & Schwarz, N. (1986). Not forbidding isn't allowing: The cognitive basis of the forbid-allow asymmetry. *Public Opinion Quarterly, 50*, 87–96.

Hippler, H. J., Schwarz, N., & Noelle-Neumann, E. (1990, May). *Response order effects in survey measurement: Cognitive elaboration and the likelihood of endorsement.* Paper presented at annual conference of the American Association for Public Opinion Research, Lancaster, PA.

Hippler, H. J., Schwarz, N., & Sudman, S. (Eds.). (1987). *Social information processing and survey methodology*. New York: Springer-Verlag.

Hoch, S. J. (1987). Perceived consensus and predictive accuracy: The pros and cons of projection. *Journal of Personality and Social Psychology, 53*, 221–234.

Horn, W. (1960). Reliability survey: A survey on the reliability of response to an interview survey. *Het PTT-bedrijf, 10*, 105–156.

Hunt, M. (1993). *The story of psychology*. New York: Doubleday.

Huttenlocher, J., Hedges, L. V., & Bradburn, N. M. (1990). Reports of elapsed time: Bounding and rounding processes in estimation. *Journal of Experimental Psychology, Learning, Memory and Cognition, 16*, 196–213.

Hyman, H. H. (1954). *Interviewing in social research*. Chicago: University of Chicago Press.

Hyman, H. H., & Sheatsley, P. B. (1950). The current status of American public opinion. In J. C. Payne (Ed.), *The teaching of contemporary affairs* (pp. 11–34). New York: National Education Association.

Jabine, T., Straf, M., Tanur, J., & Tourangeau, R. (Eds.). (1984). *Cognitive aspects of survey methodology: Building a bridge between disciplines.* Washington, D.C.: National Academy Press.

Jobe, J. B., & Loftus, E. F. (Eds.). (1991). Cogition and survey measurement [Special issue]. *Applied Cognitive Psychology, 5*(1).

Jobe, J. B., White, A. A., Kelley, C. L., & Mingay, D. J. (1990) Recall strategies and memory for health-care visits. *Milbank Quarterly, 68,* 171–189.

Johnson, E., & Tversky, A. (1983). Affect, generalization, and the perception of risk. *Journal of Personality and Social Psychology, 45,* 20–31.

Kahneman, D., & Miller, D. (1986). Norm theory: Comparing reality to its alternatives. *Psychological Review, 93,* 136–153.

Katz, D. (1960). The functional approach to the study of attitudes. *Public Opinion Quarterly, 24,* 163–204.

Kemp, S. (1988). Dating recent and historical events. *Applied Cognitive Psychology, 2*(3), 181–188.

Kish, L. (1965). *Survey sampling.* New York: Wiley.

Klein, S. B., & Kihlstrom, J. E. (1986). Elaboration, organization, and self-reference effect in memory. *Journal of Experimental Psychology: General, 115,* 26–38.

Klein, S. B., Loftus, E. J., & Burton, H. A. (1989). Two self-reference effects: The importance of distinguishing between self-descriptiveness judgments and autobiographical retrieval in self-referent coding. *Journal of Personality and Social Psychology, 56*(6), 853–865.

Knäuper, B., & Whittchen, H. U. (1994). Diagnosing major depression in the elderly: Evidence for response bias in standardized diagnostic interviews? *Journal of Psychiatric Research, 28,* 147–164.

Kolodner, J. L. (1984). *Retrieval and organizational strategies in conceptual memory.* Hillsdale, NJ: Erlbaum.

Krosnick, J. A. (1991). Response strategies for coping with the cognitive demands of attitude measures in surveys. *Applied Cognitive Psychology, 5,* 213–236.

Krosnick, J. A. (1992). The impact of cognitive sophistication and attitude importance on response order and question order effects. In N. Schwarz & S. Sudman (Eds.), *Context effects in social and psychological research* (pp. 203–220). New York: Springer-Verlag.

Krosnick, J. A., & Abelson, R. P. (1992). The case for measuring attitude strength. In J. M. Tanur (Ed.), *Questions about questions* (pp. 177–203). New York: Russell Sage Foundation.

Krosnick, J. A., & Alwin, D. F. (1987). An evaluation of a cognitive theory of response order effects in survey measurement. *Public Opinion Quarterly, 51*, 201–219.

Krosnick, J. A., & Schuman, H. (1988). Attitude intensity, importance, certainty and susceptibility to response effects. *Journal of Personality and Social Psychology, 54*(6), 940–952.

Krueger, R. A. (1994). *Focus groups*. Newbury Park, CA: Sage.

Kuiper, N. A., & Rogers, T. B. (1979). Encoding of personal information: Self-other differences. *Journal of Personal and Social Psychology, 37*, 499–514.

Lachman, R., Lachman, J. T., & Butterfield, E. C. (1979). *Cognitive psychology and information processing*. Hillsdale, NJ: Erlbaum.

Lackner, J. R., & Garrett, M. F. (1972). Resolving ambiguity: Effects of biasing context in the unattended ear. *Cognition, 1*, 359–372.

Larsen, S. F., & Plunkett, K. (1987). Remembering experienced and reported events. *Applied Cognitive Psychology, 1*, 15–26.

Lessler, J. T., & Forsyth, B. H. (1995). A coding system for appraising questionnaires. In N. Schwarz & S. Sudman (Eds.), *Answering questions*. San Francisco: Jossey-Bass.

Levinson, S. C. (1983). *Pragmatics*. Cambridge, England: Cambridge University Press.

Lichtenstein, S., Slovic, P., Fischoff, B., & Combs, B. (1978). Judged frequency of lethal events. *Journal of Experimental Psychology: Human Learning and Memory, 4*, 551–578.

Lieberman, P. (1963). Some effects of semantic and grammatical context on the production and perception of speech. *Language and Speech, 6*, 172–187.

Lieury, A., Aiello, B., Lepreux, D., & Mellet, M. (1980). La role des reperes dans la datation des souvenirs. *L'Anee Psychologique, 80*, 149–167.

Lindquist, E. F. (1953). *Design and analysis of experiments in psychology and education*. Boston: Houghton-Mifflin.

Linton, M. (1975). Memory for real-world events. In D. A. Norman & D. E. Rumelhart (Eds.), *Explorations in cognition* (pp. 376–404). New York: W. H. Freeman.

Linton, M. (1978). Real-world memory after six years: An in vivo study of very long-term memory. In M. M. Gruneberg, P. E. Morris, & R. N. Sykes (Eds.), *Practical aspects of memory* (pp. 69–76). London: Academic Press.

Linton, M. (1982). Transformations of memory in everyday life. In V. Neisser (Ed.), *Memory observed: Remembering in natural contexts* (pp. 77–91). New York: W. H. Freeman.

Linton, S. J., & Gotestam, K. G. (1983). A clinical comparison of two pain scales: Correlation, remembering chronic pain, and a measure of compliance. *Pain, 17,* 57–65.

Linton, S. J., & Melin, L. (1982). The accuracy of remembering chronic pain. *Pain, 13,* 281–285.

Loftus, E. F. (1975). Leading questions and the eyewitness report. *Cognitive Psychology, 7,* 560–572.

Loftus, E. F., & Fathi, D. C. (1985). Retrieving multiple autobiographical memories. *Social Cognition, 3,* 280–295.

Lombardi, W. J., Higgins, E. T., & Bargh, J. A. (1987). The role of consciousness in priming effects on categorization: Assimilation and contrast as a function of awareness of the priming task. *Personality and Social Psychology Bulletin, 13,* 411–429.

McClendon, M. J. (1986). Response order effects for dichotomous questions. *Social Science Quarterly, 67,* 205–211.

McFarland, C., Ross, M., & DeCourville, N. (1988). *Retrospective vs. current reports of menstrual distress.* Unpublished manuscript, University of Waterloo, Ontario.

MacGregor, D., Lichtenstein, S., & Slovic, P. (1988). Structuring knowledge retrieval: An analysis of decomposed quantitative judgment. *Organizational Behavior and Human Decision Processes, 42*(3), 303–323.

MacLachlan, J., Czepid, J., & LaBarbera, P. (1979). Implementation of response latency measures. *Journal of Marketing Research, 16,* 573–577.

Markus, G. B. (1986). Stability and change in political attitudes: Observed, recalled, and explained. *Political Behavior, 8,* 21–44.

Marslen-Wilson, W. D. (1984). Function and process in spoken word recognition. In H. Bouma & D. G. Bouwhuis (Eds.), *Attention and performance* (Vol. 10). London: Erlbaum.

Martin, L. L. (1986). Set/reset: Use and disuse of concepts in impression formation. *Journal of Personality and Social Psychology, 51,* 493–504.

Martin, L. L., Seta, J. J., & Crelia, R. A. (1990). Assimilation and contrast as a function of people's willingness to expend effort in forming an impression. *Journal of Personality and Social Psychology, 59,* 27–37.

Martin, L. L., & Tesser, A. (Eds.). (1992). *The construction of social judgment.* Hillsdale, NJ: Erlbaum.

Mathews, C. O. (1929). The effect of the order of printed response words on an interest questionnaire. *Journal of Educational Psychology, 30,* 128–134.

Means, B., & Loftus, E. F. (1991). When personal history repeats itself: Decomposing memories for recurring events. *Applied Cognitive Psychology, 5,* 297–318.

Means, B., Mingay, D. J., Nigam, A., & Zarrow, M. (1988). A cognitive approach to enhancing health survey reports of medical visits. In M. M. Gruneberg, P. E. Morris, & R. N. Sykes (Eds.), *Practical aspects of memory: Current research and issues (Vol. 1), Memory for everyday life.* Chichester, England: Wiley.

Menon, G. (1991). *Judgments of behavioral frequencies: An information processing perspective.* Unpublished doctoral dissertation, University of Illinois at Urbana–Champaign.

Menon, G. (1994). Judgments of behavioral frequencies: Memory search and retrieval strategies. In N. Schwarz & S. Sudman (Eds.), *Autobiographical memory and the validity of retrospective reports* (pp. 161–172). New York: Springer-Verlag.

Menon, G., Bickart, B., Sudman, S., & Blair, J. (1995). How well do you know your partner? Strategies for formulating proxy-reports and their effects on convergence to self-reports. *Journal of Marketing Research, 32,* 75–84.

Menon, G., Raghubir, P., & Schwarz, N. (in press). An accessibility-diagnosticity framework for behavioral frequency judgments: The use of response alternatives versus rate-of-occurence as sources of information. *Journal of Consumer Research.*

Menon, G., Sudman, S., Bickart, B. A., Blair, J., & Schwarz, N. (1990). *The use of anchoring strategies by proxy respondents in answering attitude questions.* Paper presented at the meeting of the American Association for Public Opinion Research, Lancaster, PA.

Mingay, D. J., & Greenwell, M. T. (1989). Memory bias and response order effects. *Journal of Official Statistics, 5,* 253–263.

Mingay, D., Bickart, B., Sudman, S., & Blair, J. (1994). Self and proxy reports of everyday events. In N. Schwarz & S. Sudman (Eds.), *Autobiographical memory and the validity of retrospective reports* (pp. 235–250). New York: Springer-Verlag.

Moore, J. C. (1988). Self-proxy response status and survey response quality: A review of the literature. *Journal of Official Statistics, 4,* 155–172.

Morton-Williams, J., & Sykes, W. (1984). The use of interaction coding and follow-up interviews to investigate comprehension of survey questions. *Journal of Market Research Society, 26,* 109–127.

Morwitz, V., Johnson, E., & Schmittlein, D. (1993). Does measuring intent change behavior? *Journal of Consumer Research, 20,* 46–61.

Moss, L., & Goldstein, H. (Eds.). (1979). *The recall method in social surveys.* London: NFER Publishing Co., Ltd.

Mosteller, F., Hyman, H., McCarthy, P. J., Marks, E. S., & Truman, D. B. (1949). *The preelection polls of 1948.* New York: Social Science Research Council, Bulletin 60.

Moxey, L., & Sanford, A. (1992). The communicative functions of quantifiers and their use in attitude research. In N. Schwarz & S. Sudman (Eds.), *Context effects in social and psychological research* (pp. 279–296). New York: Springer-Verlag.

Mueller, J. E. (1970). Choosing among 133 candidates. *Public Opinion Quarterly, 34,* 395–402.

Neisser, U. (1982). *Memory observed: Remembering natural contexts.* New York: W. H. Freeman.

Neisser, U., & Winograd, E. (Eds.). (1988). *Remembering reconsidered: Ecological and traditional approaches to the study of memory.* Cambridge, England: Cambridge University Press.

Neter, J., & Waksberg, J. (1964). A study of response errors in expenditure data from household interviews. *Journal of the American Statistical Association, 59,* 18–55.

Nisbett, R. E., & Bellows, N. (1977). Verbal reports about causal influences on social judgments: Private access versus public theories. *Journal of Personality and Social Psychology, 35,* 613–624.

Nisbett, R. E., & Ross, L. (1980). *Human shortcomings of social judgments.* Englewood Cliffs, NJ: Prentice-Hall.

Nisbett, R. E., & Wilson, T. D. (1977). Telling more than we know: Verbal reports on mental processes. *Psychological Review, 84,* 231–259.

Noelle-Neumann, E. (1970). Wanted: Rules for wording questions. *Public Opinion Quarterly, 34*, 191–201.

Ostrom, T. M., & Upshaw, H. S. (1968). Psychological perspective and attitude change. In A. C. Greenwald, T. C. Brock, & T. M. Ostrom (Eds.), *Psychological foundations of attitudes*. New York: Academic Press.

Ottati, V. C., Riggle, E. J., Wyer, R. S., Schwarz, N., & Kuklinski, J. (1989). The cognitive and affective bases of opinion survey responses. *Journal of Personality and Social Psychology, 57*, 404–415.

Paarek, U., & Rao, T. V. (1980). Cross-cultural surveying and interviewing. In H. Triandis & J. G. Draguns (Eds.), *Handbook of cross-cultural psychology* (Vol. 6, pp. 127–180). Boston: Allyn & Bacon.

Parducci, A. (1982). Category ratings: Still more context effects. In B. Wegener (Ed.), *Social Attitudes and Psychological Measurement* (pp. 89–105). Hillsdale, NJ: Erlbaum.

Parducci, A. (1983). Category ratings and the relational character of judgment. In H. G. Geissler, H. F. J. M. Bulfart, E. L. H. Leeuwenberg, & V. Sarris (Eds.), *Modern issues in perception* (pp. 262–282). Berlin: VEB Deutscher Verlag der Wissenschaften.

Parducci, A., & Perrett, L. F. (1971). Category rating scales: Effects of relative spacing and frequency of stimulus values. *Journal of Experimental Psychology Monograph, 89*, 427–452.

Payne, J. D. (1971). The effects of reversing the order of verbal rating scales in a postal survey. *Journal of the Marketing Research Society, 14*, 30–44.

Payne, S. L. (1949). A case study in question complexity. *Public Opinion Quarterly, 13*, 653–658.

Payne, S. L. (1951). *The art of asking questions*. Princeton, NJ: Princeton University Press.

Pepper, S. C. (1981). Problems in the quantification of frequency expressions. In D. W. Fiske (Ed.), *Problems with language imprecision*. New directions for methodology of social and behavioral science, Vol. 9. San Francisco: Jossey-Bass.

Petty, R. E., & Brock, T. C. (1981). Thought disruption and persuasion: Assessing the validity of attitude change experiments. In R. E. Petty, T. M. Ostrom, & T. C. Brock (Eds.), *Cognitive responses in persuasion* (pp. 55–79). Hillsdale, NJ: Erlbaum.

Petty, R. E., & Cacioppo, J. T. (1986a). The elaboration likelihood model of persuasion. In L. Berkowitz (Ed.), *Advances in experimental social psychology* (Vol. 19, pp. 123–205). New York: Academic Press.

Petty, R. E., & Cacioppo, J. T. (1986b). *Communication and persuasion: Central and peripheral routes to attitude change*. New York: Springer-Verlag.

Petty, R. E., Ostrom, T. M., & Brock T. C. (Eds.). (1981). *Cognitive responses in persuasion*. Hillsdale, NJ: Erlbaum.

Pillemer, D. B., Rhinehart, E. D., & White, S. H. (1986). Memories of life transitions: The first year of college. *Human Learning, 5,* 109–123.

Poulton, E. C. (1989). *Bias in quantifying judgments*. London: Erlbaum.

Quinn, S. B., & Belson, W. A. (1969). *The effects of reversing the order of presentation of verbal rating scales in survey interviews*. London: Survey Research Centre.

Reiff, R., & Scheever, M. (1959). *Memory and hypnotic age regression*. New York: International Universities Press.

Reiser, B. J. (1983). *Contexts and indices in autobiographical memory* (Cognitive Science Tech. Rep. No. 24). New Haven, CT: Yale University.

Reiser, B. J., Black, J. B., & Abelson, R. P. (1985). Knowledge structure in the organization and retrieval of autobiographical memories. *Cognitive Psychology, 17,* 89–137.

Reiser, B. J., Black, J. B., & Kalamarides, P. (1987). Strategic memory search processes. In D. C. Rubin (Ed.), *Autobiographical memory* (pp. 100–121). Cambridge, England: Cambridge University Press.

Ring, E. (1974). Wie man bei listenfragen einflüsse der reihenfolge ausschalten kann. *Psychologie und Praxis, 17,* 105–113.

Ring, E. (1975). Asymmetrical rotation. *European Research, 3,* 111–119.

Robinson, J. A. (1987). Autobiographical memory: A historical perspective. In D. C. Rubin (Ed.), *Autobiographical memory* (pp. 159–190). Cambridge, England: Cambridge University Press.

Rogers, T. B., Kuiper, N. A., & Kirker, W. S. (1977). Self-reference and the encoding of personal information. *Journal Personality and Social Psychology, 35,* 677–688.

Ross, M. (1989). The relation of implicit theories to the construction of personal histories. *Psychological Review, 96,* 341–357.

Ross, M., & Conway, M. (1986). Remembering one's own past: The construction of personal histories. In R. M. Sorrentino & E. T. Higgins (Eds.), *Handbook of motivation and cognition* (pp. 122–144). New York: Guilford.

Ross, M., & Sicoly, F. (1979). Egocentric biases in availability and attribution. *Journal of Personality and Social Psychology, 37*(3), 322–336.

Rubin, D. C. (Ed.). (1986). *Autobiographical memory.* Cambridge, England: Cambridge University Press.

Rubin, D. C., & Baddeley, A. D. (1989). Telescoping is not time compression: A model of the dating of autobiographical events. *Memory and Cognition, 17*(6), 653–661.

Rugg, D. (1941). Experiments in wording questions: II. *Public Opinion Quarterly, 5,* 91–92.

Rugg, D., & Cantril, H. (1942). The wording of questions in public opinion polls. *Journal of Abnormal and Social Psychology, 37,* 469–495.

Russell, B. (1921). *The analysis of mind.* London: Allen & Unwin.

Russell, B. (1948). *Human knowledge: Its scope and limits.* London: Allen & Unwin.

Schuman, H., & Duncan, O. D. (1974). Questions about attitude survey questions. In H. L. Costner (Ed.), *Sociological Methodology 1973–1974.* San Francisco: Jossey-Bass.

Schuman, H., & Kalton, G. (1985). Survey methods. In G. Lindzey & E. Aronson (Eds.), *Handbook of social psychology* (Vol. I). New York: Random House.

Schuman, H., & Ludwig, J. (1983). The norm of evenhandedness in surveys as in life. *American Sociological Review, 48,* 112–120.

Schuman, H., & Presser, S. (1981). *Questions and answers in attitude surveys.* New York: Academic Press.

Schwarz, N. (1990a). Assessing frequency reports of mundane behaviors: Contributions of cognitive psychology to questionnaire construction. In C. Hendrick & M. S. Clark (Eds.), *Research methods in personality and social psychology* (pp. 98–119). Newbury Park, CA: Sage.

Schwarz, N. (1990b). Feelings as information: Informational and motivational functions of affective states. In E. T. Higgins & R. Sorrentino (Eds.), *Handbook of motivation and cognition: Foundations of social behavior* (Vol. 2, pp. 527–561). New York: Guilford Press.

Schwarz, N. (1994). Judgment in a social context: Biases, shortcomings, and the logic of conversation. In M. Zanna (Ed.), *Advances in experimental social psychology* (Vol. 26, pp. 123–162). San Diego, CA: Academic Press.

Schwarz, N., & Bienias, J. (1990). What mediates the impact of response alternatives on frequency reports of mundane behaviors? *Applied Cognitive Psychology, 4*, 61–72.

Schwarz, N., & Bless, H. (1992a). Constructing reality and its alternatives: Assimilation and contrast effects in social judgment. In L. L. Martin & A. Tesser (Eds.), *The construction of social judgment* (pp. 217–245). Hillsdale, NJ: Erlbaum.

Schwarz, N., & Bless, H. (1992b). Scandals and the public's trust in politicians: Assimilation and contrast effects. *Personality and Social Psychology Bulletin, 18*, 574–579.

Schwarz, N., Bless, H., Bohner, G., Harlacher, U., & Kellenbenz, M. (1991). Response scales as frames of reference: The impact of frequency range on diagnostic judgment. *Applied Cognitive Psychology, 5*, 37–50.

Schwarz, N., Bless, H., Strack, F., Klumpp, G., Rittenauer-Schatka, H., & Simons, A. (1991). Ease of retrieval as information: Another look at the availability heuristic. *Journal of Personality and Social Psychology, 61*, 195–202.

Schwarz, N., & Clore, G. L. (1983). Mood, misattribution, and judgments of well-being: Informative and directive functions of affective states. *Journal of Personality and Social Psychology, 45*, 513–523.

Schwarz, N., & Clore, G. L. (1988). How do I feel about it? Informative functions of affective states. In K. Fiedler & J. Forgas (Eds.), *Affect, cognition, and social behavior* (pp. 544–620). Toronto: Hogrefe International.

Schwarz, N., & Clore, G. L. (in press). Feelings and phenomenal experiences. In E. T. Higgins & A. Kruglanski (Eds.), *Social psychology: A handbook of basic principles*. New York: Guilford.

Schwarz, N., & Hippler, H. J. (1991). Response alternatives: The impact of their choice and ordering. In P. Biemer, R. Groves, N. Mathiowetz, & S. Sudman (Eds.), *Measurement error in surveys* (pp. 41–56). Chichester: Wiley.

Schwarz, N., & Hippler, H. J. (1995). Subsequent questions may influence answers to preceding questions in mail surveys. *Public Opinion Quarterly, 59*, 93–97.

Schwarz, N., Hippler, H. J., Deutsch, B., & Strack, F. (1985). Response categories: Effects on behavioral reports and comparative judgments. *Public Opinion Quarterly, 49,* 388–395.

Schwarz, N., Hippler, H. J., & Noelle-Neumann, E. (1992). A cognitive model of response order effects in survey measurement. In N. Schwarz & S. Sudman (Eds.), *Context effects in social and psychological research* (pp. 187–201). New York: Springer-Verlag.

Schwarz, N., Hippler, H. J., & Noelle-Neumann, E. (1994). Retrospective reports: The impact of response alternatives. In N. Schwarz & S. Sudman (Eds.), *Autobiographical memory and the validity of retrospective reports* (pp. 187–202). New York: Springer-Verlag.

Schwarz, N., Knäuper, B., Hippler, H. J., Noelle-Neumann, E., & Clark, F. (1991). Rating scales: Numeric values may change the meaning of scale labels. *Public Opinion Quarterly, 55,* 618–630.

Schwarz, N., & Münkel, T. (1988). *Asymmetic contrast effects: A perspective theory account.* Unpublished manuscript.

Schwarz, N., Münkel, T., & Hippler, H. J. (1990). What determines a perspective? Contrast effects as a function of the dimension tapped by preceding questions. *European Journal of Social Psychology, 20,* 357–361.

Schwarz, N., & Scheuring, B. (1988). Judgments of relationship satisfaction: Inter- and intraindividual comparison strategies as a function of questionnaire structure. *European Journal of Social Psychology, 18,* 485–496.

Schwarz, N., & Scheuring, B. (1991). Die erfassung gesundheitsrelevanten verhaltens: Kognitionspsychologische aspekte und methodologische implikationen [The assessment of health-relevant behaviors]. In J. Haisch (Ed.), *Gesundheitspsychologie. Zur Sozialpsychologie der Prävention und Krankheitsbewältigung* (pp. 47–63). Heidelberg, Germany: Asanger.

Schwarz, N., & Schuman, H. (1992). Unpublished research.

Schwarz, N., & Strack, F. (Eds.). (1991a). Social Cognition and Communication: Human judgment in its social context [Special issue]. *Social Cognition, 9*(1).

Schwarz, N., & Strack, F. (1991b). Evaluating one's life: A judgment model of subjective well-being. In F. Strack, M. Argyle, & N. Schwarz (Eds.), *Subjective well-being* (pp. 27–47). London: Pergamon.

Schwarz, N., & Strack, F. (1991c). Context effects in attitude surveys: Applying cognitive theory to social research. In W. Stroebe & M. Hewstone (Eds.), *European Review of Social Psychology* (Vol. 2, pp. 31–50). Chichester, England: Wiley.

Schwarz, N., Strack, F., Hippler, H. J., & Bishop, G. (1991). The impact of administration mode on response effects in survey measurement. *Applied Cognitive Psychology, 5,* 193–212.

Schwarz, N., Strack, F., & Mai, H. P. (1991). Assimilation and contrast effects in part-whole question sequences: A conversational logic analysis. *Public Opinion Quarterly, 55,* 3–23.

Schwarz, N., Strack, F., Müller, G., & Chassein, B. (1988). The range of response alternatives may determine the meaning of the question: Further evidence on informative functions of response alternatives. *Social Cognition, 6,* 107–117.

Schwarz, N., & Sudman, S. (Eds.). (1992). *Context effects in social and psychological research.* New York: Springer-Verlag.

Schwarz, N., & Sudman, S. (1994). *Autobiographical memory and the validity of retrospective reports.* New York: Springer-Verlag.

Schwarz, N., & Sudman, S. (1995). *Answering questions.* San Francisco: Jossey-Bass.

Schwarz, N., & Wellens, T. (1994). *Cognitive dynamics of proxy responding: The diverging perspectives of actors and observers.* (Report to the Census Bureau). Ann Arbor: ISR.

Schwarz, N., & Wyer, R. S., Jr. (1985). Effects of rank ordering stimuli on magnitude ratings of these and other stimuli. *Journal of Experimental Social Psychology, 21,* 30–46.

Scott, W. A. (1966). Measures of cognitive structure. *Multivariate Behavior research, 1,* 391–395.

Shank, R., & Kolodner, J. L. (1979). *Retrieving information from an episodic memory.* (Research Rep. No. 159). New Haven, CT: Yale University, Department of Computer Science.

Sherman, S. J. (1980). On the self-erasing nature of errors of prediction. *Journal of Personality and Social Psychology, 39,* 211–221.

Sherman, S. J., & Golkin, L. (1980). Attitude bolstering when behavior is inconsistent with central attitudes. *Journal of Experimental Social Psychology, 16,* 388–403.

Sherman, S. J., Zehner, K. S., Johnson, J., & Hirt, E. R. (1983). Social explanation: The role of timing, set, and recall on subjective likelihood estimates. *Journal of Personality and Social Psychology, 44,* 1127–1143.

Simon, H. A. (1957). *Models of man.* New York: Wiley.

Sirken, M. (1989). *A cognitive approach to designing survey questions.* Paper presented at the winter conference of the American Statistical Association, San Diego, CA.

Smith, E. E. (1990). Categorization. In D. N. Osherson & E. E. Smith (Eds.), *Thinking: An invitation to cognitive science* (Vol. 3, pp. 33–54). Cambridge, MA: MIT Press.

Smith, T. W. (1992). Thoughts on the nature of context effects. In N. Schwarz & S. Sudman (Eds.), *Context effects in social and psychological research* (pp. 163–186). New York: Springer-Verlag.

Smyth, M. M., Morris, P. E., Levy, P., & Ellis, A. W. (1987). *Cognition in Action.* London: Erlbaum.

Sperber, D., & Wilson, D. (1986). *Relevance: Communication and cognition.* Oxford: Basil Blackwell.

Stewart, D. W., & Shamdasani, P. N. (1990). *Focus groups.* Newbury Park, CA: Sage.

Stouffer, S. A., & DeVinney, L. C. (1949). How personal adjustment varied in the army—by background characteristics of the soldiers. In S. A. Stouffer, E. A. Suchman, L. C. DeVinney, S. A. Star, & R. M. Williams, Jr. (Eds.), *The American soldier: Adjustment during army life.* Princeton, NJ: Princeton University Press.

Strack, F. (1992). Order effects in survey research: Activative and informative functions of preceding questions. In N. Schwarz & S. Sudman (Eds.), *Context effects in social and psychological research* (pp. 23–34). New York: Springer-Verlag.

Strack, F. (1994). Zur Psychologie der standardisierten Befragung. Heidelberg, Germany: Springer-Verlag.

Strack, F., & Martin, L. L. (1987). Thinking, judging, and communicating: A process account of context effects in attitude surveys. In H. J. Hippler, N. Schwarz, & S. Sudman (Eds.), *Social information processing and survey methodology* (pp. 123–148). New York: Springer-Verlag.

Strack, F., Martin, L. L., & Schwarz, N. (1988). Priming and communication: The social determinants of information use in judgments of life-satisfaction. *European Journal of Social Psychology, 18*, 429–442.

Strack, F., & Schwarz, N. (1992). Implicit cooperation: The case of standardized questioning. In G. Semin & F. Fiedler (Eds.), *Social cognition and language*. Newbury Park, CA: Sage.

Strack, F., Schwarz, N., Bless, H., Kübler, A., & Wänke, M. (1993). Awareness of the influence as a determinant of assimilation versus contrast. *European Journal of Social Psychology, 23*, 53–62.

Strack, F., Schwarz, N., & Gschneidinger, E. (1985). Happiness and reminiscing: The role of time perspective, mood, and mode of thinking. *Journal of Personality and Social Psychology, 49*, 1460–1469.

Strack, F., Schwarz, N., & Wänke, M. (1991). Semantic and pragmatic aspects of context effects in social and psychological research. *Social Cognition, 9*, 111–125.

Strube, G. (1987). Answering survey questions: The role of memory. In H. J. Hippler, N. Schwarz, & S. Sudman (Eds.), *Social information processing and survey methodology* (pp. 86–101). New York: Springer-Verlag.

Suchman, L., & Jordan, B. (1990). Interactional troubles in face-to-face interviews. *Journal of the American Statistical Association, 85*, 232–241.

Sudman, S. (1976). *Applied sampling*. New York: Academic Press.

Sudman, S., & Bradburn, N. M. (1974). *Response effects in surveys: A review and synthesis*. Chicago: Aldine.

Sudman, S., & Bradburn, N. M. (1982). *Asking questions*. San Francisco: Jossey-Bass.

Sudman, S., Finn, A., & Lannom, L. (1984). The use of bounded recall procedures in single interviews. *Public Opinion Quarterly, 48*, 520–524.

Sudman, S., & Schwarz, N. (1989). Contributions of cognitive psychology to advertising research. *Journal of Advertising Research, 29*, 43–53.

Sudman, S., et al. (1993). Cognitive aspects of reporting cancer-prevention examinations and tests. *Proceedings, Survey Research Methods Section, 153rd Annual Meeting of the American Statistical Association*.

Tanur, J. M. (Ed.). (1992). *Questions about questions: Inquiries into the cognitive bases of surveys*. New York: Russell Sage Foundation.

Thompson, C. P., Skowronski, J. J., & Lee, D. J. (1988). Telescoping in dating naturally occurring events. *Memory and Cognition, 16*, 461–468.

Thorndyke, P. W., & Hayes-Roth, B. (1979). Integration of knowledge from text. *Journal of Verbal Learning and Verbal Behavior, 18*(1), 91–108.

Tourangeau, R. (1984). Cognitive science and survey methods: A cognitive perspective. In T. Jabine, M. Straf, J. Tanur, & R. Tourangeau (Eds.), *Cognitive aspects of survey methodology: Building a bridge between disciplines* (pp. 73–100). Washington, DC: National Academy Press.

Tourangeau, R. (1987). Attitude measurement: A cognitive perspective. In H. J. Hippler, N. Schwarz, & S. Sudman (Eds.), *Social information processing and survey methodology* (pp. 149–162). New York: Springer-Verlag.

Tourangeau, R. (1992). Attitudes as memory structures: Belief sampling and context effects. In N. Schwarz & S. Sudman (Eds.), *Context effects in social and psychological research* (pp. 35–47). New York: Springer-Verlag.

Tourangeau, R., & Rasinski, K. A. (1988). Cognitive processes underlying context effects in attitude measurement. *Psychological Bulletin, 103,* 299–314.

Tourangeau, R., Rasinski, K. A., & Bradburn, N. M. (1992). *The consistency of attitude responses.* Unpublished manuscript.

Tourangeau, R., Rasinski, K. A., Bradburn, N. M., & D'Andrade, R. (1989a). Belief accessibility and context effects in attitude measurement. *Journal of Experimental Social Psychology, 25,* 401–421.

Tourangeau, R., Rasinski, K. A., Bradburn, N. M., & D'Andrade, R. (1989b). Carryover effects in attitude surveys. *Public Opinion Quarterly, 53,* 495–524.

Tourangeau, R., Rasinski, K. A., & D'Andrade, R. (1991). Attitude structure and belief accessiblity. *Journal of Experimental Social Psychology, 27,* 48–75.

Tulving, E. (1972). Episodic and semantic memory. In E. Tulving & W. Donaldson (Eds.), *Organization of memory* (pp. 381–403). New York: Academic.

Tulving, E. (1983). *Elements of episodic memory.* Oxford: Clarendon Press.

Turner, C. F., & Martin, E. (Eds.). (1982). *Surveys of subjective phenomena.* Cambridge, MA: Harvard University Press.

Tversky, A., & Kahneman, D. (1973). Availability: A heuristic for judging frequency and probability. *Cognitive Psychology, 5,* 207–232.

Tversky, A., & Kahneman, D. (1974). Judgment under uncertainty: Heuristics and biases. *Science, 185,* 1124–1131.

Tyebjee, T. T. (1979). Response latency: A new measure for scaling brand preference. *Journal of Marketing Research, 16,* 96–101.

Uhlenhuth, E., Haberman, S. J., Balter, M. D., & Lipman, R. S. (1977). Remembering life events. In J. S. Strauss, H. M. Babigan, & M. Roff (Eds.), *The origins and course of psychopathology.* New York: Plenum Press.

Wagenaar, W. A. (1986). My memory: A study of autobiographical memory over six years. *Cognitive Psychology, 18,* 225–252.

Watkins, M. J., & Kerkar, S. P. (1985). Recall of a twice-presented item without recall of either presentation: Generic memory for events. *Journal of Memory and Language, 24,* 666–678.

Weinberg, E. (1983). Data collection: Planning and management. In P. H. Rossi, J. B. Wright, & A. B. Anderson (Eds.), *Handbook of survey research.* New York: Academic Press.

Weitz, B., & Wright, P. (1979). Retrospective self-insight on factors considered in product evaluations. *Journal of Consumer Research, 6,* 280–294.

White, R. T. (1982). Memory for personal events. *Human Learning, 1,* 171–183.

Whitten, W. B., II, & Leonard, J. M. (1981). Directed search through autobiographical memory. *Memory and Cognition, 9,* 566–579.

Williams, M. D., & Hollan, J. D. (1981). The process of retrieval from very long-term memory. *Cognitive Science, 5,* 87–119.

Wilson, T. D., LaFleur, S. J., & Anderson, D. E. (1995). The validity and consequences of verbal reports about attitudes. In N. Schwarz & S. Sudman (Eds.), *Answering questions.* San Francisco: Jossey-Bass.

Wilson, T. D., & Hodges, S. D. (1992). Attitudes as temporary constructions. In A. Tesser & L. L. Martin (Eds.), *The construction of social judgment.* Hillsdale, NJ: Erlbaum.

Withey, S. B. (1954). Reliability of recall of income. *Public Opinion Quarterly, 18,* 31–34.

Wyer, R. S., & Srull, T. K. (1989). *Memory and cognition in its social context.* Hillsdale, NJ: Erlbaum.

Name Index

Subject Index

A

Asking Questions, 258

Attitude, defined, 123–124

Attitude reports, 251–253, 257; context dependency of, 123–128; judgmental perspective in, 123–125; self-reports versus proxy reports, 228–231, 233; stability over time, 125–126

Attitude theory: attitude accessibility in, 127–128; attitude strength in, 126–127; attitudes as memory structures in, 124–125; file-drawer versus construal model, 124

Autobiographical reports. *See* Memory, autobiographical

Availability heuristic strategy, 89–90, 181, 210

B

Behavioral effects, of survey questioning, 77

Behavioral reports, 253–257; and multiple events, 255–256; self-reports versus proxy reports, 228–231, 232; and specific event, 255

Belief sampling model, 101

Bounded recall, 194–195

Bureau of Social Science Research, 12

C

Coding categories, cognitive difficulties, 24–30

Cognitive laboratories, 17

Committee on National Statistics, 13

Computer-assisted personal (CAPI) interviewing, 268

Computer-assisted telephone (CATI) interviewing, 268

Context effects, 80–129, 263–265; and ambiguous questions, 83–84; cognitive process involved in, 82–83; at comprehension stage, 71–72, 82, 83–85; and concept of error, 81; and content of preceding questions, 113–116; and crystallization, 126–127, 133–134; at editing stage, 98; at formatting stage, 92–96; and general norms, 86–87; and generality of target question, 117–120; implications for attitude theory, 123–128; at judgment stage, 82–83, 85–92, 149–153; and number of preceding questions, 105, 116–117; and previously formed judgments, 85–86; and question order, 71–72; and questionnaire introductions to item blocks, 122–123; and questionnaire item spacing, 120–122; and questionnaire layout, 122–123; and respondents' expertise, 103–105; and subjective experiences, 87–92. *See also* Inclusion/exclusion model

Contrast effects, 100, 105–107; asymmetric, 151–153

Conversation, cooperativeness principle in, 62–63